TODAY'S HANDBOOK
OF
BIBLE TIMES & CUSTOMS

William L. Coleman

BETHANY HOUSE PUBLISHERS
MINNEAPOLIS, MINNESOTA 55438
A Division of Bethany Fellowship, Inc.

TODAY'S HANDBOOK
OF
BIBLE TIMES
& CUSTOMS

Scripture quotations are taken from the *New International Version* of the Bible, unless otherwise noted.

Published by Bethany House Publishers
A Division of Bethany Fellowship, Inc.
6820 Auto Club Road, Minneapolis, MN 55438

Printed in the United States of America

Library of Congress Cataloging in Publication Data

Coleman, William L.
  Today's handbook of Bible times and customs.

  Includes indexes.
  1. Bible—Handbooks, manuals, etc.   2. Sociology,
Biblical—Handbooks, manuals, etc.   I. Title.
BS417.C72   1984   220.9′5   84-4303
ISBN 0-87123-594-3

PHOTO SOURCES

Each photo is keyed to this index by initials at the close of that photo's caption. The publisher gratefully acknowledges the cooperation of these persons and organizations.

AJW   Courtesy of the *American Jewish World*, Minneapolis

AR   Ann Roth

BAS   Biblical Archaeology Society

CD   Charlette Dillon

CGI   Consulate General of Israel

DM   Photo by Dever/Mull, courtesy of the Archaeological Institute of America

EHLE   Eye-ographic Holy Land Exhibit

ICI   Italian Cultural Institute

JJ   Jacquelyn Johnson

JLAT   Photo from *Jewish Life in Art and Tradition*, published by Hechal Schlomo, courtesy of World Zionist Press Service, Jerusalem; and the *American Jewish World*, Minneapolis

KM   Photo by Kook-Magnes, courtesy of World Zionist Press Service, Jerusalem; and the *American Jewish World*, Minneapolis

LB   Photo by Lev Borodulin, courtesy of World Zionist Press Service, Jerusalem; and the *American Jewish World*, Minneapolis

REI   Religion and Ethics Institute

RI   Robert Ibach, Jr.

RN   Photo by Richard Nowitz, courtesy of World Zionist Press Service, Jerusalem; and the *American Jewish World*, Minneapolis

TW   Terry White

WB   Photo by Werner Braun, courtesy of World Zionist Press Service, Jerusalem; and the *American Jewish World*, Minneapolis

WZPS   Courtesy of World Zionist Press Service, Jerusalem; and the *American Jewish World*, Minneapolis

CONTENTS

INTRODUCTION

Do you fully understand the person who lives next door? Probably not. You therefore can imagine how difficult it would be to piece together a personality who lived thousands of years ago in a different culture. Such a task must be approached with thoroughness, humility and an open mind. Even then successes can be only partial. The final conclusion will be only a sketch of the true picture. Reality is too far removed for us to see all the colors in all their shades.

This book is an attempt to help us better understand the people of the Bible. I had little difficulty describing the schools, jobs, houses and governments, but *feelings* were another matter. What made a Jew of the biblical period laugh, hope, pray or cry? What made him hate? What were the smells that prickled his senses? What symbols made him stand erect with patriotism and pride? Which expressions, solemn ceremonies or pastoral scenes made him want to praise God?

The better we know the emotions, mindsets and lifestyles of the Jews, the better we will understand the Bible. Some scripture passages will mean little unless we visualize a face turning red with anger; hear a voice shouting in indignation, or whispering with tenderness; feel the aching muscles after a day of pulling wet, fish-laden nets.

The better we know the ancient Jews, the better we will know Jesus Christ, for Jesus was a Jew. He wore the clothes, tasted the food, laughed at the jokes and sang the songs of Palestine.

Writing this book was a pleasure. It gave me the opportunity to delve into matters I have often wanted to investigate. It was a chance to grow spiritually, a chance to be surprised, and a chance to gain insight on how God has worked among His chosen people.

As you venture through this volume, either by reading chapter after chapter, or by picking through the index, keep certain principles in mind:

1. *There is no typical Jew*. It has been too easy to stereotype and say Jews did this or that. The effects of culture certainly ensure many similarities between persons, but each is nonetheless different, in appearance and temperament.

2. *There was great pluralism*. Throughout most of their history,

the Jews were not a closed, airtight society. The cultures, languages, foods, sports, governments, clothing, and religions of other nations greatly affected them. They frequently adopted the ways of others.

3. *Do not judge them by their laws.* Too frequently this type of book has been written with the assumption that Jews kept the biblical laws. If a law declared they were to feed the poor, it is not safe to imagine that everyone did. In many cases a law was the ideal but not necessarily the reality.

The same should be said of the teaching of the rabbis. They frequently contradicted each other on many subjects; therefore the average person often paid them little heed.

4. *Jewish culture was not static.* The lives of Abraham and Peter were different from each other. Avoid the trap of reading about an act in Genesis and then extrapolating that concept into the Gospel of John. Life among the Jews did change, and over a span of thousands of years it changed drastically. Many mistakes are made by equating present-day Jews or Palestinians with New Testament characters. This leads to shoddy interpretation of Scripture.

My search for the facts and the feelings of Bible people sent me far afield. I have rifled through library catalogs from Princeton Seminary to Hastings College and many schools in between. I have perused with admiration the works of Jeremias, Daniel-Rops, Deissmann and too many more to mention. I have spent long hours scrutinizing photographs in archaeological journals, enjoying the fruits of contemporary scholarship. Hopefully some of that satisfaction and delight I felt will be conveyed on these pages to you.

Much of the credit goes to my wife, Pat. Not only did she expend Trojan effort in editing, researching and typing, but Pat also supplied the warm love and encouragement that was crucial to my completing this project.

William L. Coleman
Aurora, Nebraska

CHAPTER 1

AT HOME IN ISRAEL

First-century Jews enjoyed security and family closeness amidst the sounds, smells and sights of their modest homes. Fresh bread baked in the clay oven, uncles played music in the courtyard, and the dim light from the oil lamp frustrated the night shadows. Life at home was filled with activity, togetherness and solid traditions.

Houses could be found in a variety of shapes and sizes, for there was a great gulf between rich and poor. There was no typical home in Palestine, but certain characteristics were common among those of average citizens. In most cases the structures were simple and fairly small. The majority of an Israelite's activities were outdoors

The small, simple homes that covered the hillsides of ancient Jerusalem are depicted in this model of Jerusalem at the time of Christ. TW

so his house was built to provide shelter and a place to eat and sleep.

The average home in the time of Christ was a one-room dwelling with minimal decor and fixtures. Many homes were only 10 feet square with a couple of windows and a dirt floor. But even the poorest home had at least one staircase leading to the flat roof. Most of the social and family activities took place on the roof and in the yard. Especially during the oppressive heat of the summer the family slept on the roof under a spectacular starlit sky. They sometimes erected a tent or "booth" for privacy.

FLAT ROOFS □ The closest facsimile to a recreation room was the ingeniously designed roof which consisted of heavy beams reinforced with brushwood and covered with mud mixed with chopped straw. Smoke escaped through the windows of a Jewish home. Wealthy families used tiles to strengthen their roofs.

A mud roof required careful upkeep. Because rain would erode the surface, it often had to be patched with more mud. Grass was allowed to grow and thus retard erosion. Such a "lively" roof needed regular stone-rolling to keep it flat and reasonably watertight. But despite regular care, leaks were common and thus became a laughing matter (Prov. 19:13).

On a warm afternoon women could be seen on their roofs weaving fabric; baking bread; drying figs, flax, dates; or cleaning grain. Laundered clothing was spread out there to dry.

Since flat roofs were so practical and accessible, they were used for a large variety of activities. Peter used a roof as a place to pray (Acts 10:9) as did many others. Special announcements blared loudly across the neighborhood (Matt. 10:27; Luke 12:3). Rooftop activities were such a normal part of life that rails were required by Mosaic law (Deut. 22:8). These rails were often made of lattice work.

Two-story buildings were rare among common people during this period, though structures were frequently built on the roofs. Everything from makeshift lean-to's to fully enclosed guest rooms could be found. Such a room was used as a summer residence or as a prayer closet called *alliyah*. Jesus told His followers to enter this prayer closet

The flat roofs of the old city of Jerusalem provided a place to pray (Acts 10:9) and a place from which to make announcements (Matt. 10:27; Luke 12:3).　　CD

instead of pompously displaying their piety in public (Matt. 6:6).

Jesus and His disciples met in a well-furnished upper room for the Passover Supper (Luke 22:12). This room was large and probably belonged to a wealthy follower. One hundred and twenty of His disciples met in a similar room after Christ's ascension into heaven (Acts 1:13). It seems several of Jesus' followers were people of means.

Booths were often built on the roofs for various functions. During the Feast of Booths or Tabernacles, a hut was constructed as part of the celebration. It was copied after the shelters farmers built in their fields during harvest. This feast was similar to Thanksgiving Day in the U.S. (Ex. 23:14–17; Lev. 23; Deut. 16).

This was a pilgrim feast which brought thousands of people into Jerusalem. Hastily constructed booths stood in the streets and on the squares; any vacant space might be claimed. Such booths may be what Peter had in mind when he offered to build shelters of tribute to Moses, Elijah and Jesus on the Mount of Transfiguration (Matt. 17:4).

Homes in some cities were built wall-to-wall and their roofs made a convenient street. The rabbis referred to them as a "road of roofs" and people often traveled across them.

Jesus said we should not take time to come down off the roof in the days of judgment (Matt. 24:17). He probably meant that we were not to take time to come down inside the house and collect our belongings.

While plumbing is as old as cities, by the time of Christ strides were again being taken to install toilet facilities in homes. The Romans commonly built bathrooms with running water. Depending on the era and

These pillars are a portion of the floor of the hot-bath area of Herod's sumptuous desert palace at the fortress Masada, near the Dead Sea's western shore. The pillars supported an intricately-decorated floor (a portion may be seen at right), and hot water circulated underneath the floor and exited through the conduit in the rear.   TW

the location, cesspools, running gutters and sand ditches were used. Clay pipe, similar in design to modern sewer pipe, had also been used from ancient times. In the homes of the wealthy full bathrooms were becoming popular in the first century. Tubs were used in some homes and a few people had even devised hot-water systems. ∎

THE DOORWAY □ The front doors of homes in this era differed greatly, even as ours do today. Most doors were narrow, short and hinged on stone sockets. The door would swing open easily. Country dwellers in the daytime would probably leave their door standing wide open. In cities people would be more cautious. A Hebrew's door held great spiritual significance. The stone threshold was considered sacred, and during the Passover blood was sprinkled on it to remind the Jew of his miraculous deliverance during the plagues in Egypt. Every door had a tubular metal or wood box, called a *mezuzah*, fixed to the doorpost. Inside the mezuzah was a parchment bearing the words of Deut. 6:4–9, the credal statement of Judaism called the *Shema*: "Hear, O Israel: the Lord our God is one Lord: and thou shalt love the Lord thy God with all thine heart, and with all thy soul, and with all thy might. And these words, which I command thee this day, shall be in thine heart: and thou shalt teach them diligently unto thy children, and shalt talk

of them when thou sittest in thine house, and when thou walkest by the way, and when thou liest down, and when thou risest up. And thou shalt bind them for a sign upon thine hand, and they shall be as frontlets between thine eyes. And thou shalt write them upon the posts of thy house, and on thy gates." Mezuzah parchments are

The mezuzah is often attached to a doorpost by Jews as a reminder of God's presence and the redemption of the Jewish people from Egypt. The original, more elaborate versions of the mezuzah contained a piece of parchment which was inscribed on one side with the passages Deut. 6:4–9 and 11:13–21, and on the other side with the word "Shaddai," a name applied to God. EHLE

still produced today by specially trained scribes. The parchment is precisely rolled and placed in the box so the Hebrew word meaning "almighty" can be seen through a hole in the box.

Often, before entering or leaving his home, a Jew would kiss his fingers and place them on the mezuzah. The mezuzah served several purposes: a testimony to the neighborhood, a sign of faith in God's protection, and a reminder of Israel's history.

The door was usually not locked but it could be. Some locks were opened with large wooden keys. These keys, though often huge, were sometimes worn around the person's neck. The house could also be secured by a wooden bar behind the door.   ■

FLOORS □ Most floors were made of either brushed earth or clay, though some were of packed mud or plaster. An affluent home owner may have used limestone slabs which were easy to maintain and keep clean.

The foundation which stabilized and supported a house was extremely important (Matt. 7:24–27). Heavy, fast rainstorms, which can quickly erode the ground, and strong earthquakes presented a continual threat to a foundation. If a builder was careless and placed the home on an unsteady base such as sand, the results could be disastrous. When possible the builder tried to dig down to hard clay or bedrock. Ancient homes deteriorated with age and were torn down, but their replacements often were built on foundations of previous buildings.   ■

WINDOWS □ Most houses had only a couple of windows located high along the walls for ventilation during the hot summers. Glass was not used though the material was available; in order to keep out hot sunlight, wooden lattice work in clever designs was often used. Shutters could be closed as protection against the cool evenings. Since these windows also functioned as chimneys, they probably were blackened by smoke.

If a house stood along the city wall, its windows made good escape hatches (2 Cor. 11:33). They were, however, dangerous if someone fell asleep listening to a long sermon (Acts 20:9).   ■

LIGHTING □ Due to the few windows and the absence of electricity, the interior of the average home was quite dark. An indoor oven would give a dim glow, but lamps provided most of the minimal illumination.

The King James Bible often mentions candlesticks, but that is really a mistranslation. There were no candles during Bible times. Even the seven-stemmed *menorah*, similar in appearance to a candelabra, actually held olive oil and wicks. Each stem had a small cup for oil but no socket for a candle.

Early lamps were small, open bowls, like saucers with one side pinched to form a groove for the wick. Others had enclosed tops like modern teapots. The saucer-like lamps held a pool of oil which fed a cotton or flax wick that lay in the groove. The principle is similar to that employed in old-fashioned American kerosene lamps. The most common lamps were made of clay. More expensive lamps were created from bronze or other metals and often sported elaborate decorations on their sides. Gentile families had lamps with animal-shaped handles. The Jews refused to use these because they disdained idolatry.

If there was no light in a house, you could be sure no one was home, for since oil was readily available and cheap, lamps were kept burning. Another reason for letting a lamp burn was the difficulty of lighting it. Sticks had to be rubbed together or stones struck for sparks. Only the poor were careful in their use of oil.

With oil being continuously burned, a sweet scent hung in the house and greeted every visitor.

When Jesus told the story of the lost coin, His listeners immediately could identify with it. They could picture a woman carrying her lamp into the shadowy corners of the room as she searched (Luke 15:8). The people could readily understand the predicament of the virgins who failed to carry enough oil (Matt. 25:1–4). By discussing lights and lamps, Jesus explained the gospel in the language of everyday, practical experience.

Even a faint light of an oil lamp was a discouragement to potential thieves. Darkness worked to the advantage of criminals but light promoted honesty (John 3:20). The duty of a conscientious wife included keeping a lamp burning (Prov. 31:18).

Lamps were placed in several places in a room. Many times stone shelves were attached to the wall, with portable lampstands used in corners or where needed. The clay or wood stands were tall enough to allow the light to cover a wide area. In wealthier homes lampstands were made of metal.

When Jesus said we should not hide our light (Matt. 5:15), His audience most likely saw the humor in the statement. Would *we* hide a lighted flashlight under our coat or in a pocket? He told us to place a lamp on the lampstand where it can do some good. To correctly understand Jesus' illustration, our modern mind has to forget our present method of lighting.

Lamps had to be maintained constantly, so needed supplies, such as oil, wicks and lamps, were

Small clay lamps, like this Herodian lamp from the first or second century A.D., illuminated the homes of ancient Jews. Used with oil and a wick, these lamps gave off a continuous sweet scent of oil being burned.   TW

stored and kept ready because running out could be very disappointing (Matt. 25:1–10).

Olive oil was plentiful and also useful for a huge assortment of practical purposes, including lamp fuel. Everything from soap to cooking to cosmetics to worship called for oil. The oil was crushed from olives which grew plentifully in the region.   ■

WALLS □ Interior walls were usually stark. Israelites were commanded not to use any figures as decoration. All likenesses to people or animals were considered idolatrous and were strictly forbidden, although the discovery of a synagogue with an elaborate wall shows there were exceptions to this rule.

Walls were constructed of dried mud or clay bricks. The bricks were made by digging a pit, pouring in water and chopped straw, then stomping them with bare feet into the clay. The mixture was then shoveled into wooden molds of uniform size and shape—either rectangular or square. After drying in the sun, the bricks were ready for use. For wealthier homes or palaces the bricks were kiln-baked and sometimes decorated with ornaments.

Bricks were mortared together with mud, though for more expensive dwellings sand and lime, or gypsum, were used. Bitumen or pitch could also be used (Gen. 11:3). The walls were then covered with whitewash of lime or gypsum.

Most walls required considerable upkeep, for wind and rain took their toll on the soft material. The snake on the wall in Amos 5:19 could have wriggled through a crack in the mortar.

Despite their vulnerability many of these homes stood for centuries. A solid foundation and good bricks aided longevity. Some homes had kiln-fired bricks in the foundation.   ■

Furnishings □ Most homes in Israel had a utilitarian appearance, for there was little furniture to clutter the room. The dinner table was usually a straw mat or animal skin spread on the floor. Tables and chairs were luxuries reserved for the wealthy. Even a simple three-legged stool was a rarity.

The Last Supper may have been quite different than the picture painted by da Vinci. It is possible that a table was used, but only if the house belonged to a wealthy person. If that were the case, the table was probably lower and the disciples most likely reclined on pillows and mats rather than sitting up in chairs. It is also unlikely that everyone was sitting on one side of the table. Reclining was the usual posture at a meal in biblical times. When not eating, people sat upright with legs crossed.

The amount of furniture found in the rest of the room or rooms depended on the family's wealth and preference. Generally a chest stood in a corner to hold a variety of provisions.

Most beds (thick mattresses, straw mats or animal skins usually served the purpose) were rolled up each morning and stored along a wall. However, at the time of Christ bedsteads were becoming popular for those who could afford them. Blankets were easy to keep track of since most people merely slept in their street clothes, possibly pulling an extra tunic over themselves when the air turned chilly.

Pillows, often covered with goatskin and stuffed with wool or feathers, cushioned sleepers' heads. Jesus used such a pillow when He slept in a boat (Mark. 4:38). The cushion must have been comfortable, for He slept during the raging storm.

Sometimes carpets covered the floor and occasionally a divan stood against the wall. Several jars, pitchers and bowls lined the low ledges on the walls, storing foods, medicinal substances and other supplies.

Most of these descriptions cover an average to poor income family. The more prosperous added a room or two. Floors were probably stone and had more expensive carpets, brass pots and possibly an extra divan. However, most people were of limited income. Some of the homes described in the New Testament were elaborate since Jesus had wealthy followers as well as those of modest income and beggars.   ■

OPEN COURTYARDS □ The courtyard was a favorite part of

a house. Its size and appearance depended, of course, on the fam-

ily's financial condition. In larger homes the courtyard was surrounded by the house on three sides, but the more common one-room homes had a small yard. Here was the center of activity for practically every Jewish family.

Some yards were tiled and decorated with shrubs, flowers or even trees, and possibly a cistern to catch rainwater, although most of the family's water had to be carried from a nearby well or river. Water was piped into a few of the better homes and sewers were constructed in large cities

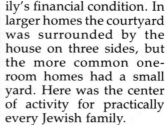

Water, even today, is frequently transported by means of skin or rubber bags strapped to the back of a donkey.   TW

Several ancient olive trees still stand in the Garden of Gethsemane, the site where Jesus was betrayed. This lovely garden is nestled at the foot of the Mount of Olives.

TW

such as Jerusalem and Caesarea. The extensive sewer system at Caesarea by the Sea was a credit to Roman engineering.

Gardens were seldom grown at home. Except for a few plants, serious gardening which produced much of a city's food was done outside the city walls in plots like the garden next to the tomb of Jesus (John 20:15). Christ was betrayed in a garden of olive trees outside the walls of the city near the Brook of Kidron (John 18:1). That garden evidently was fenced in with stones.

The yard was often used for meal preparation. Family celebrations were held there; relatives and friends would bring musical instruments and play, dance, sing and eat together. ■

HOSPITALITY □ Whenever visitors entered a house they were treated with great warmth. Hospitality was at the heart of Jewish living and carried over into primitive Christianity. This doesn't suggest that some Jews were not rude or even hostile, but the basic attitude was one of open generosity. Jesus taught His followers to open their homes even to the poor and the handicapped (Luke 14:13). Jewish homes were friendly, sharing places. In spite of unprincipled people who plotted to exploit such openness, generous hospitality was part of the fabric of both the Jewish faith and the teaching of Jesus Christ.

If a total stranger stopped at the door, he was treated as a friend and fed, lodged, protected, and clothed if necessary. The Greek word for hospitality means a lover of strangers (Rom. 12:13; Titus 1:8; 1 Pet. 4:9). A breach of hospitality was considered a pagan act (Luke 16:19–25). This attitude carried over into the Christian faith so strongly that three short books in the Bible address this subject: Philemon, 2 and 3 John.

One notable act of hospitality was the washing of guests' feet. In wealthier homes a servant performed the task, while among the common people the host's wife washed feet. Jesus gave this function spiritual significance (John 13:3–16). Widows who washed feet were considered of special importance (1 Tim. 5:10). Jews always took their sandals off when entering a house. This kept dirt out of the house and also prepared the guest to have his feet washed by his host (Luke 7:38, 44). Footwashing was a tradition from very ancient times.   ■

VILLAGES, TOWNS AND CITIES □ Not many homes were

isolated. Most were grouped around springs or wells to form the many towns and villages of Israel. During the time of Christ, there were 240 towns in Galilee.

Villages were small and usually had no synagogues, courts or judges. Nazareth and Nain were towns, while Bethlehem and

Emmaus were villages. In post-New Testament times, Jewish law stated a wife was not obligated to follow her husband if he moved from a town to a village, or vice versa, because her lifestyle would change so drastically. A village offered fresh air, a garden and greater privacy. A town offered more consumer goods and social activities.

A community surrounded by a wall was usually defined as a city. Entry to the city was afforded by various large doorways, or gates. The busiest places of a city were

The busiest part of any village was at the gates. Today a bustling scene of commerce is at the Damascus Gate to the Old City of Jerusalem.   TW

its gates. They served as marketplaces and trade centers (e.g., Sheep Gate or Fish Gate of Jerusalem). Gossip was exchanged and day laborers were hired at the gates. At night these gates were closed and guarded carefully.   ■

LIFE IN TENTS □ One of the richest descriptions of the incarnation tells us that the Word became flesh and pitched His tent among us (John 1:14). The Greek word *skēnóō*, which is translated "dwell," had a deep meaning rooted in Israel's wilderness experience.

During the time of the patriarchs, they often lived in tents as they sought grazing lands for their flocks and herds. During Israel's wilderness wanderings, they even built their place of worship inside the temporary walls of a tent-like tabernacle.

Generally the word "tent" meant temporary to the Jew as it does to us. They would use one for a while but eventually hope to return to something permanent. While a major part of a shepherd's life may have been nomadic, for most, living in a tent would have been as undesirable as it would be for us.

The Jew of Christ's day saw life as only a temporary stay with a permanent home awaiting after death. Peter applies this imagery when he describes his life, equating his body with a tent (2 Pet. 1:13). He knows he will be moving on.

With almost artistic use of language, Paul contrasts a tent and a permanent building (2 Cor. 5:1–4). He assures the believer that if

The entire nation of Israel lived in tents at one time as they wandered in the deserts.
TW

the tent he lives in is destroyed, he has a building made by God
waiting for him.   ∎

EARLY TENTS □ The Israelites were not naturally nomads or
tent dwellers. From their earliest history we find them a mixture of
both. From before Abraham some of them were dependent on tents.
In fact, Jabal, who lived before the Flood, is called "the father of
such as dwell in tents and of such as have cattle" (Gen. 4:20). It is
assumed that he was the first nomad. The text implies that people
did not live in tents before him.

Many generations later Abraham changed the course of history
by leaving the city of Ur of the Chaldeans and pitching a tent (Gen.
12:8). This indicates that ancient peoples did not live in tents and
progress to city life, for archaeological evidence shows Ur was a
large, flourishing city in Abraham's day. His obedience to God
marked him as a nonconformist, in both spirituality and lifestyle
(Heb. 11:9, 10).

Abraham was a wealthy man and his tent and other possessions were probably quite elaborate (Gen. 13:2). He employed a
large complement of herdsmen as did his nephew Lot. Tents of
such wealthy leaders (possibly chiefs or sheiks) were large and often
contained separate rooms. Some families had several tents to accommodate everyone.

Most tents were constructed of animal skins which were sewed
together and stretched over wooden poles. Cords were tied to the
skins and held in the ground with wooden pegs which were
pounded into the ground with mallets (Judg. 4:21).

When compared to our modern homes, the furnishings of an
ancient nomadic tent seem sparse. It held some carpets, cushions,
cooking utensils and a lamp. Food was stored in skins or goat-hair
bags. Every item was compact and light enough to be transported
on a donkey's back. When a nomad pitched his tent, he required
two things of the site: shade from the hot sun and water for his
people and animals.   ∎

THE WILDERNESS WANDERINGS □ The patriarch's luxurious tent life ceased when Israel, in the midst of famine moved
into Egypt because of God's provision through Joseph. During the
ensuing centuries, they were reduced to slavery.

When Moses led the Israelites out of Egypt, they commenced
their second stage of tent living, en masse. Their 40 years of wandering before beginning their conquest of Canaan were hard times,
and tent living was a meager existence. Their nomadic existence
came to an end when the land was apportioned to the tribes (Josh.
15).

Tent life provided a rich part of Israel's spiritual heritage. Their
tabernacle in the wilderness, the "tent of meeting" (Ex. 26), was
built according to God's specific instructions from exotic materials,

Goat hair is good material for tents, for when exposed to rain, the goat hairs swell, creating a less porous and more insular shelter for those living inside. This Bedouin tent-dweller family lives in Jordan, several hours from Amman.   TW

including woven goat's hair, sea-cow skins and ram skins dyed red (Ex. 36:14–19). Only after King David realized the ark of God should not dwell in a tent (while the king lived in a palace of cedar—2 Sam. 7:1–11) were steps taken to gather materials for constructing a permanent temple.

After Israel occupied the land some people continued to live in tents while most had shifted to permanent dwellings, but tents remained a part of Israel's spiritual imagery. When the psalmist thought of going to be with God, he spoke of dwelling in God's tent forever (Ps. 61:4; 78:60). Eliphaz spoke of God's judgment by saying that he would tear up the cords of a man's tent (Job 4:21, NIV).

The Rechabites were a unique group who rejected prosperous living and chose to live in tents and drink no wine as an act of protest (Jer. 35). They desired to regain the spiritual purity of the wilderness. However, during the attacks by Nebuchadnezzar, king of Babylon, the Rechabites sought refuge in the city of Jerusalem. ∎

PAUL THE TENTMAKER □ In New Testament times tents were still being used by some pastoral nomads and keepers of livestock, and in traveling and for festivals and special occasions. However, the great majority of the population lived in houses.

There obviously was enough need for tents to keep Paul, Aquila and Priscilla busy making them (Acts 18:3). This trade supplemented their income while the apostle preached the gospel.

The exact meaning of the word "tentmaker" remains a little unclear. It actually means "leather-worker," so Paul may have made more than tents. Paul had come from Tarsus of Cilicia which was famous for its goat-hair cloth called *cilicium*. The apostle may not have been a tanner who made the cloth and the leather but merely a craftsman working with them. Being a tanner would have made him unclean because of frequent contact with animal carcasses. His job would have been to sew tents out of *cilicium.*

In Paul's famous discussion of the thorn that would not go away, he uses the tent metaphor as he speaks of the sufficient grace of God. The apostle brags about his weaknesses so that Christ's power could spread its tent ("rest") over him (2 Cor. 12:9). Whether he had a common tent in mind or the ancient tabernacle, the concept of tents was part of his thinking. In times of hardship he found comfort in the thought that God could surround him with His tent. The metaphor is lost in the English translation but vivid in the Greek.

Other New Testament writers used the imagery of tents to describe our future hope. One pictured Jesus Christ as the high priest sitting on the right hand of God in the tabernacle, or tent, "which the Lord pitched" (Heb. 8:2). The one who sits on the throne will "spread his tent" over His people (Rev. 7:15, NIV).

To the Jewish mind the word tent signified protection, comfort and hope. This is why the Scriptures so often equate God's presence with a tent.   ∎

CHAPTER 2

FAMILY AT THE CENTER

Throughout Bible history the family was held in high esteem and its strength was at the heart of Israel's survival and success. The normal setting for most was a household complete with a husband, a wife and some children.

When Paul wanted a warm, friendly word to describe the special relationship Christians had, he called them members of the "household of faith" (Gal. 6:10). "Household" conjured up feelings of security, acceptance and love.

This is not to say that Israelite homes fit the ideal. In Scripture we see the variety of extremes and abuses that exists seemingly in every society. We see polygamy, parent-child estrangement and sibling rivalry at its worst. However, these exceptions do not distort the rule. Over the centuries the family was usually well-defined, stable and vibrant.

In the family of Jesus we find parents who are caring and tender even under the most difficult conditions. In the story of the prodigal son, we discover one of pressure, conflict, and forgiveness. It would be easy for most families to identify with the feelings portrayed in either case.

During the first century the family was undergoing several changes in attitudes. (The Jewish family had faced the trials of change many times before.) Greek and Roman influences disrupted many traditional values. Often parent and child found themselves in disagreement over cosmetics, clothing styles, athletic events, intermarriage, religious practices and a host of other issues.

The orthodox Israelite was having trouble maintaining his system in a "modern" world. Successive occupations by a series of foreign armies bombarded his sense of values. In addition, improved travel and communication increased the mobility of new ideas. Many merchants, soldiers, laborers, philosophers, drifters and prophets were moving up and down the Roman highways.

Into these troubled waters came Jesus Christ, whose ideas about the family and society, about women, divorce, forgiveness and children were startling to both the narrow-minded and the liberal. Jesus called people back to the best and foundational values of family, and forward to more compassionate understanding of the individual. A person's preconceived notions had to die if superior principles were to live and reign.

His disciples were surprised to find Him conversing with a

woman at the well (John 4:27). His welcoming attitude toward children was in distinct contrast to the desire of the disciples to dismiss them (Mark 10:13). Jesus' stands concerning forgiveness (Matt. 18:22) and divorce were markedly different from what most were used to (Matt. 19:8).

The choice of following Jesus Christ would bring new pressures on some families, just as He said it would. One brother would believe while another rejected the Son of God. Persecution would splinter families. Standing for Christ and righteousness could mean the loss of one's job. But central to this revolutionary faith was the sanctity of the family.

THE HUSBAND/FATHER □ A Jewish family in the first century was not necessarily a tranquil cove of contented souls. Family tensions were normal. However, overall, the family remained the foundational support of the Jewish community.

A husband and father was considered by most families as a compassionate leader, though a few men saw themselves as ruling despots to whom everyone must bow. However, most Jews loved their fathers and felt a deep, sincere allegiance to them. A common Jewish expression for death was to go and sleep with one's fathers (1 Kings 2:10). The thought was no doubt appealing to them.

Discipline and respect were due the head of a home. In fact, the Hebrew word for husband was *baal*, or lord. He had the option to exercise absolute authority in his household. He could divorce his wife at his pleasure, though she had no such easy privilege (Deut. 24:1).

Fathers worked in the fields along with their families. This family harvests wheat near Bethlehem.
TW

Despite his exalted status the husband was not to act as a despot. The apostle Paul reminded fathers to avoid heavy-handedness (Eph. 6:4). While a man could have been a dictator to his wife, God's principles of love would lead him to release her to be her own type of woman (Prov. 31).

The frequent picture we see of fathers in the New Testament is of those who love their families. The story of Joseph, father of Jesus, is one of long-suffering and kindness (Matt. 1:18–20); he was loving and protective in the face of circumstances nearly impossible to comprehend. The father of the prodigal son (Luke 15) was a man who let his son make wrong decisions, then, without rancor welcomed him back without hesitation. The epileptic son was brought to Jesus by a father who had too often seen him fall into the fire (Matt. 17:15). His love for his child was rewarded.

The Jewish concept of a caring father related directly to their picture of God. They saw God as firm, fair and compassionate. Jesus addressed God as Abba (Mark 14:36), which corresponds to our "papa" or "daddy," one of a child's first words. It reflects respect, intimacy, affection and trust. Paul continued the theme by saying our sonship allows *us* to call God papa (Rom. 8:15; Gal. 4:6). The word gives us a better understanding of God and first-century fatherhood.

The head of a home was expected to supply the needs of his family. If he was neglectful, he was considered worse than pagan (1 Tim. 5:8) unless he was physically incapable. He also bore the main responsibility for his children's education and was obligated to make sure his sons learned a trade. This often required the direct involvement of the father.

In the normal activities of life a father conveyed his religious, political and social values to his children. As they ate in the home, worked in the field, repaired roofs or walked to the lake, his outlook on life was easily and naturally communicated to his family.

It would be a mistake to imagine the first-century family as mechanical and unloving in their relationships. While not all spouses loved each other, many did and such a relationship was expected (Eph. 5:25; Titus 2:4). And when love between child and parent was at low ebb, respect and honor were still expected to remain firm (Ex. 20:12; Eph. 6:1).

When changes came to their society, as changes invariably do, some Jewish men expressed their insecurities. These few saw certain freedoms exercised by Roman and Greek wives and feared the same might occur with their wives, whom they considered as mere property. (They had twisted Ex. 20:17 to mean that their wives were like houses or oxen.)

Husbands, as always, varied in character. Many of them were good men who would lead a family well. As in all ages, how these duties were carried out depended much on their personalities and character.   ■

THE WIFE/MOTHER □ A Hebrew woman had been trained from childhood to become a wife and a mother. During most ages her life purpose and fulfillment depended on her success in that role. Consequently, she learned to cook, sew, tend children and work in the field so that she could be the best possible wife.

The amount of freedom and creative self-expression she could employ as a wife depended partially on her own initiative as well as her husband's disposition. Some wives were totally involved in domestic duties, while others were outgoing self-starters who made waves in the waters of society.

The woman of Proverbs 31 illustrates the latter type. The woman described here is far from docile. Even by our present standards she was a wife who uniquely expressed her personality and pursued her opportunities. This exalted wife managed servants in her home, carried on profitable trade and cared for the poor and needy. She even dealt in real estate.

While some wives functioned only within the realm of the family, this was not by divine commission. Many of the limitations placed on wives were constructed by dictatorial husbands and by some women who welcomed them.

In biblical society wives were not always given equal treatment with men. If a wife committed adultery, her husband could bring charges against her (Num. 5:12ff.). However, if he committed adultery, it appears she had little legal recourse. If a husband chose to divorce his wife for any cause, he could merely issue her a bill of divorcement (Deut. 24:1). According to certain rabbis, food or an untidy home were just grounds for divorce. However, the wife could not instigate such action. Jesus restored equality by refuting a husband's right to do this (Matt. 19:9).

Because of her closeness to the children, a mother was usually loved greatly by her offspring. Some of the most touching stories in the Bible center on the affection and understanding between mother and child. This explains the conversations at the Cana wedding (John 2). Mary asked her son for a favor and He balked at the suggestion, but without another word she turned to the servants and in effect said, "Do whatever my son says; he'll take care of it." It seems she assumed her son would not disappoint His mother.

New Testament teaching maintained the high dignity of a woman and her work. At the time her basic, but not sole, function was still within the home. Paul reminded women that taking good care of their homes would bring honor to God (Titus 2:5) as much as anything a church officer could accomplish.   ∎

CHILDREN □ Couples desired children and considered them a status symbol. Those who did not have them were treated with pity and some suspicion. Why had God not blessed them with offspring? Childlessness was assumed as the woman's fault, so a barren woman was looked on as incomplete and somehow out of God's favor. Not only did they want children but they continued to feel unfulfilled until they had produced a boy. Therefore, a girl was bound to feel that she was not as special as a son. In fact, some Jews had a prayer in which men thanked God for not making them women.

Divorce was not widespread among Jews in the first century, but when it did occur the mother usually took custody of the girls and the father the sons. In some cases a judge might overrule that tradition.

When their children were born, most parents took seriously their responsibility to train them correctly. The average Jew considered the proper nurturing of a child as an obligation to God and a reflection on his own ability. Many parents succeeded in their goals, though as always, some failed.

During a child's earliest years, the mother met his basic needs of life. As a boy grew older he came under the general instruction of the father. The mother oversaw the daughter's domestic training, while the father made certain his son learned a trade. The rabbis believed a father cursed his son if he failed to teach him a trade.

Most children learned skills and responsibility by performing regular chores. There were animals to care for, gardens to tend, clothing to sew, food to cook. Daily needs required a great deal of time and parents were careful to pass on the skills.

However, life was not dreary. Children kept pets and enjoyed a wide variety of games. They even playacted funerals, weddings, and other ceremonies (Matt. 11:16, 17) in imitation of adult activities. A child was not likely to own many toys but probably had a few made by either the mother or father. Rattles and whistles were plentiful. Some had wooden pull toys with wheels. Children owned several types of balls and made up games with which to use them. They may have had a swing hanging from a tree branch. Dolls were created of cloth or shaped from wood. Some dolls had moveable arms attached from the inside by strings, while others had openings for inserting fingers in the back to control arms and legs. Children also had an assortment of small pots and furniture to accommodate these dolls. Knucklebones may have been similar to our game of jacks. Some children owned clay marbles. From the markings found on ancient pavement stones, it would appear that they played something similar to our hopscotch. Some children also owned hoops (large circles to either roll or turn around their limbs). Often a family owned a board game or two. Chess existed at the time, as well as a dice game.

Children made up athletic events. They often participated in archery and wrestling. Many became excellent with the sling, no doubt emulating David.

We cannot be certain how much they engaged in Greek games. Boxing and a form of field hockey were played, and possibly many Jewish children participated. Gentile nations pursued athletic

Today, as in biblical times, children assist in the family chores. Here children and their mothers haul straw on the backs of donkeys near Heshbon. RI

programs quite seriously as we will see later (see *Athletics*).

Parents took a great deal of pride in their children so they wanted them to mature properly. Parents wanted children badly (Ps. 127:3–5) but were nonetheless willing to discipline them if the occasion warranted (Prov. 22:15). The book of Proverbs testifies to both the concern parents had and the difficulty some faced in training a child. It has never been easy to nurture children, as the account of Cain and Abel shows (Gen. 4:8); however, it is possible by God's grace.

Children could even be put to death by parents (Lev. 20:9, etc.). It appears, though, that this practice was not followed. However, some children may have been sold (Ex. 21:7; Gen. 31:15).

Jewish children grew up in a pluralistic society. They were pulled from several sides and had to choose which lifestyle they would follow. Paul is a good example of a person caught in the middle. The apostle carried two names: To his Jewish friends he was Saul, a respected Hebrew name, yet, his Gentile friends called him Paul, a suitable Greek name.

Timothy as a child experienced this dilemma. His father was Greek but his mother Jewish (Acts 16:1–3). His parents probably could not agree on how to raise their son. Happily, he daily spent more time with his Christian mother.

Children were prized by their parents, but not everyone enjoyed having them around. The disciples displayed this attitude when they tried to brush the children away from Jesus (Luke 18:15–17). Christ, however, welcomed the children and held them up as examples of true faith.

The Bible places strong emphasis on a good start for a child. If parents are dishonest and undependable, too often that influence persists for generations (Ex. 20:5). Consistent, loving training for children was the key to the success of the Jewish family (Prov. 22:6).   ■

RELATIVES □ The closest relatives a child had were his own brothers and sisters. Some siblings got along well, as did James and John, while others' relationships were strained. Such was the case between Jesus and His four half brothers and an unknown number of half sisters (John 7:5; Matt. 13:55); they generally distrusted Jesus, although later they believed He was the Son of God (Acts 1:14). (Catholic theology usually assumes these to be cousins or other relatives.)

During much of Jewish history most families were large, extended families in the same locale. From 586 B.C. a series of deportations and persecutions began scattering the Jews, but most remained in Palestine until the destruction of the temple in A.D. 70 and the expulsion of Jews from Jerusalem in A.D. 135. Despite such hardships the family remained central in Jewish life.

When possible, grandparents made preparations to be self-supporting, but if those plans failed the children were responsible for their support (2 Cor. 12:14).

The closeness of relatives may have accounted for a more stable family, or the stability of family life may have encouraged relatives to remain close together.   ■

WIDOWS □ A family sometimes had to aid in the support of a widowed grandmother. Some widows were extremely poor but others received a considerable inheritance. When a father died, the inheritance normally passed to his eldest son, who in turn was responsible to support his widowed mother. Biblical laws gave stern warnings against anyone who tried to cheat a widow (Ezek. 22:7); God considered himself the defender of each widow (Ps. 68:5).

Nevertheless people did cheat widows. Some of the worst offenders were those who pretended to be the most religious. Jesus bluntly accused the Pharisees of concocting religious schemes to defraud widows of their estates (Mark 12:40). The same Pharisees refused to support their own widowed mothers. Instead they pled "*Corban,*" meaning they had contributed to the temple so the temple should support their parents (Mark 7:11).

In most situations the best thing a widow could do was remarry and thus reduce her vulnerability. If she was childless, her deceased husband's brother was obligated to marry her, and if possible father a son who was to take the name of the deceased husband. This law seems to have endured into the time of Christ (Deut. 25:5–10; Matt. 22:23, 24).

Whatever provisions had been made for widows must have been insufficient or neglected, for the early church had to assume the task of supporting them (Acts 6:1). Unfortunately, this led to abuses and division among the believers.

When Paul told Timothy how best to help the widows, he included some regulations (1 Tim. 5:11): An "official" widow had to be at least 60 years old, have a good reputation and no family to support her. Clearly a family was to view their widowed grandmother's needs as of paramount importance. To reject such responsibility was pagan (James 1:27).

In ancient days Tamar, Judah's daughter-in-law, wore a specific "widow's garment" after her husband died (Gen. 38:14). However, we do not know what the garment was and find no evidence that such a garment was worn during New Testament times. ∎

HOUSEHOLD CHURCHES

□ For most Jews the concept of household was sacred. It constituted their personal domain no matter how humble or extravagant it might have been. When the New Testament Church began, the household maintained its prominence. Many people who came to believe in Christ did so with their entire households. Cornelius' household was quite large and the officer invited all of the members plus his relatives and close friends to hear Peter explain the gospel (Acts 10:7, 24). All of Lydia's household became believers (Acts 16:15) as did the Philippian jailer's household (Acts 16:31–34). If a family was affluent, their "household" also included servants, employees and possibly slaves. Sometimes Christianity divided a household, but nonetheless it was common for an entire family unit to respond favorably to the gospel.

Though it was difficult, the early Christians worked hard to maintain the sanctity of the household. They centered their activities in individual homes whenever it was practical (Acts 2:46). When Paul remembered the few people he had baptized in Corinth, he recalled the household of Stephanas (1 Cor. 1:16). When he wrote to Timothy, he wanted especially to greet the household of Onesiphorus (2 Tim. 4:19). The household church continued for centuries and still exists in many forms today.

Jesus used the familiar term of the householder or father when He taught His disciples about heaven (Luke 13:25). He reminded them that the Householder of heaven would eventually lock the door. Those who had become Christians would be inside the household of God (Gal. 6:10; Eph. 2:19). Few terms could have better described the relationship between God's people. ∎

DEDICATION TO FAMILIES

□ Within one generation after the life of Christ, many Jewish and Christian families would be thrown out of their homeland. Many would be tortured and murdered, especially during the fall of Jerusalem in A.D. 70 and the persecutions under Nero. It would be difficult to maintain family unity under such horrendous circumstances. In the shadow of these and other pressures early Christian teachers gave needed instruction to guide families. Men were reaffirmed as leaders of the home (Eph. 5:22); husbands and wives were reminded to love each other (Titus 2:5; Eph. 5:25); children were exhorted to obey their parents (Eph. 6:1); parents were instructed to treat their children fairly (Col. 3:21).

In addition, guidance was given to the leaders of the church. They were warned not to become so involved in God's work that they would ignore their families. If they had major problems at home, they would be disqualified from their position as overseers or deacons in the church (1 Tim. 3:4, 5, 12).

The principles given by Christ were crucial in strengthening the family; love, acceptance, patience and forgiveness made kind parents and respectful children.   ■

CHAPTER 3

FOOD AND DRINK

The Jewish lifestyle was not a stereotype, and by the first century there were many ways for a family to gather their food. Gardens were common but often could not supply all of a family's needs. Families often kept small livestock or some form of fowl, and a fruit tree or a small vineyard. When possible they supplemented their larder by buying from or trading with merchants and farmers. Fish, grain, fruit and other commodities could easily be acquired. For those who could afford them, other imported delicacies were available. The large amount of commerce in those days shows us that even 2,000 years ago people liked to add variety to their basic diets.

Jewish food laws dictated what they could eat and what they had to reject. Strict Jews often tried to follow these laws with extreme exactness.

However, the dietary laws of the Old Testament took a serious blow from the teachings of Jesus (Mark 7:14–23). And after Peter testified of his vision of the sheet lowered from heaven (Acts 10:9–16; 11:1–10), Christians had new freedom in their selection of food,

Since fish was a regular part of the Jews' diet, fishing was a viable industry. These fishermen, moored near the shore of the Sea of Galilee, work on repairing their nets after a catch.
CD

although this new liberty was a stumbling block to many Jewish believers who felt strongly tied to their heritage.

Good food and drink was considered one of the great joys of life. While some of the religious practiced an austere, ascetic lifestyle, they were in the minority. Even Jesus appreciated a hearty meal, a feast or a party. His critics did not approve of this attitude, but they did not deter Him (Matt. 11:19; Luke 7:34).

Fish, fruit, meat and poultry are still sold in abundance at the Mahane Yehuda Market just off Jaffa Road in Jerusalem. It is an especially interesting and colorful place to visit on a Friday before the start of the Sabbath. TW

The following provide a quick look at some of the more common or significant foods consumed by the people of the Bible.

SALT □ Salt was used in the Jewish diet not only for flavor but to help preserve food due to the absence of refrigeration.

Seasoning and preservation were not the only uses for salt, but they were primary. The Bible commands that salt be included in the cereal and burnt offerings (Lev. 2:13; Ezek. 43:24). Salt was also rubbed on newborn babies (Ezek. 16:4); some think it had genuine medicinal purpose but others believe it was related to superstition. This is still practiced by some Arabs who consider it antiseptic.

One unusual use of salt in the Old Testament remains unsolved. Did Abimelech really spread salt on the earth at Shechem? (Judg. 9:45). If so, he would have ruined the ground for farming. There are precedents for this in the history of war; however, another possibility is that this is a figure of speech, which actually means he devastated the area.

Food without salt tended, as now, to be bland

Salt from the Dead Sea encrusts the rocks, twigs and fences along its shore. The Dead (or "Salt") Sea lies 1286 feet below sea level, and its water, which is about 25 percent salt and other minerals, is a rich source of sodium, calcium, potash, and other salts. TW

The Sea of Galilee was a major source of freshwater fish. These modern Israelis man their small fishing boat near Tiberias, on the western shore.
TW

and tasteless. Salt therefore was added to bread and was sprinkled over boiling meat. In addition to salt, the people seasoned food with mustard, mint, cumin, anise and coriander seed, as well as other substances. We find no use of pepper in the Bible, though it could have been imported from India.

Israelites could have secured salt from several sources, but the most obvious source was inside their own country. The Dead Sea offered much salt merely for the harvesting.

Jesus' profound truths were often explained by illustrating from everyday experiences. Because salt was familiar to adult and child, He used it often to clarify a teaching (Matt. 5:13; Mark 9:50; Luke 14:34, 35).

Christ's statement about salt losing its flavor (Luke 14) raises some fascinating questions which are not easily answered. For instance, how does salt lose its flavor or tang? Under normal conditions it doesn't. There are cases, though unlikely explanations in this case, where chemicals have been added or unusual storage procedures (such as adding gypsum) have been employed. Jesus may not have been speaking of such processes at all, so there may be no need to find a historical precedent. Christ may simply have meant, "What good is salt without flavor?" (Eugene Deatrick, *The Biblical Archaeologist*, Vol. XXV, argues for chemical change). There certainly is no practical way to restore flavor to salt. Therefore, Jesus was probably using a figure of speech. Whatever the case, if salt had lost its flavor, it was no longer fit for the manure pile (Luke 14:35). Salt, in small amounts, was sometimes added to dunghills in Egypt and Palestine, presumably to slow fermentation. "Dead" salt would have no effect. Consequently, the owner might as well dump the salt in the street and let people walk on it (Matt. 5:13). Jesus may also have been referring to rooftops where salt was added to the soil there to harden the surface and thus be resistant to leaks.

Paul alluded to salt's seasoning function when he wrote to the church at Colosse and told them to season their speech with salt (Col. 4:6). This figure of speech would cause his readers to picture their mothers sprinkling salt into bread dough or on meat and to recall how delightful the finished product tasted. ∎

FISH □ Through the use of salt, fish could be cleaned, dried and sold across the country. *Muries* was a popular salt seafood prepared in Palestine and sold as far away as Rome. The term *muries* is too broadly used to distinguish if the word refers to shellfish, sea mammals or crustaceans, although these would have been prohibited by Jewish dietary laws.

One of the most plentiful fish in the Sea of Galilee is the *musht*, or Saint Peter's Fish, served here at a restaurant in Tiberias on the western shore.

TW

The Sea of Galilee was a major source of fish, as were the Mediterranean Sea and the Jordan River. The Jews ate a wide variety of fish, but the law forbade the eating of any fish without scales (Lev. 11:9–12). Thus catfish, eel, sharks, rays and lampreys were off-limits. In their zeal some rabbis prohibited putting salted fish in water over the Sabbath because the fish would begin to de-salt, and that would constitute work.

Fish were so plentiful in Palestine that one gate in Jerusalem was named the Fish Gate. This was located near the flourishing fish market. Since the average person could afford little meat, fish was a regular part of his diet.

While there are many references to pearls in the New Testament (Matt. 7:6; 13:45, 46), it is unlikely that many Jews ate oysters, for shellfish were forbidden under Old Testament law (Lev. 11:9–12), probably because of the difficulty in keeping them fresh. By New Testament times Gentiles in Palestine were eating them and possibly some Jews were also.

Roasting on an open fire was a common way to cook fish and we do know Jesus prepared fish in this manner (John 21:9). The tiny sardine type of fish caught in the Sea of Galilee, which was used to feed the multitudes, was widely sold (Matt. 14:17; 15:36).

Possibly seven of Jesus' disciples were fishermen (Peter, Andrew, Philip, James, John, Thomas, Nathanael). This fact, plus the people's frequent use of fish in their diet, led Jesus to speak often of fish in His teaching. Christ's audiences would have understood the thoughtfulness of a father giving a fish to his son (Luke 11:11). This was to furnish good, nutritious food. A snake would have been insulting, as well as dangerous.

Several of Jesus' miracles involved fish. One of His most spectacular miracles was the coin found in the fish's mouth (Matt. 17:27); Peter caught the fish with a hook, though nets were normally used in commercial fishing. Twice Jesus fed multitudes with fish (Matt. 14:15ff. and Matt. 15:38). These fish were the small sardines and were accompanied by barley bread eaten usually by the poorer

This remarkable mosaic, 1600 years old but still brilliant, was found on the floor of the Church of the Multiplication of Loaves and Fishes at Tabgha, about eight miles north of Tiberias. It is the traditional site of Jesus' feeding of the multitudes and depicts the fish and loaves of bread which He used.   TW

classes. We are not certain if these were the boy's lunch or if he was an enterprising young vendor (Lenski, John 6:9).   ■

HONEY □ One of the favorites among Jewish foods, honey had a number of excellent uses. Besides being used as a medicine, the sweet liquid was used in food as a sweetener. As a treat honey often appeared in cakes or other rich pastries (Ex. 16:31).

In most cases in the Scriptures the word honey represents the product of bees, but sometimes refers to a sweet nectar made from grapes and dates. These were probably the honey exported as trade.

We have no idea how many bees existed in Israel at the time of the Exodus, but we do know that it was described as a land "flowing with milk and honey" (Ex. 3:8), although this may have been only a figure of speech. Since the land did not literally flow with milk, there may not have been honey dripping from trees either. Nonetheless it was a rich, prosperous land.

Most of Palestine's honey came from wild bees, but domestic bees were certainly possible (2 Chron. 31:5). Today many domestic bee colonies are kept in Israel.

Since honey was widely appreciated in Israel, we can see why the writers of the Psalms (19:10) and of Proverbs (16:24; 24:13) used it as an illustration. The reader readily understands when he reads that the righteousness of God is sweeter than honey or the honey-comb.

John the Baptist used honey as well as locusts to fill his empty stomach (Matt. 3:4; Mark 1:6).

Jesus probably ate honey often in one form or another. Some Scripture versions indicate He had honey with His fish after the resurrection (Luke 24:42). However, the word "honeycomb" does not appear in the better manuscripts (Geldenhuys, Lenski, Robertson).   ■

FIGS □ The fig was one of the best-liked and most easily available fruits during the time of Christ. The succulent fruit was cultivated by farmers but also grew wild across the countryside. Because of their taste, they were sometimes eaten at the end of the meal as a dessert. The fig tree's leaves furnished clothing for Adam and Eve (Gen. 3:7). The tree which Zacchaeus climbed was actually a fig-mulberry (Luke 19:4).

Figs were eaten in several forms: fresh, dried like raisins or fermented into wine. Abigail gave 200 cakes of figs to David (1 Sam. 25:18). These presumably were figs pressed together.

A fig tree can grow to 30 feet tall and because of its sprawling branches offers comfortable shade. They were frequently planted in the corners of vineyards for shade. A person was considered well off if he could rest under the shade of a fig tree (John 1:48).

When the fig trees in Israel fared poorly, a large portion of the economy suffered (Hab. 3:17).

The presence of fig trees made easy object lessons. When James wrote that fig trees do not give olives and grapevines do not pro-duce figs (James 3:12), his readers could readily picture the small, pear-shaped fig.

Jesus spoke of fertilizing a fig tree by digging around its roots and filling in dung (Luke 13:8). He implied that a tree would likely be barren if it had been neglected, but if it continued to bear no fruit after proper care, it should be cut down and replaced.

The fig trees in Palestine bud in February, give leaves in April and produce ripe figs in May and June. A second crop develops in August and September. Jesus used this cycle to teach the parable of the fig tree (Luke 21:29, 30). He said in effect that as the coming of summer could be predicted by certain signs, so also could the coming of the Kingdom be expected by observing certain events.

There may be no perfect explanation of why Jesus withered the fig tree (Matt. 21:19–21) on the Mount of Olives at Passover time. Jesus and His disciples passed a fruitless fig tree growing independently by the road and Jesus caused it to wither by speak-ing to it. The most plausible explanation is that Jesus used the

This ancient olive press near the Galilean town of Capernaum shows the rotating stone used to crush the olives and the trenched stone (standing, in back) through which the squeezed oil was collected for usage.   TW

incident as a parable to show that Israel's fruitlessness would be punished. This was a common teaching technique among the prophets. ∎

OLIVES □ Olive oil was an all-purpose product which could be found in practically every home in Israel for cooking, bathing, curing an illness or lighting (in a lamp).

Olives could be eaten whole, but more often they were crushed for their oil. The oil was added to salads or used in frying. When bread was baked, oil was kneaded into the dough and spread on the pan.

Olive trees were plentiful and the Mount of Olives, where Jesus spoke, was covered with them (Matt. 24:3). These slow-growing trees might take 15 years to begin producing, but once they started they could grow olives for hundreds of years. They needed little water and thrived on the rocky hillsides of Israel.

The need for wood may have led to the destruction of many olive trees over the centuries. From the number of ancient stone olive presses found in Palestine, it would appear that there once were many more trees.

Olive trees have always been plentiful in Palestine, and were flourishing even before the conquest under Joshua. This grove, in the fertile Jezreel Valley, is typical. The olive tree is approximately the size of an apple tree and often survives for hundreds of years.   TW

Paul used the olive branch and tree as an illustration of God grafting Gentiles into Israel (Rom. 11:17, 24). The analogy does not find its exact counterpart in the cultivating of olive trees. Although it was possible to graft young olive branches into an old tree, it was not widely done. However, the reader could easily get the point. Gentiles were once nonbelievers and consequently not part of the tree. Now they believed and God had grafted them in. This was uncommon among olive trees and unheard of among men, except by the grace of God.   ■

LOCUSTS □ The ancient recipe for cooking locusts was as follows: Collect a panful of locusts (they look much like grasshoppers and are related to cockroaches and katydids) and pull off the wings, legs and heads. Depending on the eater's tastes, they can be stewed, roasted or boiled. If the eater prefers, they can be eaten raw or dried. They also can be covered with honey. When cooked in salt water they taste like shrimp. Locusts may also be ground to powder and added to bread dough for flavor.

John the Baptist enjoyed locusts (Matt. 3:4) as do many people in Palestine today.

Locusts are frequently associated with destruction, for they can strip a tree of its leaves in a few minutes. When faced with crossing a river, they have been known to bridge it with their bodies and walk across. The prophet Joel (1:1–12) wrote of their merciless destruction as had Moses centuries before (Ex. 10:15). In mass movements they are capable of darkening the sky.   ■

MILK □ Cows, sheep, goats and camels were the primary sources of milk for drinking in Israel.

One of the common methods of serving milk was to curdle it. The milk was cultured to make a food similar to yogurt, thus making refrigeration unnecessary. This Kefir is still sold, even in American health food stores, and those who drink it consider it highly nutritious. This was probably the same drink Abraham served to the visiting angels (Gen. 18:8), and Jael served to Sisera before murdering him (Judg. 4:19).

The promise of a land flowing with milk and honey (Ex. 3:8) suggested a place of good grazing for the milk-producing livestock.

It was unlawful to boil a kid in its mother's milk (Deut. 14:21), a practice associated with the sacrifices of the Canaanites.

Cheese was also popular during Bible times, but the word is difficult to translate. In some cases it really means curdled milk. ∎

EGGS □ Though seldom mentioned in the Bible, eggs were a common food. They were collected from the nests of wild fowl since early times and from domestic birds starting around 500 B.C. Chickens were plentiful by the time of Christ (Matt. 23:37; Mark 13:35).

There were several ways to prepare and serve eggs, including boiling and frying. Some people cooked fish under a layer of egg.

Jesus referred to an egg while discussing the generous nature of God as our Father (Luke 11:12).   ∎

DATES □ This delicious fruit frequently found its way into the Jewish diet as a wine, honey, syrup, or compressed cakes. Some groups ate dates as a primary food source.

The area around Jericho was famous for producing dates. The

Jericho is set in a broad and spacious valley near the Dead Sea and the Mountains of Moab in the Transjordan Valley. Wide tracts of land are covered with date palms, and from this Jericho became known as the "City of Palms." Jericho was the first city to be taken by the tribes of Israel (Josh. 6).   TW crop was dried and exported to other nations.

As with many other foods, dates are not mentioned in the Bible; however, it is likely that Jesus ate them often.   ■

Dates on a date palm near the Wailing Wall in Jerusalem.   TW

MEATS □ Meat was not abundant in the Jewish diet but was usually reserved for weddings, special feasts and holidays. People avoided slaughtering animals because they produced wool, milk and more animals.

When they did eat meat it could have been beef, goat, lamb or veal. They also enjoyed wild and domestic fowl, such as pigeons, chickens, partridges, quail and geese.

The Pygarg, or ibex, a type of bearded wild goat (Deut. 14:5), was one of the wild game animals available for food. This buck is part of a herd on a game preserve near En Gedi.   TW

Wild game, including deer, ibex, gazelle, and roe deer, may have been on the table of a hunter.

Under the old laws the Jews were not to eat swine, camel, hare or rock badger.
■

VEGETABLES □ During the time of Christ people ate a wide selection of vegetables, including onions, leeks, garlic, lettuce, beets, cucumbers, beans and lentils (pea family). The Jews ate them raw, boiled or mixed with other foods.
■

WINE □ Wine was a favorite beverage in most households. Though usually made from grapes, it also was made from pomegranates, dates, or figs. The first wine each year was made from grapes and later from other bases.

The wine made from grapes was definitely fermented. It is the

normal use of the word in both the Old and New Testaments, for the wine-making process resulted naturally in a fermented drink. Whatever we think about drinking wine, we cannot allow our opinion to alter the facts (*Unger's Bible Dictionary*, etc.).

These ruins near Avdat in the Negev are of a 1500-year-old vat for stomping out grape juice.   JJ

This large vat was where ancient Israelites, while singing and shouting, stomped juice from warm grapes (Isa. 63:3). The squeezed juice ran off into the smaller vat at left and then was permitted to ferment for six weeks.   RI

The Jews produced a red wine but lack of a special name for white wine implies they may have had only red. Many Jews considered wine as a gift from God and some rabbis believed God taught Noah how to make wine. Grapes were brought in from the vineyard and left in the sun which dehydrated them, thus increasing the sugar content by volume. The grapes were then put in a vat and stomped with bare feet (Isa. 63:3). Workers often held onto an overhead rope and sang and shouted as they stepped (Jer. 25:30). The squeezed juice ran off into a smaller vat where it was allowed to ferment for six weeks. The juice was then put into jars (John 2:6) or fresh goatskin flasks (Matt. 9:17).

Jesus showed no hesitation about using the beverage (Matt. 26:29) and even made it (John 2:6ff.). However, its consumption was not universal. John the Baptist did not drink it and Christ was criticized for His practice (Matt. 11:18, 19), although it seems He was criticized for what the Pharisees considered drunkenness, not for the act of drinking.

Despite the general acceptance of wine, many did not handle it well. There are admonitions against its abuse (Eph. 5:18) and frequent stories of drunkenness (Gen. 9:21).

Because wine played such an obvious role in Jewish life, Jesus used wine as a source of illustrations in His teaching (Matt. 9:17).   ■

FRUIT AND NUTS □ A home may have had several fresh fruits

for the family to enjoy. Mulberries, grapes, almonds, pomegranates, pistachio nuts, figs and dates were common. Several varieties of melons were eaten, possibly both the watermelon and the cantaloupe.   ■

GRAIN □ Wheat, rye, barley and millet were staple items. However, these names may not directly correspond to our use of the words. The word corn is used in the King James Version, though it almost certainly was not grown in Israel during Bible times, for corn was a New World grain.   ■

HERBS AND SPICES □ A great deal of seasoning was applied to food. Garlic, mustard, mint and cinnamon are only a few. The Pharisees were careful to tithe of their herbs and spices (Matt. 23:23).   ■

MEALTIME □ Most religious Jews made a practice of giving thanks to God for their meals. It was deeply ingrained in their worship experience. Not only did they pray before they ate, but they were expected to pray afterward (Deut. 8:10). There was no set method for praying and from house to house there was considerable variety. At one home the father would pray, at another the guest would be asked. A third home might have all its members pray in unison.

Some prayers were spontaneous but others were formal and memorized. One of the common prayers still in use today is, "Blessed are Thou, Jehovah our God, King of the world, who causes to come forth bread from the earth."

The Scriptures give many examples of Jesus praying before He ate: at the Last Supper (Matt. 26:26); with the disciples from Emmaus (Luke 24:30). He also prayed before feeding the 5,000 (John 6:11) and the 4,000 (Matt. 15:36). In these cases Jesus was not praying for the miracle but giving thanks for the food. It would appear that this was His mealtime habit. Late in the book of Acts we find Paul continuing this practice (Acts 27:35).

Usually the food was served in the bowl in which it was prepared. Our type of silverware wasn't necessary because they used

Prayer and the reading of prayers continue to be an important part of Jewish life. The goal of Jews the world over is to stand and pray at the Wailing (Western) Wall, the holiest shrine in the Jewish world.
TW

bread in the same way some Westerners sop gravy. Each person tore off a piece from the loaf and dipped it into the dish, thus picking up some food. Eating from common dishes was a sign of friendship. The host would pick out a piece of fish or meat and hand it to his guest as a special gesture of hospitality. There is particular irony in the fact that the person who betrayed Jesus was one who dipped his hand into the same food dish (Matt. 26:23). ∎

WASHING HANDS □ In a society where people ate with their hands, it was especially important that people wash before eating. Not only did they wash before the meal but they also washed afterward to cleanse sticky, oily hands.

One of the debates in the Gospels centered around this simple practice. The Pharisees insisted on elaborate ceremony when someone washed his hands before a meal. According to their regulations water had to be poured on the hands and allowed to run down from the fingers to the wrists. If not, it had to be done again. Water had to be poured from a container no smaller than one and a half eggshells in size. The Pharisees were indignant that Jesus did not wash His hands according to their rules (Luke 11:38) and thus complained about it (Mark 7:5). Jesus attached little importance to their rules (Matt. 15:2), for He recognized the higher law of love for God and man. ∎

THE COOKING PROCESS □ Weather permitting, food was cooked outside the house in the courtyard, thus allowing smoke to

This outdoor oven, still in use today for baking bread, is similar to outdoor ovens used in biblical times.   BAS

escape and keeping cooking odors out of the house.

Cooking fuel varied, but dried dung led the assortment. It is used by peasants in Palestine even today. Wood was scarce and when the average person had some, he was likely to sell it to a wealthy household. Twigs, thorns and grass were often used for fuel. Grass was thrown into ovens to give a fast, hot fire (Matt. 6:30). Charcoal, made from wood, may have been used by Jesus to cook breakfast after His resurrection (John 21:9).

Stoves or ovens were small. They had a wide opening at the front to receive fuel and on top was a large hole where pots were placed. Only one pot at a time could be used. The light, movable stove had small holes in the back to allow air to circulate freely. It could easily be moved outside for cookouts.

Insects, such as flies, fleas and mosquitoes, were a serious problem in the ancient world. If water for cooking or drinking was kept in the house, the mouth of the jar had to be covered. This, however, did not prevent all intrusions. Consequently the people were frequently straining gnats or other tiny creatures out of the water or wine. Jesus' listeners were well acquainted with this practice when He spoke about gnats and camels (Matt. 23:24). ■

CHAPTER 4

KEEPING UP APPEARANCES—
CLOTHING AND COSMETICS

While the people of the ancient world did not enjoy our wide selection of styles and fabrics, it would be a mistake to think of their clothing as drab. Many wore garments with distinctive colors, some with elaborate embroidering. Most clothes were simple and homemade.

Most Jews did not limit themselves to a certain set of clothing, for the influences of the Greeks and Romans shaped what they wore. And despite some strict guidelines in their law, many Jews dressed as they pleased. ∎

Weaving of sheep's wool continues today as it did in biblical times. BAS

BASIC WARDROBE □ The basic wardrobe in first-century Israel, aside from such items as a money bag and extra shawl or shoes, consisted of four or five essential items. They were as follows:

The outer garment. Often termed a cloak, this served as a covering, like a sport coat or jacket. It possibly was little more than a square of fabric with a hole in the middle for the wearer's head. Cloaks could be dyed in any of a variety of vivid colors or stripes and were made from fine linen or a coarser material, depending on the wearer's financial status. A gentleman would not enter the temple without wearing a proper cloak, since to do so would be like our going to church wearing a tee shirt.

A prized garment, the cloak was often the focus of considerable personal pride. When someone fell into financial difficulty, he could surrender his cloak as collateral. However, the cloak had to be returned by nightfall to its original owner, for it was used as a blanket at night. When Jesus made His triumphant entry into Jerusalem, those who lined the streets spread their garments along His pathway as a gesture of honor (Matt. 21:8).

Some outer garments were of high quality and sported fringes along the borders. Later the fringes were moved to the inner garments and finally to the prayer shawls. Initially fringes were on a blue border and were intended to remind the wearer of God's commandments (Num. 15:37–41). As time passed this became an abused practice. Some of the Pharisees enlarged their fringes so everyone would be impressed with their devotion to the commandments. Jesus called this pretentious enlargement putrid (Matt. 23:5).

When Paul wrote to Timothy he asked for some of his cherished personal possessions, including a few parchments and his cloak (2 Tim. 4:13). On cold evenings in a Roman prison, it would prove welcome.

The cloak of the first century became a robe of larger and better material as the wealthy of that day displayed their affluence by the number and quality of their robes (James 5:2), for the average probably had only one simple cloak.

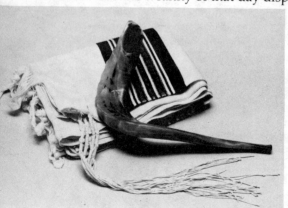

A correct understanding of the outer garment increases our appreciation of what Christ said about it. He told us in Matt. 5:40 that if anyone sued and took one's coat (inner garment),

A shofar resting on a prayer shawl.   KM he should then offer the cloak (outer garment). Interestingly, in Luke 6:29 the sequence is the opposite. He said this despite the fact that the law protected the outer garment (Ex. 22:26, 27). Jesus knew how much the cloak meant as a personal possession, but nevertheless, He taught His followers to surrender theirs voluntarily. Jesus' law of love made "personal rights" secondary to other people's needs and desires.

The temptation to strut around in impressive robes was too much for some to resist. Jesus therefore criticized the religious scribes

Paul's parchments were probably much like these sections of Isaiah from the Dead Sea Scrolls. Parchments were rolled into scrolls rather than folded. CGI

for resorting to ostentatious outer garments (Luke 20:46) in the form of long robes because the wearers looked so good and cared so little for other people.

History's most cruel cloak was no doubt the purple robe placed on Jesus in mockery (John 19:2). Purple indicated royalty, but in Christ's case the crown of thorns and the draped purple robe were the soldier's demonstration of contempt for the Messiah.

Purple was a prized color of the Israelites as it was of the Canaanites before them. The dye which was valued throughout the world was extracted from the murex shellfish (a snail) and manufactured in various shades. Solomon sent to Tyre for men skilled in the making of purple fabrics (2 Chron. 2:7).

Two of the most notable outer garments in the Old Testament were worn by Joseph and Goliath. Joseph's outer garment earned its reputation partly from a mistranslation. Strictly speaking it was not a coat of many colors but rather a robe of large sleeves (Gen. 37:3). The long sleeves indicated that he was too important to do ordinary labor. His brothers, of course, resented this and plotted against him.

The huge jacket worn by Goliath was a coat of mail, possibly weighing 125 pounds (1 Sam. 17:5). This was an early form of armor, containing hundreds of metal scales sewn together to deflect weapons. Two hundred such coats were captured at the battle of Megiddo.

The inner garment. The most basic piece of Jewish clothing was the coat or tunic which functioned as a long shirt, open at the bottom like a dress or nightgown. Like the cloak it was often made from wool or linen.

It is often difficult to distinguish between the outer and inner garment when clothes are mentioned in the Bible. Any discussion of them, therefore, contains a mixture of fact and conjecture.

The tunic could be plain or decorated with beautiful colors and could be embroidered as the outer cloak often was.

Since many people considered their clothing a status symbol, the words of John the Baptist were disturbing; he told the crowds that if any had two inner garments, they should give one away to someone who had none (Luke 3:11). Jesus also felt it was easy to become enslaved by a desire for good clothing. He assured us that if the flowers did not worry about what to wear, neither should we (Matt. 6:28–33).

When Jesus told the story of the rich man and Lazarus (Luke 16:19ff.), it appears He placed special emphasis on the selfish, wealthy man's attire of purple and fine linen, for He usually did not mention a person's clothing. The term purple may have referred to one of several shades ranging from deep violet, deep scarlet or crimson to a deep blue. The man's linen inner garment was woven from Egyptian yellowed flax called *byssus*, so luxurious that the Egyptians named it "woven air."

When the high priest tore his clothes in disgust at Christ, we are not certain which garment he ripped. The word in Mark 14:63 indicates an inner garment, but Matt. 26:65 suggests an outer one; Josephus insists it would have been an inner garment. It is possible that the priest tore both.

The clothing which Jesus had worn and was taken by the soldiers at His crucifixion (John 19:23) was evidently an inner garment (the purple robe had been put on Him and taken off again earlier).

Jesus' inner garment was seamless, and therefore of good quality. It was not extravagant, however, but it was special. The high priest always wore a seamless inner garment. To divide the cloth into four pieces would have meant ruining an excellent garment. The parting or division of the apparel fulfilled Ps. 22:18.

The belt. The loincloth, girdle and belt are probably different forms of the same type of garment. Over the centuries it seems to have changed in size and name but remained identical in function—holding up long clothing to permit ease of movement. Long robes or coats were not good for working vigorously or hurrying through the countryside. In such instances the wearer pulled his clothes above his knees and secured the excess fabric with the loincloth.

Sometimes a loincloth was a shirt which was tied tightly around the waist. Elijah may have made the most famous use of a loincloth when he tightened his up before running to the entrance at Jezreel (1 Kings 18:46).

When a person was in mourning he would use a loincloth made of sackcloth (1 Kings 20:32). A sackcloth was made of goat hair and when worn next to the skin, it practically guaranteed misery to the wearer (Jon. 3:6). Sometimes the sackcloth was worn on top of other clothes.

Belts were popular during the first century. Their most obvious use was to hold loose fitting inner garments close to the body. Most belts were made of cloth fitted and wrapped around the waist. However, wealthy men had silk or leather belts. These often had colorful embroidering and some even sported a gold buckle. The fabric of the belt itself might have been a lively shade.

During the time of Christ belts served practical purposes. Sometimes they held daggers, knives, swords or inkhorns. They also functioned as purses to carry money. When Jesus told His disciples not to stock their belts with gold, silver or copper as they toured preaching (Matt. 10:9), He was referring to the belt or girdle.

This belt is the same item Agabus took from Paul (Acts 21:11) and used to tie his own hands and feet as a sign of future events.

To "gird up one's loins" or gather the loose hem of the robe into the belt became a colloquialism in Israel which indicated hard times. Elisha told one of the children of the prophets to gird up his loins and deliver a message (2 Kings 9:1). In the light of this usage Peter told Christians to gird up the loins of their minds (1 Pet. 1:13).

Headgear. Headdress is rarely mentioned in the Bible, but practically everyone wore some kind of covering. Though we see few pictures of Jesus wearing a covering on His head, it is almost certain that He did.

One of the most popular headdresses was the head-square. Although often white, it came in many colors. Folded in a triangle with a pointed end stretched down the back of the wearer's neck like a scarf, it was held in place by a piece of rope or cord which circled the top of the head. On a hot day it protected the neck from rays of the sun. As with most Jewish clothing this hat had considerable versatility. It could shade the eyes from bright sunlight and quickly be converted into a face mask if a dust storm developed.

Most likely this was the type of headdress Jesus would have worn. He also would have owned a prayer shawl to cover His head in the synagogue. Skull caps, known today as *yarmulkes*, were also worn in the synagogue and probably were optional.

It may be that headdresses were not used by Israelites prior to the Exile, except on special occasions.

Many Jewish women wore a veil which wrapped around the head but was not essentially a headdress. Women of neighboring countries were more fond of headwear.

Headdresses could be of several shapes (including turbans), colors and materials. Except for a few instances, headdresses were of minimal significance in the New Testament writings (1 Cor. 11:15; 1 Tim. 2:9; 1 Pet. 3:3), and in those instances hair seems to be the main issue.

The "kaffiyah," or head-square, is a multi-purpose headgear worn universally throughout the Middle East. It offers protection from the sun, the wind, and blowing sand.

TW

Footwear. Ancient footwear was of two types: sandals and shoes. Sandals were simple, much like modern sandals. The soles were made of a hard material such as palm-bark or rush, and leather straps secured the sole to the wearer's foot. Occasionally people wore socks, but sandals were usually worn on bare feet.

John the Baptist declared himself unworthy to tie the straps on Jesus' sandals (John 1:27). Removing the sandals of a guest was the job of a slave or another lowly figure in the house, or someone humbled himself to assume that role. John was thus saying that by comparison he was lower than such people.

Ancient shoes were similar to our high ankle boots. These were made of soft leather, usually from camel, jackal or hyena hide. It is likely the people wore sandals in good weather and shoes on cold or damp days.

Some shoes were of the hobnail variety. Constructed well with nails they were used for long journeys and may have approximated our hiking boots, although not as well made. Traveling seems to have been their major purpose, and consequently it was forbidden to wear them on the sabbath. Presumably if one wore them he might be tempted to walk farther than he should.

Sandals and shoes play a large role in the Bible. Shoes had to be removed at a sacred occasion or when someone entered a holy place such as the sanctuary of the temple (Ex. 3:5; Acts 7:33). In ancient Israel, Boaz closed the deal by offering the shoe provided by the Kinsman-redeemer (Ruth 4:7, 8). Amos tells us that God's people had become so corrupt that a judge would rule against the poor if he was bribed with a mere pair of shoes (2:6).

When Jesus sent out the 70 disciples, He warned them not to carry many possessions since it was important to move quickly. An extra pair of sandals would only slow them down (Matt. 10:10; Luke 10:4). The sandals on their feet would suffice.

Footwashing was a natural companion to the wearing of sandals. Abraham offered this gesture to the Lord when He appeared at Abraham's tent (Gen. 18:4). Throughout the Bible the act seems to carry a double meaning. In the first case feet were washed as a sign of hospitality and comfort, an appropriate treatment for dirty, sore feet. However, the act of washing sometimes had little to do with physical aid; in this case it was fundamentally an act of reverence and respect.

When the woman washed the feet of Jesus in the home of the Pharisee, she appears to have been majoring in reverence (Luke 7:38). Abigail may have been doing both for David (1 Sam. 25:41), as did widows for believers in the early church (1 Tim. 5:10). By washing the feet of His disciples, Jesus was emphasizing humility and respect, though no doubt their feet needed washing (John 13:4–10).

We have been fairly silent about the apparel worn by women, basically because there appears to be only minimal differences between what men and women wore. Veils were a major difference and some of the clothes may have been more colorful, and some pictures indicate finer sandals on the feet of some ladies. Women wore the same five basic garments as men. But if the distinctions between male and female apparel were subtle, they were nonetheless real. The law forbade men and women to wear the other sex's clothes (Deut. 22:5).

The materials used to make clothing can be divided into two groups: animal and vegetable. The animal materials were mostly wool taken from sheep and goats. Hides and some camel hair also were used. Silk was also used, but because it was brought from the Far East, it was usually too expensive for all but the wealthy.

Flax was the major vegetable source of textiles and it was woven into linen. A limited amount of cotton was introduced into Palestine after the Captivity.

Colorful clothing was possible because of the many dyes ancient people developed. Crimson came from insects, pink from pomegranate, yellow from the saffron crocus, to name a few. The production of dyed textiles became a formidable industry. Archaeologists have found large collections of vats to support this theory. In most cases thread was dyed then woven together into fabric.

Lydia, an early convert to Christianity at Philippi (Acts 16:11–15), sold purple garments. Her name meant "woman from Lydia." This area was noted for its production of purple dye from the murex shellfish found in the Mediterranean.

Some dyers identified themselves by hanging red or blue threads from one ear and possibly a green or pale thread from the other.

One of the most notable clothiers of early Christianity would have been Dorcas (Acts 9:36–41). She was skilled with a loom and used her talents to clothe many needy people.   ■

Perfumes and Incense □ In a hot land which was short on water, such as Israel, perfumes often took the place of a good bath. Consequently after a day of heavy work, a person might rub himself with liquid deodorant to make himself socially acceptable. Even after a bath a healthy application was recommended.

Perfumes and ointments served not only to sweeten body odors but also to soften the skin which, in a hot, dry climate, often dried and cracked. Jewish men and women were concerned for their health, comfort and appearance, so their use of oils and perfumes made the heart glad, which is affirmed by Scripture (Prov. 27:9).

The use of incense as an air freshener had also been developed by the time of Christ. Many homes burned incense to keep the air tolerable as well as hold flies, fleas and mosquitoes at bay. A Jewish home would have been filled with distinct fragrances.

Before going out or hosting company, a lady might oil her skin and then stand by the incense burner. The rising scents would permeate her hair, clothing and skin. Some women hid a small bag of perfume beneath their clothing.

Frankincense and myrrh were considered suitable offerings for God. (Whether this is the reason the magi brought them to Christ is open to question.) Frankincense was used in the tabernacle as part of a mixture of scents (Ex. 30:34–38). It was also used in the meal offering (Lev. 2:15–16). Both frankincense and myrrh are named in the romantic scenes depicted in the Song of Solomon (3:6; 4:6; 4:14, etc.). The reader can almost smell the enchanting fragrances in these passages.

But not every use of fragrant ointment was honorable. The prostitute described in Proverbs perfumed her bed with aromatic myrrh, as well as aloes and cinnamon (7:17).

And Nicodemus mixed myrrh with aloes in order to prepare the body of Christ (John 19:39). This was done not only as a gesture of respect but also to counteract the stench of a decomposing body.

One of the most memorable uses of ointment was the sacrifice made by Mary at Bethany (Matt. 26:6–13; Mark 14:3–9; John 12:1–8). Few perfumes would have been more expensive than her spikenard, taken from pink-blossomed plants in northern India and possibly the Himalaya Mountains.

She took this small alabaster jar full of spikenard, broke the neck to open it and poured the magnificent liquid on the head of Jesus. Apart from the natural greed of Judas, it is no wonder the treasurer was appalled. The amount of spikenard Mary poured out equaled the year's salary of a laborer. To appreciate what was happening, merely imagine your annual income being poured out at one time.

Aloes were one of the many perfumes made from flowers and other plants. Aloes were taken from the lily family and added to myrrh. Some perfumes were made by dipping flowers into hot fats.

Because perfumes, ointments and other cosmetics were so widely used in Bible times, their production was a large industry. A dig at Ugarit has unearthed 1,000 vessels filled with perfumes, indicating a huge business which supplied fragrances to many areas.   ∎

OINTMENTS □ When guests visited, the host might pay them special honor by anointing their heads with oil (Luke 7:46). This could be done at feasts by placing a small, oil-based cone of perfume on the head of the guest. Body heat would slowly melt the cone causing perfume to drip onto the person's clothing (Ps. 23:5).

Even the poor had perfume and ointment in their homes. Bottles, bags, boxes and jars held these valuable liquids and powders.

The most widely used ointments were made from olives, but many other ointments were available, including the two we know best: frankincense and myrrh. These were offered after the birth of

This ointment bottle, unearthed from the Roman city of Cumae, is an example of the fine glass manufactured for use as cosmetics containers.

EHLE

Christ as gifts (Matt. 2:11), and were widely used as medicines and perfumes.

In order to control the market on these products, the merchants tried to keep their origins a secret. Today we know frankincense comes from a shrub and myrrh is extracted from a small tree. The bark of each plant is peeled back in several strips. Just beneath the bark, resting in the crevices, are the gum resins which make these perfumes. Slices in the bark cause the juices to run (evidently trying to heal the wound) and form bulges on the side of the tree or shrub. The bulges or tears harden in position during the next three or four months. Once they are firm, many of the large tears fall to the ground. Harvesters then slice off the remaining lumps and gather those which have fallen. They are transported in bags. Before they are marketed, each is ground into a fine powder. They make excellent perfumes for incense burning. Since most homes probably burned incense, and the price of these perfumes was manageable, they were commonly used. They gave off a minimum of smoke and offered a pleasant aroma.

∎

COSMETICS □ Practically every cosmetic item or practice we have today was available during that era. The Israelites did not have the same love for cosmetics as the Gentiles but they dabbled in much of it.

Some of the women wore lipstick and painted their toenails and fingernails. Face powder was not uncommon and some applied a red or black rouge with a stick. Even eye paint was worn by some. Jezebel's use of cosmetics probably reflected the Phoenecian style and may have made the practice less acceptable (2 Kings 9:30). Both Jeremiah (4:30) and Ezekiel (23:40) spoke of cosmetics in disparaging terms and thus some Jewish ladies possibly felt uncomfortable about using them.

∎

JEWELRY □ When Paul wrote his epistles it seems the believers were unsure as to how a woman was to decorate herself (1 Tim. 2:9). In those times women embellished their hair with combs and hairpins, some of the more elaborate ones having carved figures and even being made of gold (1 Pet. 3:3).

Earrings were worn by women and sometimes by men (Gen. 35:4; Judg. 8:24). Often people wore them purely as decorations, but others believed they held magical powers for protection. Some Jews pierced their ears, though it may have been forbidden under

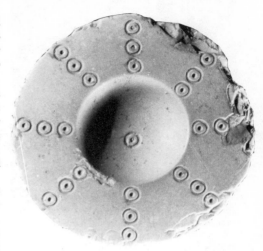

This cosmetic bowl or palette in limestone, from around 700 B.C., was used for the preparation of cosmetics, probably *kohl* for eyeshadow in this case. DM

Jewish law. Nose rings were worn by women in other nations, but Jewish ladies usually rejected them. However, there are cases in the Bible of women wearing rings in their noses (Gen. 24:47; Isa. 3:21). The ring offered to Rebekah by Abraham's servant (Gen. 24:30) was probably a nose ring. Anklets may have been a common piece of jewelry.

It is possible that the pagan emphasis on "lucky" jewelry made Jews and Christians distrustful of ornaments. Egyptians wore large, elaborate necklaces as protection from evil. The Jews carried many pieces of jewelry out of Egypt but were not entirely comfortable with the

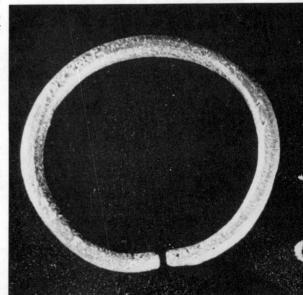

An ankle bracelet. DM

Some women today, as in Bible times, wear rings in their noses. This woman was photographed at the open-air camel market near Beer-sheba. TW

practice (1 Tim. 2:9). Rabbis often criticized the use of extravagant jewelry.

Many Jewish men bedecked themselves in a wide variety of chains, necklaces, rings and bracelets. The gold ring on the prodigal son's hand was a sign of complete acceptance and forgiveness by his father. Archaeologists have unearthed many pieces of fine jewelry dating back to this era. Rings were worn during the time of Christ as a sign of wealth (James 2:2). Many married men wore a ring on the fourth finger of the left hand because they believed a vein ran directly to the heart, which they considered the source of love for their wives. Unger tells us that rings on a man's right hand suggested effeminacy.

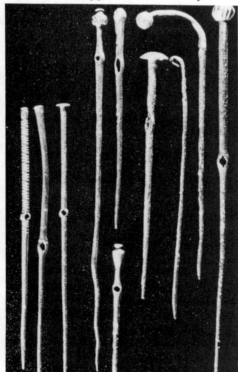

Bracelets were common among both men and women, wealthier people wearing gold ones. Some bracelets could slip over the wrist but others hinged open and were locked on the wrist with a pin. Saul wore bracelets (2 Sam. 1:10).

Necklaces were frequently worn during the time and may lead us to an interesting insight of the parable of the lost coin. A Jewish woman would collect ten coins to make a necklace for her wedding.

Copper or bronze "toggle pins" were used to hold together a common form of garment worn in Syria-Palestine during the Middle Bronze Age. In the Late Bronze Period the eye is nearer the point than the head of the toggle pin. DM

It could be that the woman had ten coins and lost one from her necklace, and so had extra reason to search thoroughly for the missing item (Luke 15:8).

First-century Jews cared for their appearance and used whatever means were available to keep themselves neat. Mirrors of metal and of glass were plentiful. The highly polished metal reflectors may not have reflected a perfect image, but they were accurate enough to be helpful. Paul refers to the dullness of a mirror, its image possibly hindered even further by the normally poor interior light (1 Cor. 13:12).   ■

HAIRSTYLES □ Although of no earthshaking theological significance, it is interesting to ask whether or not Jesus had a beard. Frankly, we don't know. However, there are several circumstantial facts as well as messianic prophecy (Isa. 50:6) which indicate He probably did.

Daniel-Rops says beards were very common among the Jews for centuries. Jeremiah stated that clipped beards were the sign of a defeated people (48:37). Those who served as priests were not to enter the temple with their curly sideburns shaved (Lev. 21:5). Wearing beards was highly acceptable among the Jews, though this may not suggest that Jesus wore a beard. Many men influenced by customs of the Greco-Roman society did not.

We do know also that hairdressers, barbers and masseurs were common during intertestamental and New Testament times, although some of the more devout Jews of the time looked on such practices with suspicion.

Beards, popular in biblical times, are still worn by a great many modern Jews. This man is an agricultural worker on a kibbutz in the northern Galilee area.   TW

Women often wore their hair piled high on the head, but several styles were in vogue. Tight curls were popular as were braiding and plaiting. Some wealthy women controlled their hair with gold nets, and many scented their hair with perfumes. The beautiful lady in the Song of Solomon had her hair woven.

Gray hair was honored in Israel (Prov. 20:29), but then, as now, some preferred the illusion of youth over the honor that came with age. Many people colored their hair. Herod the Great dyed his black. There were also some curious gentlemen who sprinkled gold dust in their hair. Josephus the historian had a low opinion of the men who followed this custom.

Hairstyles among men may have differed considerably during the time of Christ. Long hair was not unknown; slightly long hair, however, may have been more popular. At times men may have tucked it up under their headgear. Ancient statues show us that some men wore their hair in a curled fashion much like our modern permanents.

Baldness was not considered a mark of distinction. Wigs and hairpieces made from both human or animal hair were available.

With so much respect for well-arranged hair, it might have been that Mary unfurled a beautiful hairdo when she wiped the feet of Jesus (Luke 7:38), an act of deep respect and humility.

It was common to anoint or oil a person's hair for several reasons. Oiling was done as a sign of respect for another or as an attempt to beautify oneself. Jesus recommended adding an oily sheen to the hair as a sign of happiness (Matt. 6:17). He saw no merit in looking dull, sad and miserable.

In a society of changing opinions about dress, jewelry and hair, Peter and Paul both found it necessary to offer some guidelines. They feared that too much concern with style and trends could be detrimental to one's spiritual life. Peter was concerned that some women would consider their up-to-date hairdos as a sign of godliness and set that idea straight (1 Pet. 3:3). He did not tell them they could not be stylish anymore, but that godliness comes from the heart and not the hairdresser. Paul agreed wholeheartedly (1 Tim. 2:9) and also expressed a need to distinguish between male and female hairdos (1 Cor. 11:14, 15). Paul's exact meaning is presently unclear because of our inability to correctly understand their culture, but may be determined through further archaeological and historical discoveries.

We have many carvings and images of Egyptians and Assyrians who also depicted Israelite hair and clothing styles.   ∎

CHAPTER 5

THE PRACTICE OF MEDICINE

The medical community in Palestine included highly trained physicians, as well as magicians and charlatans. Thus a patient in need of help could receive anything from first-class assistance to a magic potion or absolute poison. This explains why doctors receive mixed reviews in the New Testament.

WIDESPREAD SICKNESS □ If a person desired to practice medicine, there was ample opportunity. Jesus was continuously met by great hordes of crippled, maimed, blind, diseased, and mentally disturbed and distorted people. Many sicknesses were incurable and highly contagious.

When Jesus visited a city, the people brought their sick friends and relatives (Mark 6:56). They lined the ill in rows in the marketplaces or along the streets. It was a plea for help from a population

The Pool of Bethesda (John 5:2) was a gathering place for many ill and infirm Israelites. Here they waited for the angel to trouble the water, and the first to enter the water thereafter was made whole of whatever disease he had.   TW

with severe physical suffering (Matt. 8:16; Mark 1:34; 6:13; Luke 4:40). Medical knowledge was too limited to keep up with the spreading sicknesses.   ■

LOCAL DOCTORS □ Some people appreciated doctors and paid them respect. Others considered physicians the worst crooks in creation. Because of the doctors' reputations, the rabbis invented proverbs to describe them. One said, "The best among doctors deserves *Gehenna*," or hell. Another warned, "Live not in a city whose chief is a medical man."

Jesus alluded to one well-known proverb concerning doctors. He said people would probably tell him, "Physician, heal thyself" (Luke 4:23). This was a saying not only among the Jews but also the Greeks and Chinese. It skeptically tells the doctor that if his medicine is good, he should use it on himself first; then others might try it.

Another negative remark about doctors in the New Testament is found in Mark 5:26. A lady had been sick for twelve years with a hemorrhage, and the doctors had been unable to stop the bleeding. The Bible tells us she had suffered much at the hands of many physicians who had, despite their inability to cure her, exhausted her funds. Luke, himself a physician, records the same story but omits the apparent criticism of the medical profession.   ■

MEDICAL FEES □ The question of doctor's fees has always been a sore spot. Writers in the Talmud expressed mixed feelings about fees. On one hand they condemned the profession for charging outlandishly; on the other, they warned against using a doctor who charged too little. A famous physician, Umna, refused to charge for his services. He installed a box and allowed patients to deposit in it what they could afford. One rabbi tried to discourage overcharging by saying "Ah, may blessings fall upon the doctor who does not ask too great a fee."   ■

MEDICAL SCHOOLS □ Luke is the most well-known physician in the New Testament (Col. 4:14), but we know nothing about his background or practice. He did travel with Paul, possibly as a missionary doctor caring for members of the team as well as the sick they met.

Extensive training was available and Luke possibly had acquired some formal education. Some scholars argue that Luke's vocabulary in his Gospel and Acts reflects medical training. The most famous medical school of the time was in Alexandria, Egypt, and was founded about 300 B.C. Doctors at the school offered specialized instruction for various diseases. Much of this knowledge was carried into Israel and other countries.

Egyptian medicine was not without its superstitions and folklore. However, many of their remedies are practical and useful even today. The Edwin Smith Surgical Papyrus gives us insight into

Egyptian medical knowledge. This document lists 48 cases of injury, including treatment for 10 possible injuries to the brain, etc. Broken bones were set and a special adhesive plaster cast was applied. Skeletons show evidence of well-healed fractures. Castor oil was prescribed as a laxative and many herbs were recommended to cure ailments. Doctors were often specialists and were sent throughout the known world to teach and practice. Egyptian medical knowledge, though unsophisticated in light of modern western medicine, was advanced for its time. It laid the foundations for our modern medical methods.

A license was required to practice medicine in Palestine. It is probable that many doctors ignored this. Every town was supposed to have a doctor of some description. In Israel rabbis often doubled as physicians. This practice had its roots in the Old Testament use of priests as physicians. A medical practitioner was expected to be in the temple to care for the priests during this era. Since priests worked barefooted they may have been susceptible to several illnesses. The cold flagstone floors and the repeated washings were not healthy. Priests frequently suffered from dysentery.

Many specialists resided in and around Jerusalem during the time of Christ. We know there were general physicians, mental therapists, dentists, gynecologists and obstetricians. There were also many occultists who claimed to heal.   ■

SURGERY □ Doctors had a wide range of surgical instruments at their disposal, including knives, scalpels, tweezers, saws and clamps. These made possible many surgical procedures. Jewish surgeons were able to remove cataracts. They also cut squares into the skull and performed some types of brain surgery (a process called trepanning). Skeletons have been found with healed skull wounds, suggesting the patient survived the operation. Other skulls, however, have been discovered with the openings unhealed, so we assume that those surgeries were unsuccessful. Some skulls have been found with several holes, suggesting the doctors tried more than once. Others with metal plates inserted have been unearthed.

Sleeping potions, probably opiates, were given to anesthetize the patient. A spot was then shaved on the head, the skin was cut and pulled back and a tiny saw was used to open the cranium. This was done particularly to patients who suffered from tremendous internal pressure in their heads.

Artificial legs attest to the use of amputation. However, some rabbis forbade their use on the Sabbath, probably because carrying (a limb) constituted work.

There is some evidence that a spleen was removed during surgery.

Experiments and research were common among serious doctors and surgeons, who frequently were men of vision. Mar Samuel was an accomplished physician who created a procedure to examine his own stomach. Much of a doctor's training came from observation. These men collected traditional knowledge, dissected human bodies and experimented on animals.   ■

CIRCUMCISION □ The most common surgical procedure in Israel was circumcision. At eight days of age each male had the foreskin of his penis removed. In Old Testament times the surgery was performed with a flint knife which, though seemingly crude to us, can be a very sharp instrument.

During the time of Christ metal knives were used. Jesus was circumcised in compliance with the custom (Luke 1:59; 2:21). If the eighth day fell on the Sabbath, the circumcision was still to be performed. Circumcision is frequently practiced among Jews and Gentiles today.

From a medical point of view, it is important to wait until the 8th day to circumcise. In most children it takes a week after birth before the liver has developed sufficiently to produce enough vitamin K, necessary for adequate coagulation to stop bleeding. Did the earliest Jews know this fact? (Gen. 17:12). Did they learn it from experience, or divine revelation, or was the eighth day chosen at random? Today babies are given vitamin K to allow for immediate circumcision.

If a Gentile man chose to become a Jew, he had to be circumcised. This made him think seriously before converting.

This surgical procedure became an important issue in the life of Timothy (Acts 16:3), whose father was Greek and mother Jewish. Because of his father's objection, Timothy was not circumcised at birth, so before Timothy left with Paul on their missionary journey, Paul circumcised his young friend. This surgery prevented the Jews from refusing to hear an uncircumcised half-Jew.

This simple practice became a complex issue in the early church. The question was raised whether a Gentile had to become a Jew in order to become a Christian. If so, he would have to be circumcised. The council at Jerusalem finally ruled that Gentiles did not have to keep Jewish laws (Acts 15:19)—a quantum leap forward in the history of the church.   ■

BLOODLETTING □ One of the deplorable traditions which persisted for 1800 years after Christ was the practice of bleeding. Two methods were popular: In one method leeches were placed on the body to suck blood out of the patient. In the other, the doctor would "cup" the patient by cutting the flesh and drawing out blood. If either treatment was overdone, the result could be fatal. Bleeding was based on the belief that the disease dwelt in the blood. By removing blood the physicians hoped to diminish the ailment. Some doctors recommended bleeding every 30 days for people under 40 years of age.

While this practice was crude, it did indicate an advanced concept of disease—that illness is caused by internal problems and not, external, magical influences.   ■

PRESCRIPTIONS AND REMEDIES □ If a patient complained of general ailments including unexplained weight loss, the doctor probably would prescribe goat's milk. Consumed frequently in the first century, it was purported to be extremely healthful.

Several remedies were used for most common illnesses. Although aspirin was not yet developed, some medicines were used just as frequently as we today use aspirin. Some physicians might recommend a mixture of barley porridge for physical difficulties.

Good vegetables were also considered wholesome.

In ancient days mandrake leaves were considered a dependable aphrodisiac or love potion (Gen. 30:14). This idea may have persisted into the time of Christ and beyond.

One widely accepted tonic was honey (Prov. 16:24). Not only was it used for sore throats but on some occasions was put directly on an open wound (some still do this today). It was believed that honey drew water out of the bacterial cells, thus destroying them.

The common stomachache might bring a large assortment of strange remedies, including rosemary, hyssop, rue, polygonum and certain kinds of palms. An irregular heartbeat could earn the patient a cup of barley soaked in curdled milk.

Medicines varied enormously. While one remedy may have had a sound basis, the next one might be barely one step above voodooism. To fight fever one cure called for seven splinters from seven palms, seven shavings from seven beams, seven nails from seven bridges, seven ashes from seven ovens, seven hairs from seven old dogs. These were placed in a bag and hung from the patient's throat with a white thread. We aren't told if Peter's mother-in-law had tried this magical solution (Matt. 8:14, 15).

While many people recovered, others did not. No lesser believer than Paul may have had a perplexing ailment that refused to heal (2 Cor. 12:7–9; Gal. 4:13–15). Trophimus was too sick to travel with Paul (2 Tim. 4:20) and Epaphroditus was so ill that he nearly died (Phil. 2:25–27).

Divine miracles were real but diseases, illness and suffering still persisted. Paul had to resort to dispensing kitchen remedies (1 Tim. 5:23). ∎

OILS AND WINES □ Oils and wines may have been the most popular home remedies for multitudes of sicknesses. The Good Samaritan may not have had medical training, but his first reaction was to pour oil and wine on the wounds of the beaten man (Luke 10:34). Sometimes the two were mixed and at other times were administered separately.

Though it had greater ceremonial significance than medicinal, oil was part of the healing ministry James outlined in 5:14. Anointing with oil was often part of miraculous healing as the disciples practiced it (Mark 6:13). It was also employed to refresh weary travelers; Jesus welcomes having oil poured over His tired head

(Luke 7:46). Some oils and perfumes could be tremendously expensive (Matt. 26:9), depending on the scents employed in them.

Wine was another cure-all. In many cases it was probably taken when one didn't know what else to do. If a person suffered a general ailment, he might have tried a bit of wine to improve his spirits. If someone had fainted, his friend might bring wine to stimulate him. On the other hand, if he was excited or distraught, wine was expected to relax him. During mourning periods the bereaved were given ten cups of wine. Later the amount was reduced.

Paul himself resorted to dispensing this kitchen remedy (1 Tim. 5:23). The admonition to take a little wine for the stomach probably referred to the custom of mixing wine with water to kill the numerous bacteria and organisms that still are troublesome in the Middle East. Such a folk medicine was based on observation, rather than scientific theory, for microscopes did not yet exist. ∎

TEETH AND DENTURES □ Honey, figs, dates and other sweets did their damage to the teeth of Palestinians. Cavities and false teeth were frequent. Dentists were busy trying to cure toothaches. Garlic and pellitory root were used to relieve pain. Salt and yeast were rubbed into the gums to fight aches of both the teeth and gums. If teeth were not cared for in time, replacement was necessary. False teeth were made from wood, gold or silver. ∎

BLINDNESS □ Healing is a welcomed ministry in any age and it was particularly appreciated in the first century, for the large number of sick was astounding. Blindness alone is mentioned 60 times

This inn, south of Jerusalem on the road to Jericho, is accepted by many biblical scholars to be the approximate site where the Good Samaritan could have tended the needs of one who had been beaten and robbed (Luke 10:30–37).   TW

in the Bible. Unger traveled in the area in recent years and reported it was exceptional to see a lower-income person with two good eyes. Parrot reports seeing an amazing sight in Jerusalem: often two blind men would be walking together, leading each other. Called *ulemas*, they were wearing white hatbands to identify themselves. They moved throughout the city depending on each other. While they might sometimes "fall into the ditch" (Matt. 15:14), it was seldom. If this practice existed in the first century, it is reasonable to believe that Jesus was referring to these *ulemas* when He criticized the Pharisees. ■

RESPECTED PHYSICIANS □ A number of doctors achieved deserved heights of respect and affection. Luke, for instance, was known as "beloved physician" (Col. 4:14, KJV). Some ancients called physicians the angels of God. Because of the respect they had earned, doctors were hired to testify in courts concerning criminal cases. When necessary they were also invited to watch over executions to insure they were carried out properly. Such trustworthiness enhances the credibility of Luke's gospel. ■

PHARMACIES □ If a person wanted to avoid a doctor and his fees, he could go directly to a pharmacist or apothecary. Similar in role to what we see today, their place of business might have reminded us of a modern drugstore. These people mixed and dispensed herbal medicines and also prepared perfumes and a wide range of cosmetics. They also sold such items as hair restorer, eye makeup and hair dye.

Not every remedy came from sound medical science, for many of the Jewish beliefs were little more than raw superstition. For example, if a person suffered from corns, he was told to place a piece of money under the sole of his foot. This was supposed to relieve pain. One cure for bloody flux was to have the patient sit in the fork of a road holding a glass in her hand. People would then sneak up behind the patient and try to frighten her by making sudden noises. It is hard to guess how much this treatment cost.

If this didn't work, another "wonder drug" might have been barleycorn found in the dung of a white mule. ■

CHAPTER 6

CHILDBIRTH

The Jews were family centered, so most births were a cause for special celebration. Large families, such as Jacob's, thus produced many happy events.

Families frequently worked together, worshiped together and, when the occasion warranted, laughed long into the night. It was common for fathers like Zebedee to incorporate their sons into business. Normally the mothers spent many hours cooking, sewing and cleaning next to the daughters they loved, in order to train them.

In this fallen world children, beginning with Cain, could bring grief to their parents. Some followed ideas and customs which were foreign to their bewildered mother and father. The action of the prodigal son perplexed a father who loved him deeply.

Nevertheless, parents looked at the birth of a child with hope, anticipation and happiness, and were grateful for a smooth delivery in an era when birth complications were often fatal. The relationship between child and parent gave the parent the opportunity to share his way of life and hand down a vibrant faith. Children were a blessing (Ps. 127:3–5). Their arrival was met with great rejoicing.

BIRTH CONTROL □ The historical record only hints of birth control during biblical times. However, we do know that some forms were practiced and even recommended by rabbis. Besides the obvious methods of abstinence and interruption, a few artificial controls were implemented. Some women used sponges treated with citrus juice, which is highly acidic. ∎

THE DESIRE FOR CHILDREN □ There were a number of strong motivations for women to have children. The reasons were so compelling that almost every woman was eager to become a mother and relieved when she finally accomplished her goal. Some reasons follow:

1. *Natural love for babies and offspring.* While this would not have been true of all, it usually was.

2. *Desire for personal fulfillment.* Opportunities for non-mothers were severely restricted in biblical societies (1 Sam. 1:11).

3. *Desire to please her husband.* A husband who did not become a father was looked on with pity. Many assumed he had a physical defect which was reason for scorn. Others mocked him for having an "inferior" wife. Remorse and despair were often the result and these could produce pressure to divorce.

4. *Avoidance of the curse of God.* Barrenness was considered a direct judgment from heaven. Since childbirth was accepted as normal, childlessness was deemed as abnormal. Because a punishment for adultery was to render the person childless (Lev. 20:20, 21), the barren couple was considered suspect.

5. *Wish to be blessed by God.* Children were one of the clear evidences that God had shown favor (Ps. 127:3–5). They were symbols of a full, happy and righteous life.

6. *Need for earthly immortality.* To die without children meant annihilation of the family name and their property. This was very significant in the marriage of Boaz to Ruth, for her first husband had died without fathering an heir. ■

THE IMPORTANCE OF BOYS □ In many ancient, as well as some of today's, societies people not only longed for children but particularly for boys. Girls were accepted and loved, but the family was considered incomplete without at least one male offspring. The Jews were not as fanatical as other cultures which exposed baby girls to die; nonetheless, they recognized more of their needs would be met when a boy was born.

Sons remained in the household after marriage, while daughters were given in marriage. Sons usually became partners in the business or farm. In their old age the parents looked to their sons for protection and support. ■

BIRTHRIGHT □ Girls were not treated equally but neither were all boys. The firstborn son received certain rights and privileges denied the other males, for he would be the primary recipient of the inheritance and through him the family name would be continued. His inheritance would be double what each of the others received.

The oldest boy was expected to be a spiritual leader as well as administrator for the family and property. Such a system was bound to create jealousies and hatred. The story of Esau and Jacob shows the devious means used to gain the birthright from the eldest son (Gen. 25:29–34). History is probably sprinkled with similar maneuvers and an assortment of untimely deaths over the issue.

Jacob also had trouble with his sons and thus refused the birthright to his oldest son, Reuben. Guilty of incest, Reuben was denied the status which would have been his (Gen. 49:3, 4).

Birth order is specifically stated as the reason why Jehoram was named king (2 Chron. 21:3).

There is no direct mention in the New Testament of birthright as a practice, except in Heb. 12:16 (which refers to the Old Testament). However, part of the insult felt by the elder brother in the story of the prodigal could be traced to the status of the firstborn (Luke 15:28). It was a double insult to see his younger brother blessed more than he. ■

LABOR □ Pain was very much a part of the delivery of children in biblical days. We read of women who had difficult times, including death, during birth. Rachel's delivery of Benjamin was especially agonizing and resulted in her death (Gen. 35:16–19).

Biblical writers depict mothers as writhing and crying out in pain (Isa. 26:17). However, Jesus noted that women soon forgot the pain once their child was safely born (John 16:21).

The pain involved in childbirth was accepted as part of the consequences that came from the Fall (Gen. 3:16). We are not sure if attempts were made to reduce such pain, but certain sedative potions may have been used. ∎

MIDWIVES □ The Jews would not have used doctors to deliver babies. Neither would husbands have taken part. The task fell to experienced women, called midwives. In many cases a midwife was a friend, neighbor or relative. However, there were some professional midwives available.

Rachel died during childbirth, but before her death the midwife told her she was the mother of another son (Gen. 35:17, 18). When Tamar gave birth to twins, a midwife was in service and tied a scarlet thread around the wrist of the first to emerge so they could later be identified (Gen. 38:28).

From early Jewish history we have an account of unusual bravery on the part of midwives. The Pharaoh told two midwives, Shiphrah and Puah, that when they helped Jewish mothers deliver, they were to kill male babies. The midwives did not obey and soon the Pharaoh asked them why. They insisted that the Jewish women were so healthy that they gave birth before a midwife could arrive (Ex. 1:15–21).

We have no evidence that a midwife attended the birth of Jesus. ∎

BIRTHSTOOL □ Early Jewish mothers gave birth from a sitting or squatting position, not lying down. This method, which takes advantage of the pull of gravity, may have been derived from the Egyptians (Ex. 1:16). The stool may have been little more than two stones which the woman could sit on. This method of delivery was common in several other cultures in that area. ∎

THE ACT OF BIRTH □ When the baby was born, four important procedures were followed to give it a healthy start (Ezek. 16:4).

1) The umbilical cord was tied and cut.

2) The baby was washed with water.

3) It was then rubbed with salt. It is possible that it was a salt and water solution. We are not sure why this was done but it may have had religious significance.

4) The baby was wrapped. Swaddling cloths were wrapped firmly around the infant's body. Covered with several layers, even

its arms and legs were held tightly as if in bandages. The newly born Jesus was dressed in this manner (Luke 2:12). ■

NAMING □ A large part of the joy of having a new child was being able to choose a name.

When parents named their children, they often tried to select a favorite family name; a child might inherit his grandfather's or grandmother's name.

Many parents named their children as a praise to God or a statement of faith. This explains Elijah, "My God is Yahweh," and Jonathan, "God has given."

If the occasion of the birth was unusual or eventful the child might be named in remembrance of that time. This may be the reason Barak received the name "Thunder."

Others seemed to gather names from peculiar sources which remain mysteries. Caleb means "dog." Ishbosheth means "man of shame." Miriam means "fat, thick or strong."

Most ancient people did not receive a family name and a given name, but as the population increased this presented problems. By the New Testament era many people were adding appendages to help identify a person. This accounts for names such as Joseph of Arimathea, Paul of Tarsus, Jesus of Nazareth, Jesus bar (son of) Jonah, and others. Some were known by their activities, e.g. John the Baptist; others by their political views, e.g. Simon the Zealot. ■

NURSING □ In most cases the baby was breastfed by his mother. If she was unable to nurse, a wet nurse was hired to nourish the child, as in the case of Moses (Ex. 2:9).

Nursing usually continued for two or more years before weaning. We cannot be sure how old Samuel was when he was weaned, but it was not early. When Hannah finished nursing her son, she took him to the house of the Lord at Shiloh to live (1 Sam. 1:22), so he no longer needed a mother's care.

It may not have been common but Abraham decided to throw a feast when his son Isaac was weaned (Gen. 21:8). Parents would have seen it as a definite step toward independence, but we are not sure how many actually celebrated it. ■

CIRCUMCISION □ On the eighth day after birth male babies were circumcised in Israel (Gen. 17:12; Luke 1:59). In a simple surgical procedure the foreskin of the penis was removed. Establishing it as a common practice is fairly easy—we know that this was done from early history and we also know it was followed by many non-Jewish people. But explaining why they circumcised their young is entirely another matter.

For health purposes. This is a long-standing theory which has many proponents. Indeed, historians claim that the Egyptians circumcised for the reason of hygiene. The argument carries some validity since removal of the foreskin does seem to lessen the possibility of retaining bacteria. Some medical studies have shown that there is less cancer among women with circumcised husbands. However, not every scientist agrees with this position.

Mark of identity. This purpose carries some validity. The theory is that Jews could be set apart by this peculiar surgery. However, other groups used this rite; consequently, it is suspect as a mark of distinction. Also, since it was not normally seen, circumcision made a poor badge of identification.

Acceptance into manhood. This is hard to defend since it was done on the eighth day, long before the prospect of puberty. For converts circumcision was a sign of acceptance into Judaism, but in this case it was often performed on adults as well as children.

Covenant relationship. Possibly the best explanation is that circumcision was an act of commitment between the parents and God. In this the parents indicated their dependence on their heavenly father. The fact that other people used it, and some possibly used it before Israel, does not detract from this theory.

Soon after the early Christians began to gain converts, the question of circumcision became a heated issue. The heart of the problem was whether or not someone had to become a Jew in order to become a Christian. The debate became more intense because many Jews, Christian and non-Christian, refused to listen to anyone who was not circumcised. In this context Timothy agreed to be circumcised so he would be more acceptable to Jews on his missionary journeys (Acts 16:3). The council at Jerusalem took a stand

This Egyptian relief (Old Kingdom) shows the rite of circumcision being performed. The inscription labels one of the participants a priest, so this may have been part of a priestly initiation ceremony.   AR

declaring that it was unnecessary to be circumcised as a prerequisite to becoming a Christian (Acts 15:5, 19–21). ∎

REDEEMING CHILDREN AND PURIFICATION ☐ At the end of 40 days a firstborn male had to be taken to the temple in Jerusalem to be consecrated before God (Ex. 13:2; Luke 2:22-24). In Egypt the firstborn had been saved by the blood of the Passover lamb and thus belonged to God. A new mother was also expected to be purified after childbirth.

The firstborn male was presented to the priest (Num. 18:16) and the parents paid five shekels to buy him back or redeem him. The mother was then expected to pay a yearling lamb and a pigeon or a dove for her own purification. If, however, she could not afford a lamb, two doves or pigeons would suffice (Lev. 12:8). Mary must have had little money since she offered the two pigeons (Luke 2:24). ∎

MISCARRIAGES ☐ We know very little about how the Jews viewed miscarriage. It was certainly a sad occasion accompanied with a profound sense of loss.

The law, however, made a distinction between the life of a fetus or unborn child and that of a mother. If two men were fighting and one accidentally hit a pregnant woman causing damage, there were prices to pay. Should the blow cause a miscarriage the person who inflicted the damage would be expected to pay a fine (Ex. 21:22, 23). If, however, that same blow caused the woman permanent injury the guilty person could be executed. The law placed a value on a fetus but not equal to that of the mother. ∎

HANDICAPS ☐ When children were born with deformities, there were restrictions barring them from the priesthood (Lev. 21:18); however, otherwise they were kept and helped as much as possible. Jesus healed a man who was born blind (John 9:1). The man's parents had not rejected him as a child. A crippled man was brought daily to the Gate Beautiful. Unable to walk since birth, someone continued to care for him (Acts 3:2). Doubtless there were abuses in Israel, but the attitude was one of caring for those with birth defects. ∎

SUPERSTITIONS ☐ Even devout Jewish women were not immune to seeking magical formulas to ensure childbirth. With so much pressure to have children, it is no wonder they occasionally went to extremes. Some women adopted pagan idols hoping they could cause fertility. Others believed that mandrake leaves carried special powers. It is difficult to identify exactly what they thought such leaves could accomplish. They seem to have accepted them as an aphrodisiac; however, they also may have expected them to produce conception. It is difficult to discern precisely what people anticipate from a superstition. The incident between Rachel and

Leah implies the leaves accomplished both (Gen. 30:14–18). The Song of Solomon notes the plant but emphasizes its amorous aroma rather than its direct power (Song of Sol. 7:13).

It was not uncommon for pregnant women to suspend stones from their necks as charms. Supposedly these would ward off the possibility of miscarriage.   ∎

This mold-made fertility figurine plaque is presumably identified with the Canaanite fertility goddess Asherah in her Egyptian guise as Hathor.   DM

CHAPTER 7

WOMEN IN SOCIETY

Within the history of Israel we find almost the entire gamut of opinion about the status of women. There is a strong emphasis on their worth, their equality and their excellent leadership qualities. At the same time there is an abundance of laws that kept them from total equality.

It is important to refrain from judging the people of Israel by our modern viewpoints. Harmony and cooperation were more significant to them than were liberty and individuality. This fact does not justify their behavior but does allow room for their reasoning.

Jewish law permitted enormous flexibility, though it was not literally followed in its entirety. A woman's role was largely dependent on her personality and her husband's attitude.

OLD TESTAMENT ISRAEL □ *Positive attitudes toward women.* Women were not an afterthought or a secondary product of the creation. Men and women were together the image of God (Gen. 1:26, 27). That image was not complete until Eve was created.

Some accepted that fact but others did not. Consequently many Jewish women were active, creative and vocal in relationships with their families, husbands and nation. Jochebed took the initiative and concocted a plan to save her son Moses from the Pharaoh's murderous decree (Ex. 2). Hannah aggressively made a covenant with God (1 Sam. 1:1–25) so that she might eventually be the mother of Samuel.

Women rose to places of leadership in Israel. Deborah was a judge who helped lead an army (Judg. 4:6–9). Miriam ranked second in command with Aaron under Moses and later led a rebellion against her famous brother. Esther became queen of Persia and bravely thwarted genocide of the Jews. Huldah was a prophetess who was called upon to prophesy during the reign of Josiah (2 Kings 22:14–20). Judaism did not prevent them from taking leadership roles.

It is also important to consider the ideal wife in Prov. 31:10–31. This woman oversees a household complete with servants, makes clothing, runs a business and purchases land. She is a wife with a wide range of opportunities and responsibilities.

The Bible commands equal honor to both parents. It also insists that if a couple is caught in adultery, both the male and female are to be stoned (Deut. 22:22).

Women are honored for their faith as are men. Both Sarah and Rahab are numbered in the famous list of people of faith (Heb. 11).

Restrictions of women. Israel was definitely a patriarchal society; men were usually the leaders of the families and the governments. While women may have been of equal value in God's sight, they were not deemed equal in importance by man. Some laws placed considerable restrictions on women.

A famous Jewish prayer of men in the first century thanks God for not making them women. This sentiment was widespread and led to abuses by some men.

Here are a few of the laws which appear to restrict women in their activities, legal functions or intrinsic value.

1. Normally only men could own property. A daughter could receive an inheritance but only if there were no sons (Num. 27:8).

2. A wife could keep a promise or pledge only if her husband agreed to allow her (Num. 30:10-12).

3. If a woman failed to have a child, it was assumed to be her problem and a sign of God's disapproval (Gen. 30:1, 2, 22).

4. A woman was expected to prove her virginity (Deut. 22:20, 21). Such proof for a male was impossible.

5. A woman's life was considered to have half the monetary value of a man's (Lev. 27:1–8). Those who felt women were property believed they were also simple and in need of protection. Consequently, women were not encouraged to seek education outside the home and few pursued a career. Most moved unquestioningly into marriage and those who did not remained under their father's authority and protection.

In this society the parents were more eager to see a boy born into their family than a girl. That feeling added greatly to limiting the value of women.

This does not alter the fact that wives and daughters were loved and frequently treated as equal. If a husband mistreated or shamed his wife, he might soon find himself answering to her father and brothers. It is also obvious from Jacob's fourteen years of labor for Rachel that some men loved their wives greatly (Gen. 29:15–30). ■

WOMEN IN THE MINISTRY OF CHRIST □ Not only did

Jesus minister to many women, but a large number of them made up His inner circle of followers. These women were from a wide spectrum of society and economic strata.

The four Marys and Martha are the most familiar to us. Mary, His mother, was a woman of considerable faith and of remarkable influence over Jesus. She was a frequent companion. In a spiritual sense Jesus considered many women His mother (Mark 3:35).

Mary Magdalene was formerly possessed with demons; however, there is no solid reason to believe she had been a prostitute. She was probably a woman of financial means, as a number of the women following Jesus were (Luke 8:2, 3). Mary was one of the several women who traveled with Jesus and the disciples as they evangelized from village to village.

In His hour of death Mary joined the others despite the dangers lurking in Jerusalem. Later she witnessed the empty tomb and was the first to see the resurrected Christ. From the biblical accounts it would appear that only

This mosaic, located on a church near Lazarus' grave near Bethany, depicts Mary, Lazarus and Martha, with whom Jesus had a close relationship.   TW

four or five people could be considered closer than she to Jesus and His ministry.

The sister of the resurrected Lazarus, Mary of Bethany, was a dedicated follower of Jesus. Pictured in the Scriptures as a contemplative, sensitive person, Mary sat at the feet of Jesus to learn (Luke 10:38ff.). She was also present at the resurrection of her brother (John 11). One of her most remarkable acts was her washing of the head of Jesus with a highly expensive perfume (Matt. 26:7) causing great consternation among some of the practical-minded male disciples.

Mary, the mother of James and Joseph, attended most of the major events in the latter part of the life and death of Christ as did Mary Magdalene. She also accompanied Jesus on evangelistic trips.

There are other Marys in the New Testament. At least two more appear in Acts and Romans. The ones we have discussed are not easy to identify. For instance, which one was the wife of Clopas? Was the mother of Peter and John also a Mary, and if so, was she one of the four we have already mentioned (the mother of James and Joseph)? Mary was a popular name and we know that several of Christ's close friends had it.

Martha is often mentioned with her sister, Mary, and brother, Lazarus. Her most memorable appearances in the life of Christ are her busyness when Jesus visited her home, and confrontation with Him before the resurrection of her brother.

It is noteworthy that during the most difficult hours of His arrest, death and burial, the women were daring enough to remain close to Jesus. They in turn first shared the enormous joy of seeing the evidence of the resurrection.   ■

THE ATTITUDE OF JESUS TOWARD WOMEN □ Jesus'

association with women left the doors wide open for public misinterpretation. His detractors would have been happy to charge

Him with immorality and impropriety. It appears that Jesus demonstrated remarkable courage by crossing social barriers and maintaining a vital and personal ministry among women. The greatness of the risk Jesus took is borne out by the fact that some modern critics still misconstrue His activities with women.

It is impossible to garner the whole of the emotions and prejudice toward women during Christ's time. However, a look at some of Jesus' actions will give us a feel of the revolutionary nature of the steps Jesus was willing to take.

We also need to remember that in Israel during the first century, not everyone agreed on the status of women. When a leading rabbi said women should be treated a certain way, that does not mean the majority of the population agreed. The influence of the Greek and Roman cultures also influenced Jewish views. Society was changing during the time of Christ. In that context Jesus set out to spearhead a daring new attitude toward women.

Included women in His group. Orthodox Jews excluded women from active worship and restricted them to the back of the synagogue. They were expected to keep a decent distance from men rather than share religious duties. In many synagogues women were not allowed to read or otherwise participate. This attitude did not stop women such as Anna from worshiping openly in the temple (Luke 2:36, 37). The temple did have an area called the Court of Women, but women were never permitted in the Holy of Holies.

Jesus ignored the antiwomen feelings and inaugurated a program of full involvement for women. In Christ's kingdom everyone had full access to God.

Taught spiritual truth to women. Under Christ a woman's role far exceeded working in the kitchen or keeping the children quiet. Some of His most profound concepts were addressed to women. This was done privately to the woman at the well (John 4) and to Mary and Martha concerning the resurrection (John 11), and publicly to mixed audiences on many occasions. Jesus rejected the prevalent view that women were simpleminded, whereas most ancients did not consider women worth educating beyond household duties. The disciples took Jesus' attitude seriously, for we see that one of the great prayer sessions of the early church was a group of male and female believers (Acts 1:4).

Entered their homes. This was a bold move, opening Him to ruthless accusations. In this present age most men try to avoid such a situation for fear it will damage their reputations. Jesus faced the same possible slander and chose to risk it. When Martha opened her home to Jesus and His disciples, He seemingly didn't fear wagging tongues and ugly rumors (Luke 10:38).

Met with women in public. The freedom Christ felt to speak with women did not rub off quickly onto His disciples. They were shocked that He spoke openly with the woman at the well (John 4:27). There were strong feelings among many rabbis that women should not talk to strangers in public. It was considered scandalous for an educated man to speak to a woman where they could be seen. Many leaders counted this automatic grounds for divorce. During times of festival women were expected to stay inside. Single women were to stay in the center of the house, and married women could venture only as far as the door.

Extremists even objected to men talking to their own wives in the streets. Only foolish men spoke to strange women and the irresponsible met with them alone.

These were not biblical laws but opinions of the religious leaders. However, as is often true today, opinion became stronger than law. Those who thought for themselves defied these laws, and the more liberal and Roman society piled heavy pressures on Jewish culture to change.

Allowed women to touch Him. The safest route would have been for Jesus to avoid all physical contact with women. Traveling with an entourage which included females was bad enough, allowing them to touch Him would have appeared reckless.

Kissing was part of the Jewish culture and became a significant expression in the church. It is assumed that Christians kissed people of the same sex but some evidence suggests that there was kissing of the opposite sex as well. Jesus allowed a woman to not only wash His feet but to kiss them (Luke 7:38), possibly superseding culturally acceptable behavior.

Attracted prostitutes. The love and forgiveness so evident in the ministry of Christ attracted unloved, abused prostitutes. John the Baptist also drew harlots when he preached repentance and forgiveness (Luke 3:3; Matt. 21:32). Jesus did not condone their activity but He did seem to sympathize with them. While many prostitutes were open to hope, the Pharisees believed they should be given no help (Matt. 21:31, 32). Jesus preferred to minister to promiscuous women such as the one at the Samaritan well (John 4) rather than to coldhearted religionists who were too rigid to listen to God. It is no wonder that members of this despised class were attracted to the Messiah.

Women's rights in divorce. During the life of Christ there was a prevalent view which treated women as little more than property. The popular champion of this position was the scholar Hillel. He maintained that a husband could divorce his wife at any time without having to give cause. She could be dismissed at any time the husband no longer cared for her. This view was based on an interpretation of Deut. 24:1, coupled with a reading of Ex. 20:17, which equated a neighbor's wife with oxen. Hillel's school of thought considered this evidence that women were merely property.

Even men of education were quick to embrace this view as God's truth. Despite this philosophy several things deterred divorce from becoming rampant in Israel. First, many couples did not want to divorce because they were not bound by law but by love and devotion. Second, the husband in many cases would have to return the valuable dowry if he divorced. Third, men were looked down upon if they dismissed their wives too easily.

Jesus clashed head-on with this popular notion and defended the dignity of women (Matt. 19:9). Men could not divorce their wives, except on the grounds of adultery (the translation from the Greek of "adultery" is often disputed). If a husband dismissed his wife without just cause and remarried, he committed adultery.

This statement must have been welcomed by women in a society which was taking a turn against them. It represents a clear stand on a tough social issue. Jesus' stand may partly explain why women so readily heard and followed Him.   ■

VEILS OR SHAWLS □ We should not assume that there were many veils worn at any time in Israel's history. The temptation is to look at modern pictures of Arab women and imagine that ancient Jewish women consistently dressed that way.

At times some women wore them but there are few actual cases recorded in the Bible. Rebekah pulled a veil over her face when she met Isaac, but she had not been wearing one before (Gen. 24:65). She likely pulled up her shawl to cover part of her face.

We can say with reasonable assurance that some women wore veils. We can also conclude that Paul expected women to have a head covering while at worship (1 Cor. 11:5). However, we also

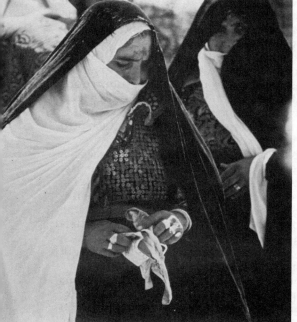

know that such a veil is almost never mentioned in the Bible.   ■

A REVOLUTION □ Paul makes a strong statement which prohibits women from being treated as property. The apostle insists that husbands must please their wives and not merely that wives must please their husbands (1 Cor. 7:1–7). He also says that husbands are to love their wives as Christ loved

The veil, or shawl, is commonly worn today among desert-dwellers such as this Bedouin woman at the Beer-sheba open-air market. Ancient Jewish women, however, did not necessarily dress as modern Arab women do today.   TW

the Church (Eph. 5:25). Peter warned husbands that if they did not honor their spouses, their prayers would not be answered (1 Pet. 3:7).

Women played a significant role as the infant churches struggled to stand. It was not a man's church, though most of the official leadership was male. Ladies such as Lydia accepted the Good News eagerly (Acts 16:14, 40). Priscilla played an important part in teaching such apostles as Apollos (Acts 18:24ff.).

Many women aided in the ministry of Jesus Christ as evidenced by the fact that Paul paid homage to eight women in the closing chapter of Romans. Women worked as deaconesses and the four daughters of Philip acted as prophetesses (Acts 21:9). We do not know the content of their prophecies, but they certainly were messages from God.

There are, of course, some unresolved difficulties in the New Testament concerning the role of women. In his letter to the Corinthians, Paul tells women to keep silence in the church (1 Cor. 14:33–36). They are also prohibited from taking positions of authority over men or from teaching them (1 Tim. 2:11, 12). We can only hope that future scholarship will provide an explanation for such passages. ∎

CHAPTER 8

WEDDINGS AND MARRIAGES

Marriage for life is the social structure which God deemed best for the human race. It has always presented problems but it has worked tremendously well.

Throughout the biblical period, the marriage of a man and a woman appears to be the normal condition for adult life. There were some people who did not marry, and in some cases celibacy was even recommended (1 Cor. 7:8, 9) for those so gifted. For most people, the needs for love, companionship, sexual satisfaction and the drive to reproduce led them to the state of marriage. Its benefits far outweighed its drawbacks.

Coupling was so normative in society that a social stigma was attached to those who did not marry. In some circles there was suspicion that those who chose to remain single possessed physical or mental defects, or practiced a deviant lifestyle. Indeed, the single woman found her social and official contacts seriously limited.

Paul's acceptance of both the single and the married helped remove that stigma for some. The solitary life of Jesus proved marriage was not absolutely necessary for a full life. Nonetheless, marriage was made for this life (Matt. 22:30) and could be enjoyed thoroughly. Despite the frequent exceptions, matrimony was the rule for the contented majority.

Over the centuries the family structures changed with shifting values, but the basic elements of lifetime partnerships generally remained the same.

POLYGAMY □ The practice of having more than one wife appears to have been widely accepted in Old Testament times. Many leading and godly men were polygamous. Not only did the practice exist in the early patriarchal period but even till after the time of David and Solomon.

This does not mean that polygamy was common among most of the population—simple economies would have prevented the common man from attempting to support more than one wife. It also does not mean that the Bible prescribes such arrangements. However, the abundance of such multiple relationships is obvious. The practice was frequent enough to cause God to offer rules to regulate it (Deut. 21:15–17; Ex. 21:10).

In a few cases a polygamistic relationship may actually have been ordered by the Scriptures, as in the instance of the levirate marriage (Deut. 25:5–10). Here a man was expected to marry his brother's widow, with no question of his current marital status. The widow was theoretically maintaining the relationship with her deceased husband, via his brother.

We find several reasons which led men to take more than one wife. Some did it because of their culture's strong demand for children. This is why Abraham took Hagar, the Egyptian maiden (Gen. 16:3). It is interesting that Sarah made the suggestion. Documents discovered at Nuzi, a Mesopotamian city, imply that this arrangement was dictated by custom. A second reason was the drive of love. Jacob was trapped and chose to take Rachel as a second wife rather than lose her altogether (Gen. 29:18). A third reason is exemplified by David (2 Sam. 5:13–16) and Solomon (1 Kings 11:1, 3), who married to seal political alliances and gain political advantages.

Polygamy still existed in Israel during the time of Christ (Herod the Great is reported to have had nine wives at once). Conservative religious leaders protested its practice in Jerusalem during this time, but probably many officials had two or more wives. As in other areas of daily living habits and religious rules, we do not see Israelites in agreement regarding polygamy. When a man weighed the possibility of taking more than one wife, he had several things to consider. More wives might provide him with more children, companionship and love and a larger work force. However, they also would create added expenses, jealousy, and angry relatives. Ironically, the Hebrew word for second wife means "rival" or "hostile."

A search for a passage which unequivocally condemns polygamy reveals that restrictions were placed only on kings (Deut. 17:17). However, several verses suggest that God's intention for marriage was one husband and one wife. The primary intent of marriage was to make a man and a wife one flesh (Gen. 2:24). This clear formula is confirmed by Christ (Matt. 19:6; Mark 10:8), showing that polygamy is not a Christian ideal.

The problem of polyandry, a woman having more than one husband, does not seem to be evident among the Jews. ■

CONCUBINES □ At times other women became part of a family and had a conjugal relationship with the male head of the home. Though not wives, they did enjoy a degree of social status. Normally concubines were taken from the slave and poor class. Their role approximated that of a modern-day mistress. In most cases the concubine was taken both for sex and to produce children, particularly boys.

Having several such women was a common practice for men who could afford them during the time of the early fathers until the beginning of the kingdom. Concubines are seen often in the Scriptures during the times of the judges. Some concubines were captured in war. Others were Hebrew slaves, gifts from wealthy men or other kings, or children of poverty-stricken families. If a concubine was Jewish, she was often treated with respect and her children could become equal heirs with the children of the wife. However, Gentile concubines were often ignored or abused by other members of the family.

Sometimes it is difficult to discern if a woman in a family actually was a second wife or a concubine. The owner of a concubine in Judges 19 is called a husband.

The law issued guidelines for concubines' protection. This may not indicate approval of the practice but merely an attempt to maintain order. Ex. 21:7–11 and Deut. 21:10–14 guarantee concubine rights.

Concubines became a way of life among many of Israel's leading figures. No lesser men than Jacob, Gideon, Saul, David, Solomon and Rehoboam had concubines.

In the Bible, Solomon possessed the most concubines. He managed to collect 700 wives of royal birth and 300 concubines (1 Kings 11:3), a figure which is mathematically staggering but possible nevertheless. Many ancient kings assembled harems of enormous sizes. Not only did concubines bring pleasure to Solomon but also helped him produce more children for the kingdom. It is impossible to redefine these ladies as housecleaners or governesses. They are clearly designated as concubines. The multiple wives were evidently part of peace treaties made with the countries of their origin, while the concubines may often have been gifts.

In humility it would be best to admit that we do not entirely understand such situations. God certainly supports the one-wife marriage; however, He obviously allowed David to keep his "master's wives" (2 Sam. 12:8).

Solomon's life was spiritually eroded by his pagan wives who turned his head toward idolatry (1 Kings 11:4). Yet Solomon did much good, for he maintained peace in Israel for 40 years. It is interesting to note that when Solomon wrote his passionate love song to the Shulamite woman, he already had 60 wives and 80 concubines (Song of Sol. 6:8, 9).   ∎

DOWRY *(Mohar)* □ There were three ways in which gifts might change hands as a dowry. The groom might pay the father of the bride for the lost value of his daughter. A present might be given from a father to the son or daughter. Or the groom might give a gift to his bride and the bride could in turn give a present to the groom. These customs do not seem to have been in equal use at all times.

The first type might be a sizable gift to the father. This present could be in the form of services, much as Jacob worked for permission to marry Rachel (Gen. 29:18). When David wanted to marry Michal, her father demanded an outrageous gift from the prospective groom (1 Sam. 18:25) in hopes that David would be killed.

It was also common for a father to give a generous present to his departing daughter. In some cases during the time of Christ, 10% of the dowry was spent on luxuries for the bride. This guaranteed her enough to purchase perfumes, jewelry and sometimes false teeth. The Pharaoh gave the devastated city of Gezer as a present to his daughter when she married Solomon (1 Kings 9:16). Solomon shrewdly rebuilt the city.

Gifts were often exchanged between the bride and groom. Abraham's servant lavished silver, gold and clothing on Rebekah, the bride-elect of Isaac (Gen. 24:53). This practice persisted into the first century A.D.

The value and number of gifts varied considerably according to place, time and families.   ■

SELECTING A SPOUSE □ Generally the bride and groom were very young. Eventually the rabbis had to fix a minimum age at 12 for girls and 13 for boys, for there are records of younger couples marrying and daughters as young as six years old being promised. In all probability Mary, the mother of Jesus, was not much older than 12 or 13. Some theorize that Joseph was older and died sooner but this cannot be proven. Under normal conditions Mary would have been little more than an early teenager when she gave birth to Jesus.

Frequently couples were matched by parents without prior consent from the boy and girl. However, this was not always the case. Some individuals did object and thus overturned the decision. The emphasis on the extended family made arranged marriages convenient. A couple's first consideration was often how the relatives felt about the marriage. In many cases the families lived close to each other and it was important that they got along well. Increased mobility eroded these factors as time went on. Children began to marry spouses of other nationalities and even other religions.

Arranged or prescribed marriages did not eliminate love. Love was expected to follow after the marriage was consummated, since they saw love as their choice and thus within their control. When they married the love would grow.

Young people did have several socially accepted ways to meet and get to know each other. Parades, festivals, harvest feasts and community dances were only a few.

In the matter of selecting a spouse for the child, especially the fathers could be quite rigid. Nevertheless, there were many young people who could venture an opinion about a prospective mate and it might be honored. Others were only too happy to have their parents do the selecting.   ■

BETROTHAL □ Great significance was placed on the betrothal or engagement period which normally lasted for one year. Often a ceremony, a feast and the exchange of gifts took place to make it official. In ancient days an engaged man was exempt from military service so he would not be killed before he could marry (Deut. 20:7).

A major part of this transaction was the negotiations over finances—how much the father of the bride was to receive, and in what form. They then discussed the dowry and determined what goods were to accompany the bride. A disaster refund was then agreed on, so if the husband were to die or the marriage were otherwise dissolved, a portion of the goods would be returned.

After the betrothal the couple were referred to as wife and husband (Matt. 1:19). However, they did not consummate the union or live together for another year.

Because of the parties involved and the monies promised, it was unusual for a couple to separate at this point. The involvement of the extended family doubtless presented difficulties to the couple, but it also provided guarantees.

If a man had sexual relations with another man's betrothed wife, the offender could be stoned to death as an adulterer (Deut. 22:23, 24). If the woman was not engaged, the man was not stoned (v. 28), but required to pay her father and marry her.

Mary and Joseph, at the time of her pregnancy, were legally betrothed and had completed whatever negotiations were necessary (Luke 2:5). In keeping with the custom they had no sexual relations (Matt. 1:25). Nevertheless Joseph was considered her husband (Matt. 1:19). Breaking the betrothal would have caused major embarrassment, not only for the couple but their families also (Matt. 1:19). Consequently, the very loving Joseph was seeking a means to dissolve their engagement which would not reveal that Mary was pregnant.   ∎

VIRGINITY □ The young bride and her family were under enormous pressure to prove she was a virgin when she married. A new husband expected to find blood on the bedding after the initial intercourse, and if no such evidence was found, he could terminate the marriage and bring horrible disgrace to the bride's family.

The practice is first described in the Old Testament (Deut. 22:13–21), but in some places it persists until today. If there was no evidence, the bride could be stoned to death. Many new wives kept the blood-stained cloth for some time in case any questions arose later. However, if the parents could prove that she was a virgin, the marriage had to stand. The elders would punish the husband and fine him a hundred shekels of silver. After this he was not allowed to divorce her no matter what the circumstances.

Because of the potential for shame to the entire family, fathers were prone to keep a careful eye on their single daughters' activities.   ∎

MIXED MARRIAGES □ Because of God's warnings, Jews were concerned about hurting their religious purity by intermarrying with pagans. Usually to their detriment, however, there was a great deal of intermarriage throughout Jewish history. Moses married a

Midianite (Ex. 2:21) and Solomon frequently acquired foreign wives as part of peace treaties (1 Kings 11:1). Nevertheless there was tremendous concern and strict teaching forbidding marriage to members of other religions (Ex. 34:15, 16). These marriages inevitably diluted the faith of the Hebrews (Ezra 9:1, 2).

Despite attempts to keep themselves pure, certain events worked against them. The Assyrian and Babylonian exiles removed Jews from their homeland, which resulted in their intermarriage with pagans. The Samaritans were a remnant of the Northern Kingdom who married Gentiles exiled in Israel by the Assyrians. Their children were no longer considered Jews.

Intermarriage was condemned under many circumstances, but it was practiced throughout biblical history. The New Testament writings denounce marriages with nonbelievers (2 Cor. 6:14, 15). ■

THE WEDDING CEREMONY □ The Jews have always been a people who enjoyed parties, festivals and elaborate celebrations. A wedding was an occasion for hearty, happy festivity that might last for a week or more. Relatives sometimes traveled from great distances and friends and neighbors poured in. Many marriages were held in the fall, after harvest, so the greatest number of people could attend.

Attendants for both the bride and bridegroom were plentiful. The groom selected a friend to be his "best man" (Judg. 14:20, RSV); he is later described as the "friend of the bridegroom" (John 3:29, KJV).

A parade preceded the wedding. The bride and her party would walk from her house and the bridegroom from a place of his choosing. Their destination was the father of the groom's house, and it is assumed that the father paid the bill. The parade was made up of friends, making music and scattering flowers. Often the entourage sang traditional wedding songs which may have included the love verses from the Song of Solomon (3:6). This parade is the procession of virgins Jesus tells us about in His parable (Matt. 25:1–13). Their function was to accompany the bridegroom to the wedding.

The bride, usually carried on a litter, was gorgeously decorated in beautiful clothing and jewelry as magnificent as the couple could afford. Often many months were devoted to making garments for this special occasion. Traditionally the bride wore a veil until the couple was alone. The guests also wore special wedding garments or festival clothes (Matt. 22:11).

A wedding ceremony was called the *huppah*, which means canopy. The bride and possibly the bridegroom sat under a canopy during some of the ceremony. It seems no official or clergyman was present for the ceremony, which parallels the ancient practice followed by Isaac and Rebekah. (Isaac merely took his bride into his mother's tent and they became married, Gen. 24:67. Any vows or promises had been made earlier.) Friends and relatives probably recited biblical passages or quoted historical wisdom as the couple stood before them. Rather than quiet and reserved, the group may have contributed to the event with gusto.

The couple was then left alone to physically consummate their marriage in a tent or room which had been specially arranged to serve as the bridal chamber. While the couple consummated their marriage, the guests continued with the party. They danced, played games, sang and played musical instruments. Food and wine were in abundance.

As odd as this sounds to western ears, the couple emerged from their bridal chamber with the evidence of her virginity and their union. This completed, the newly married couple joined the festivities which continued, mostly out of doors, for seven days or more. It was at such a party that Jesus was urged to make more wine (John 2:1–11).

The parable of the wedding banquet gives us some insight into a wedding of the wealthy (Matt. 22:1ff.). Oxen and the fatted calf were butchered in anticipation of the many guests who had been invited. In this case, when the guests refused to attend, the king was enraged.

According to one custom, seeds and fruit were tossed in front of the couple. Almost a superstition, this was to wish them many healthy, happy offspring.   ■

ATTITUDES TOWARD SEX IN MARRIAGE □ While it is difficult to understand the minds of ancient Israelites and early Christians, there are some sexual attitudes that seem quite evident. We do not know what transpired between the average couple, but we have some idea of what could have.

The tendency is to read our own sexual mores back into the Bible. In fact, however, the Scriptures are sometimes more candid about the subject than many of us. We will devote more time to the subject of sex in a later chapter.

We do know that sex was the sealing factor of the marriage. After the ceremony and gift-giving, the act of intercourse made them totally married. The bride's physical love was to be "captivating" or "ravishing" (Prov. 5:15–19). The marriage bed was to be protected from outside influences (Heb. 13:4, 5). This may reflect the principle of a husband staying home the first year to "bring happiness" to his wife (Deut. 24:5).

Because of the many pitfalls which a marriage faced, Paul encouraged sexual union in the marriage relationship (1 Cor. 7:3–5). He realized satisfying sex at home was a strong deterrent to the temptations outside the home.   ■

DIVORCE □ The problem of terminating a marriage has probably always been a clouded issue. The Old Testament provides a general rule (Deut. 24:1), but it does not resolve all the problems which might arise. Therefore, in the matter of biblical history, we know more about what did happen than what should have happened.

Marriage was considered a lifetime covenant, yet exceptions were allowed by passages such as Deut. 24:1. Debates through the centuries centered on what those exceptions might be.

By the time of Jesus Christ two viewpoints had become widespread. The school of Rabbi Shammai interpreted Deuteronomy 24 to allow divorce only on the grounds of adultery. The followers of Rabbi Hillel believed the same passage allowed divorce on practically any grounds which displeased the husband. Some teachers argued a husband could dismiss his wife if she burned soup or if he found a wife he liked better.

Jesus confronted this issue, and the church has argued since over what He said and meant (Matt. 5:27-32; 19:3-12; Mark 10:2-12; Luke 16:18). Our background and temperament play a large role in how we interpret these passages, just as they did for the Jews who tried to apply Deuteronomy 24. However, as in any matter of biblical interpretation, we must be careful not to allow our feelings or prejudices to take precedence over sound scholarship.

We do know that by the time of Christ, men, in theory, had almost unlimited freedom to divorce their wives. In contrast, the wife was almost powerless to initiate a divorce. Some observers conclude that these attitudes resulted in many divorces during the time of Christ, but others feel there were few. Many may not have divorced because they had different expectations of marital happiness than we have today. They also had close ties with their extended families which probably diminished the probability of divorce. Extended families often provided emotional support and positive reinforcement. They also would express disappointment if the marriage soured.

Many husbands would never consider divorcing their wives. Others squirmed for a way to dispose of them. By the time of Christ when divorce did occur, a written bill of divorcement from the husband was essential. This gave the woman freedom to remarry, if possible. The husband then had to repay the part of the dowry, as was agreed before betrothal.

While divorce was evidently rare in Israel, it was common among the Romans. ∎

LOVE □ In an ancient society of prearranged marriages, can we assume that married couples loved each other, or did they merely accept it as a relationship of convenience? It is safe to say that many Jewish families were filled with love. We read the expressions (Eccles. 9:9) and see the evidence (Joseph's devotion to Mary, etc.). However, we must be cautious not to romanticize their society. There must have been many Jewish couples who did not love each other.

The Jewish concept of family love differed considerably from some modern approaches. While it is popular to "fall in love" today, in those days the theory was to marry, then grow in love. This is evident from biblical commands to love (Eph. 5:25). Love was something one could choose and control. With this attitude most any marriage had great potential. Jesus assumed that even if a partner had been unfaithful, the offended person could forgive and choose to love again (Matt. 19:8, 9).   ∎

CHAPTER 9

SEXUAL PRACTICES

The average married couple in ancient times appears to have had a normal, healthy, enjoyable sex life. Unfortunately much of the biblical discussion about sex focuses on its problems.

A few of the subjects that concern us were probably considered non-issues during Bible times. For instance, since there was little time between puberty and marriage, the ancient writers ignored the question of masturbation.

The attitudes about sex differed greatly according to the times and the circumstances. There was terrific pressure for the Jews to adopt the hedonistic practices which accompanied idolatry. At times the Jews complied, and God dealt with them severely. However, their laws and moral values did not tolerate pleasure as the main goal of life. Consequently, the Israelites repeatedly rebounded and denounced debauchery as a way of life.

Despite the difficulties inherent in sex, the Jews also refused to take the opposite extreme and thus rejected asceticism. They realized that while the pleasure of sex could not be their master, neither should it be ignored. Although there was no formal sex education, there were plenty of opportunities to discuss it. The matter of circumcision certainly demanded some education as did the biblical texts which were frequently read.

EUPHEMISMS □ Sometimes the biblical writers seem quite bold by our standards and at other times they appear reluctant to directly mention sexual activity. The Bible frequently uses the words "breast" and "womb"; however, it shys away from words to describe genitals. Conception, bearing children and childbirth itself are discussed often. The term "foreskin" is used because of the heavy emphasis on circumcision. The word "loins" can mean the lower part of the body, but in some references, the genital organs are precisely intended (Gen. 35:11, KJV).

Paul uses euphemistic language when he describes parts of the body and compares them to the spiritual body. The "less honorable" parts seem to refer to genital and secretory organs (1 Cor. 12:23, 24).

The use of the word "feet" is not always clear. In many passages the meaning is literal, but in others it refers to the genitals. Several times covering the "feet" is an expression for relieving oneself (Judg. 3:24; 1 Sam 24:3, KJV). There is a difference of opinion as to what "feet" means in the story of Ruth (3:4–7).

Normally the Bible speaks directly of male prostitution, but it also refers to the practice as the activity of a dog because of the way in which dogs copulate (Deut. 23:18). This helps us understand that the major function of male prostitutes was to have sex with men, though they may have also engaged women.

Intercourse, the physical union, is the clear intention of Paul and others when they state a couple becomes "one flesh" (Eph. 5:31). The words "know" or "love" were also used to indicate sexual intercourse.

The word "flesh" could sometimes indicate sexual desire or activity; however, generally it was aimed at a wider scope, suggesting the physical experience in contrast to the spiritual. ■

MARRIED SEX □ There were two functions of sex within the marriage: to create children and to give pleasure. The Jews did not look at sex as a nuisance or a problem to be endured.

Paul's treatment of the subject is especially enlightening (1 Cor. 7:1–7), for he argued that regular sexual intercourse was essential for a married couple. Not only was it the wife's duty to please her husband but it was his duty to please her. He recommended self-control but recognized the necessity of physical satisfaction. This demonstrates that sex was appreciated as a source of pleasure. Couples frequently enjoyed sex without guilt, with no intention of having children from their union. This was especially important considering the sexual temptations present in the society around them. The text also suggests that it was perfectly acceptable for a woman to admit her need for sex. Paul discusses this as normal and expects the wise husband to honor that need.

The Song of Solomon is remarkably bold in its use of sexual expressions and imagery. Those familiar with this work were exposed to very intimate details about the subject. The author admires his lover's breasts (4:5; 7:3–7), and is enamored by her delectable kisses (4:11). She in turn loves his tender embraces (8:3), and delights in his sweet mouth (5:16) and marvelous legs (5:15).

This sensuous book speaks frankly of the sexual experience and was an accepted part of Jewish culture.

The Scriptures give some guidelines on sex within marriage which were commended to the early Christians. Couples were expected to exercise enough self-control so they could carry out their normal responsibilities. For instance, Paul acknowledged a couples' right to refrain from sex in order to devote themselves to prayer. He also insisted that a marriage partner not use sex merely for his own satisfaction. He was responsible, rather, to meet the needs of his partner (1 Cor. 7:1–7).

The Bible gives no restrictions on how a couple should go about enjoying their sex. There is no discussion or prohibitions on married sexual practices. ■

RELIGIOUS PROSTITUTION □ The pagan religions that surrounded and contaminated Israel's history frequently practiced some form of cult prostitution, usually centered on the theme of fertility. If a farmer wanted larger crops or greater flocks, he needed to appeal to the fertility gods; should a wife want to bear children the same appeal was necessary. One means of pleasing the fertility gods was to engage in sex with the female or male prostitutes available at the temple. As bizarre as this may sound, the practice was common; it endured into New Testament times and frequently was assimilated into the worship of Jehovah.

The Jews encountered religious prostitutes early in their history. In the lurid account of the death of Zimri, son of Salu (Num. 25:1–8), a Moabite woman invites the Jewish Zimri to participate in the sexual sacrifices in the tent of meeting. When Phinehas hears of what is taking place, he marches into the tent and runs a spear through both of them in a single thrust.

Pagan ceremonies and celebrations could become riotous and gruesome. A great deal of wine was frequently consumed as a tribute to Baal for good crops. The sacrifice of children to Molech, or Chemosh, the Moabite God, also occurred.

More than committing debauchery for debauchery's sake, the people who practiced these religions seemed to believe in them. Many small statues carved in the likeness of the fertility god have been found. Some are figures of pregnant women and were probably kept in the worshiper's home. Other figures are of women holding their breasts.

The degenerate religion of the Canaanites was one of the reasons why God wanted them annihilated. Because Israel did not carry out God's mandate, the religion persisted and repeatedly infiltrated the religious life of the Jews. They were continuously plagued by prostitution in their own religion despite the fact that the law strictly prohibited it (Deut. 23: 17, 18).

During the time of the judges, the Jews adopted many of the cruel, immoral

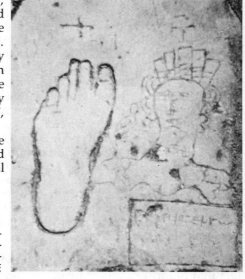

This carving of a foot in the pavement of a street in Ephesus identified as a brothel the establishment to which it pointed.   EHLE

The Acro-Corinthus rises about 1500 feet above the city of Corinth. Atop this high rock was the temple of Aphrodite, the goddess of love, where more than 1000 religious prostitutes lived and served the decadent Corinthian people.   TW

practices of the fertility cults (Judg. 8:33). However, these were only the beginning of their disobedience. Eventually half the tribe of Manasseh accepted the religion of prostitution (1 Chron. 5:25). The sons of Eli were sleeping with women, who may have been prostitutes, who served at the entrance to the tent of meeting (1 Sam 2:22). Under Rehoboam of Judah there were male prostitutes associated with the hill shrines devoted to the fertility cult (1 Kings 14:23, 24). Israel frequently fell into Baal worship which often included prostitution (2 Chron. 33:3).

Not everyone participated in the pagan worship, but everyone would have been aware of its presence. Repeatedly, godly kings would call for reform and purge out most of the fertility cult (1 Kings 15:12; 22:46; 2 Kings 23:7), but without, unfortunately, any permanent effect (Ezek. 16:5–58). These base practices remained common in certain areas of the world well through the time of Christ and Paul. One historian tells us that every woman was expected to donate some of her time as a temple prostitute for Venus.

When Paul wrote to the church at Corinth, there were 1,000 prostitutes at the temple of the goddess Aphrodite on the Acro-Corinthus. The popularity of this religion was largely responsible for the financial prosperity of the city. Corinth's reputation was so widespread that the term "Corinthian girl" became a synonym for prostitute. Consequently, when the apostle wrote to the Christians there, he was dealing with people who once had considered sex an amoral form of recreation, of little more significance than exercise. Paul's teaching that people would defile their bodies by uniting with a prostitute (1 Cor. 6:15, 16) was a fresh concept to these believers. The prevalence of prostitution also might shed light on the advice of the church fathers to new Gentile Christians that they avoid immorality (Acts 15:29). What many of us readily consider immoral, they did not.   ∎

HOMOSEXUALITY OR SODOMY □ History bears out the
fact that homosexuality is nearly as old as man and frequently be-

came commonplace during biblical times. With so much sexual activity, especially in pagan temples, it is doubtful that many Jews were naïve about the subject. The writers of the Bible seem to be mainly concerned about religious homosexuality, because this was their primary contact with the practice. Most homosexuality today is not associated with religious observances.

Homosexuality is often referred to as sodomy, taking its name from the cities of Sodom and Gomorrah (Gen. 18, 19), which were destroyed because ten righteous men could not be found in all of Sodom (18:32). "Righteous" may have meant nonhomosexual since this was the sin under discussion in the next chapter (19:5). The homosexuality which was definitely part of the city's problem may have been temple prostitution, since the practice is mentioned frequently in the rest of the Scripture.

The writer of Deuteronomy found it necessary to warn Jewish males and females to avoid participation (Deut. 23:17), but shrines which used male prostitutes became part of Jewish life during the time of Rehoboam (1 Kings 14:24) and had begun to be eradicated by King Asa (1 Kings 15:12). These homosexual males were not finally removed until King Jehoshaphat (1 Kings 22:46). However, the corruption reappeared during the time of Josiah.

Paul's condemnation of male and female (lesbianism) homosexual activity may also be addressing religious homosexuality, which was undoubtedly widespread (Rom. 1:23–27; 1 Cor. 6:9). Barclay tells us that the Roman Empire was so corrupt that Roman writers despaired for its future. Even the Roman empress Agrippina, wife of Claudius and mother of Nero, is reported to have relieved her boredom by departing the palace for an evening and entertaining herself in the local brothel. There is some evidence that several of the early emperors were homosexuals. Later, Domitian (A.D. 81–96) tried to quell the practices by charging a fine of 10,000 sesterces against those who performed homosexual acts.

Transvestism, wearing clothes of the opposite sex, was forbidden by God (Deut. 22:5). Some of these differences in dress have been lost to us.   ∎

NUDITY □ The Jews dressed modestly and considered nakedness degrading. There may have been no specific law prohibiting it, but it was generally treated with disdain. One of the humiliating acts of war was to strip prisoners before returning them (Isa. 20:4). When Hanun rejected David's servants, he shamed them by cutting off their garments at the waist (2 Sam. 10:4). Shem and Japheth expressed horror at the drunken nakedness of their father Noah after their term on the ark (Gen. 9:21–23).

Nevertheless, there does not appear to be an insane fear of nudity that some seem to adopt. God commanded His prophet Isaiah to walk without clothes or shoes as a sign of the destruction to come (Isa. 20:2–4). Isaiah went without clothes for three long years. The general abhorrence of nudity increased the impact of this act.

The question of nudity became particularly acute under the Greek games. There was tremendous controversy over whether or not the Jewish youth should participate in athletic contests since the games were conducted in the nude.   ■

INCEST □ Marriage to close relatives was a recurring problem throughout Israel's history. Usually the Jews adopted the practice from neighboring pagans.

A case of incest mentioned by Paul in his letter to the church at Corinth concerns a man in the congregation who was living with his father's wife (1 Cor. 5:1). Paul rebuked the assembly for not being shocked and immediately expelling the man from their group.

Incest occurred only rarely among Jews, Christians, and even pagans. Roman law, in fact, prohibited a marriage of the type Paul described. We do have accounts of Roman emperors marrying whomever they pleased, but this was an affront to the general public.

In the Old Testament, when Amnon raped his reluctant half-sister Tamar, he committed incest, among his other crimes. King David was furious and Absalom refused to speak to Amnon afterward (2 Sam. 13).

Biblical law forbids several marital relationships because of their incestuous nature (Lev. 18:6ff.; Deut. 22:30). One of the rare exceptions was the levirate marriage between brother and widowed sister-in-law. People who violated these laws could be executed. It is obvious, however, that the immediate descendants of Adam and Eve married siblings. Also, during the time of the patriarchs, first cousins were often chosen as spouses.   ■

BESTIALITY □ The Jewish horror of humans having sex with animals possibly has some roots in pagan mythology which tells of the mating of humans and animals. They also had great respect for God's design in creation. In the Scriptures bestiality is ruthlessly condemned. Those who practice it are to be executed (Ex. 22:19).   ■

RAPE □ In the Scriptures there were three major laws addressing rape:

1. If a man rapes a single woman outside her home, he is to be executed (Deut. 22:25–27).

2. The rapist of a married or engaged woman is also to be executed.

3. If a man rapes a virgin, he must pay her father 50 shekels, marry the girl and never be free to divorce her.   ■

THE PROBLEM OF ONAN □ There have been several attempts to make statements concerning sex from the story of Onan

(Gen. 38:1–11). In many cases the interpreters have missed the point. Onan's brother died leaving his wife Tamar childless. Judah, Onan's father, ordered him to fulfill his levirate marriage duty and father a child by Tamar. In half-obedience, Onan had intercourse with Tamar but each time spilled his semen on the ground, preventing her from becoming pregnant. God took his life because of this disobedience. The punishment deals with Onan's refusal to obey the command of levirate marriage and infers nothing about masturbation, coitus interruptus, or any other sexual practice. ■

MENSTRUATION □ Biblical laws considered a woman unclean during her menstrual period. How much the Jewish attitude was determined by hygiene knowledge and how much by pagan fertility myths remains a secret. Nevertheless conditions were dictated to regulate sexual behavior during this time. Couples were forbidden to have intercourse during the seven-day cycle (Lev. 18:19). There were laws governing even the furniture in her house. Anything she touched or sat on during her period was considered unclean, and anyone who in turn touched it was likewise unclean (Lev. 15:19–24). ■

LUST □ Self-control is a major theme in the Bible, and lust is one of the passions which is to be held in check. The word "lust" or strong desire can be applied to a wide range of subjects, including food and ambition (1 Tim. 3:1), as well as sex. In ancient society, as today, there were multiplied invitations to surrender to illicit sexual desires. Jesus warned His followers against capitulating to those lusts (Matt. 5:28). ■

ADULTERY □ As with many biblical subjects, we know more about what the laws said than we do about the attitude toward them. Since there were many prostitutes in Israel, we can assume there was a measurable amount of extramarital sexual activity. It is, however, doubtful that many people were executed for the adultery they committed.

Under the Old Testament an unusual test was used to determine whether a woman was guilty of adultery. The priest made a drink of holy water and dust from the tabernacle floor (Num. 5:16–31). He then declared that after she drank it, if she was guilty, her thighs were to waste away, her abdomen was to swell, she would suffer terribly (v. 24) and probably become infertile. However, if she was innocent, she would be unharmed and still be able to bear children. God was expected to oversee and guarantee the outcome of this procedure.

There was no such test for a man, but should a man and a wife be caught in adultery, they were both to be executed (Deut. 22:22).

Without restrictions on marriage fidelity, Jewish society would have had difficulty maintaining the family. It was essential to guarantee that the couple knew the father of the child and that jealousies be deterred rather than having couples living under the uncertainties of suspicion. The boundaries of a marriage were therefore clearly defined. Yet, men such as King David were willing to kill in order to violate those restrictions.

By the time of Christ the feelings about adultery and its penalty had shifted drastically. Due partially to the attitude of other nations, the Jews no longer considered it a matter of life and death, so were no longer executing people for adultery.

This is part of the reason why the incident of Jesus and the woman who was caught in adultery held great significance for those involved. Since the law was part of their moral code, yet was not being enforced, Jesus' response would have raised controversy no matter what His reply. Suggesting that anyone who was innocent throw the first stone defused the argument and caused the accusers to slink away in embarrassment. (Sparse manuscript evidence for this passage has led some conservative scholars to think that it was not originally part of the Canon.)

Jesus addressed the discussion of adultery, thus giving us some ability to handle the problem. Some of His contribution is lost in the rigid disagreement by Christians over what He meant. He seems to teach that a man can divorce his wife on the grounds of fornication (Matt. 5:31, 32). In doing so Jesus may have supplied a safety valve which made execution unnecessary. To save face a husband could divorce his wife rather than seek harsher action. On another occasion Jesus suggests that it would be better if a couple remained together even under the pressure of adultery (Matt. 19:8, 9). In stating this He advocated the healing powers of forgiveness. ■

PREMARITAL SEX □ Chastity before marriage was of prime importance to Jewish families and young couples. Legally, a woman was expected to be a virgin on her wedding night and capable of proving it (Deut. 22:15). It may have been easier to remain a virgin in those days than now, since there were apparently fewer years between puberty and marriage.

Paul's admonition to avoid fornication (1 Cor. 6:9) is a broad use of the word which prohibits all forms of sexual immorality. ■

CHAPTER 10

EDUCATION AND LITERACY

The primary force in Israel's quest for knowledge was their strong desire to follow God. They recognized the need to read if they were to pass on their faith from generation to generation. The history and laws of Israel were of the highest priority to many of its leaders.

Consequently, they probably did not have as deep a passion for general knowledge as many of their contemporary nations. Israel had minimal interest in current or ancient philosophy and their interest in mathematics and engineering was hardly at a fever pitch.

Many Jews, especially around the first century A.D., received a good "liberal arts" education, thanks to the influence of Babylon, Greece and Rome. Nonetheless, they spent much of their energies in maintaining their religious heritage. To this extent, education was vital and the people received an excellent education. They were literate early in their history because of a simple alphabet and that literacy was among the masses at least by the time of Joshua.

We may be tempted to assume that populations 2,000 years ago were fairly ignorant. Regarding some subjects this was true, but in many areas they had amazing knowledge and

There is a great desire to learn and a love for books in modern Israel. This bookbinder practices his craft in the charming, cobbled streets of the ancient city of Safed. The first printed Hebrew book was manufactured here, in 1578, and for many years Safed was the center of learning for all of Galilee. TW

This reproduction depicts the oldest known library catalog. It lists the titles of 62 Sumerian literary works current in Babylonia in the first half of the second millennium B.C.   EHLE

ability to apply that knowledge. When we mention the Jews of the first century, we are talking about an intelligent people with a keen appreciation for education.

LIBRARIES □ The people of the Old and New Testaments were literate and had a love for learning and literature. Their respect for manuscripts and scrolls (their books) is evidenced repeatedly throughout their history. This was also true of many of the nations surrounding them. Volumes by the tens of thousands were available and used.

If our definition of a library is either a small or large collection of volumes, then libraries were fairly plentiful. Many of those discovered are archives, where letters, contracts, histories and literature were kept. They were probably not the same as our concept of the free lending library, but the books were available and they were used. The large amount of documents, letters and records of transactions gives us reason to believe there were far more libraries than have been unearthed.

The oldest library yet discovered belonged to Sargon, king of Assyria, from 722-705 B.C. (Isa. 20:1). Twenty-five thousand volumes were excavated from this site. A library of 20,000 tablets was owned by Ashurbanipal (662 B.C.). The huge library at Nippur contained 50,000 volumes 400 years before Christ. The library at Alexandria, Egypt, housed an estimated quarter million volumes in 246 B.C. This library was the work of Ptolemy.

Under the Romans, libraries seem to have multiplied and were organized. Here reading rooms began to appear.

The famous Dead Sea Scrolls were evidently kept in the library of the Essenes, then hidden in jars and secreted in a cave when Titus crushed Israel in A.D. 66–70. The discovery of this library has been a great asset to modern biblical studies, for it has verified the accuracy of many Old Testament manuscripts.

A library per se is not mentioned in the New Testament, but there are many references to books, and the apostles seem to have been bibliophiles (2 Tim. 4:13).   ∎

Cave 4 at Qumran, on the northwest shore of the Dead Sea about eight miles south of Jericho, yielded a great treasure for biblical scholars when a shepherd discovered, in 1948, a number of huge clay pots containing the Dead Sea Scrolls.   TW

The Jews' diligence in studying the Torah led to their becoming known as "the people of the book."   TW

LITERACY □ There are several good reasons to believe that most of the people of Israel could read and write. From their earliest history, easy alphabets, basic training in the home, schools and an emphasis on the written law made literacy important.

Archaeologists have found clear evidence of schools at Ur, Egypt and Mesopotamia during the time of Abraham. Clay tablets with lessons in arithmetic, grammar and geometry have been discovered. These schools trained a professional class of scribes.

Throughout Israel's history there was little difficulty finding someone to read and write. Moses was capable of reading to the nation (Ex. 24:7), but so was the average person. Everyone was expected to write on the doorpost of his home (Deut. 6:9). Joshua assumed that he could readily choose three men from each tribe who could record a survey of the land (Josh. 18:4, 8, 9).

By New Testament times many homes contained copies of the Torah and the laws were taught regularly by fathers who could read them. It is safe to assume that among the Jews and neighboring nations literacy was quite high. Part of the reason why Christianity spread so rapidly was the population's ability to read—not only their native tongue but Greek and even Latin as well.   ■

SCHOOLMASTERS □ Some Greek, and later Roman, families had dependable male slaves who watched over their sons. Their specific duties are not clear, but in a general sense they saw to it that the boys were educated.

In many instances this meant the slave walked the boy to and from school. Others did this and then supplemented the child's education. Some, as private tutors, provided all of a boy's education.

Paul uses the "schoolmaster" to describe the role played by the law. He says the law was the schoolmaster, or custodian, which took us to Christ (Gal. 3:24, 25, KJV). He also uses the same word as he clarifies his relationship with the believers at Corinth (1 Cor. 4:15).   ■

SCHOOLS □ There is little proof that formal schools existed in early Israel. Yet, there is an abundance of material to suggest that education took place well before the time of Moses, for people were literate as early as the time of Abraham. It is also obvious that some classes were held. The real question is, were these special classes for the elite or for the average person?

The Gezer Calendar provides strong evidence of formal education during the time of Solomon (ca. 925 B.C.). Macalister found a small limestone plaque merely 4½ by 3½ inches. It had been used often and scraped clean to be used again. On it was a description of the Jewish harvest seasons. It is believed that this calendar was used to teach Hebrew children.

Schools that appeared in Israel during their his-

This replica of the Gezer calendar, which probably dates from the ninth or tenth century B.C., was found at the devastated city of Gezer which was given by the Pharaoh to his daughter when she married Solomon. The calendar was apparently a schoolboy's exercise for memorization and until recently it was our earliest known specimen of Hebrew writing.   EHLE

tory were probably for the education of the upper class. The education of the general population came from fathers who taught the laws of God to their children. A father would teach them well enough that the child could in time teach them to his own children.

At some time between the Exile and the 4th century B.C., a special kind of school began to appear. Some feel these schools were devised early by a group who later became the Pharisees. Hebrew was being replaced by Aramaic, and religion was shifting from the temple to the law. Therefore, afraid that their children would lose their traditions of faith and history while in captivity, some leaders may have organized schools not unlike Sunday schools.

Ezra trained scribes to fulfill the role of teachers (Ezra 7:6) of the law. It is indeed possible they held formal classes. Ezra conducted classes to teach the laws of God to the Levites. They in turn explained them to other groups (Neh. 8:2–8).

When the Greeks took over, Israelite education took on new

significance out of necessity. The Greeks placed great stock in learning and began to impose their knowledge and philosophy on the Jews. As a counter move the Jews established (or possibly reestablished) schools in connection with the synagogues. A Greek school was located in Jerusalem, near the temple, in 175 B.C., and some Jews began attending. This caused panic among other Jews and soon they had begun schools across the nation.

Rabbi Simon ben Shetach is credited with being the father of this newly developed school system. At first called "House of the Book" the concept spread quickly. Eventually school became compulsory and children who were frequently absent were punished. They were expected to begin their education when five years old, and some students remained in school until they were fifteen. After their studies were completed, advanced education was often available.

In times of oppression the synagogues were looked upon as havens of strength for the Jews. They not only supplied spiritual reenforcement but were educational institutions and places to test ideas.

We see, therefore, that schools were common during the life of Christ, and that not only was literacy a factor but so were advanced discussions of philosophy, language, mathematics and other subjects.   ■

TEACHERS □ Parents were the earliest teachers in Israel. They apparently took seriously their role to pass along the basics of their faith as well as the rudimentary skills of a trade. For many parents it was a matter of pride as they would have felt it a disgrace to produce ignorant children.

Much of their teaching rose naturally out of daily circumstances. Parents used the religious festivals as teaching tools. They told the stories their parents had told them. Many illustrations were given as father and son, and mother and daughter worked together. When Scriptures became available, these too were read and discussed.

Eventually a special group of Levites became formal teachers established to instruct Israel. They appear to have been the major teachers of Israel, outside the home, until the time of the Exile. After this the scribes assumed a dominant role in education. They were key figures in interpreting and teaching the law.

Soon the word "rabbi" became a popular title which applied to many varieties of people. It meant "master" but was often used in place of "teacher." In some cases it referred to people who held official teaching positions but at other times was an honorary title. In either use rabbi designated respect for wisdom, intelligence and experience.

When the disciples called Jesus teacher or rabbi (John 1:49), it was in recognition of His leadership role over those who followed and respected Him, for He had not formed a class that met regularly. Jesus was called rabbi and called himself teacher (Matt. 23:8). The original word for master in the KJV is teacher. Like a parent, Jesus gave much teaching in response to everyday events. Others also referred to Jesus as teacher. Half of the occurrences of the word teacher in the New Testament refer to Jesus Christ. At this time the term teacher was held in high esteem and one felt honored to be called such.

The title continued to have significance as the early church formed. Few functions could have been more important in the establishing of young believers (Acts 13:1).

Christian schools were not founded by the first-century believers. Persecution and a desire to be included in the synagogues made this impossible.   ■

FAMOUS TEACHERS □ During the era of Christ some teachers were treated with great respect as scientists or writers might have been at other times. A few of their names have endured to the present.

Hillel. Born in Babylon, Hillel came to Palestine to propagate his stories and soon became known for his mental abilities. He devised seven principles to be applied when interpreting the Scriptures. Eventually, Hillel taught at his own school, Bet Hillel. He held the title of *Nasi,* designating him as the chief teacher of the temple. Historians consider Hillel a liberal interpreter of the law.

Shammai. Shammai was a respected teacher who frequently opposed Hillel's views and took a more conservative or strict interpretation of the Scriptures. While Hillel felt almost any cause justified divorce, Shammai believed there were very few legitimate grounds for divorce. These two teachers thus became the first of the series of famous "pairs"as they were called.

When Jesus was asked about divorce (Matt. 19:3), He was being wedged between these two men's positions.

Gamaliel. A famous teacher of the first century, many of Gamaliel's sayings are preserved to this day in the Mishnah. In all probability he followed the teachings of Hillel. As a teacher his most famous student was the apostle Paul (Acts 22:3). His wisdom and authority convinced the Sanhedrin not to kill the apostles (Acts 5:34–39). Gamaliel's views were pragmatic and widely accepted. When he died, some said the glory of the law ceased.   ■

LANGUAGES □ It would appear that a person living in Israel in the time of Christ was conversant in three languages and knew a few words of a fourth.

Aramaic. The language with which Jesus was most familiar was Aramaic. In all probability He spoke it daily and did most, if not all, of His teaching in it. Aramaic was the language of the region and had experienced a revival by the time of Christ.

When Jesus was dying on the cross He cried out in Aramaic,

not in Hebrew or Greek (Matt. 27:46).

Each synagogue may have had an interpreter to translate the service for those who did not understand Hebrew, which, centuries before Aramaic, had been the common language of the synagogue.

To accommodate the population some copies of the Old Testament existed in Aramaic. This caused great consternation in the first century. Gamaliel resented the Aramaic translation and even had a copy buried in a wall.

In the case of Jesus, not only did He speak Aramaic but also the Galilean dialect of Aramaic, as did Peter (Matt. 26:73). Consequently, much of His education may have been in this language.

Hebrew. In practice this became the language of holiness. The Jews fought to keep the law and its interpretation in Hebrew, though they were not always successful. Normally Hebrew was read in the synagogues, in the temple and in private at home. In all probability the Israelites' proverbs and ancient sayings endured in Hebrew.

Knowledge of Hebrew differed drastically from family to family. How much it was used at home was as important as how much it was taught at school.

When Jesus stood to read Isaiah in the synagogue, it is safe to assume that the text was in Hebrew (Luke 4:16). We may assume He had no difficulty reading it.

Greek. During the time of Christ, Greek was the most widely accepted language of people throughout the Near East. The Greek that was used to write the New Testament, Koine, is not as pure and precise a language as many have been led to believe. Koine Greek is a diluted form of classical Greek. It was a language of the common and basically unlettered man. There is no established standard of Koine language, for it differed considerably from place to place. It was flexible enough to include foreign words and to allow writers such as Paul to coin new words or phrases. The flexibility of the language made it particularly suitable for the New Testament, for as the language of international trade it was an excellent vehicle for rapid communication of new ideas.

Paul and other writers of the New Testament were well versed in the language. This fact, plus its widespread use, suggest that Jesus had a command of it. Peter and John, from the same section of the country as Christ, spoke it well.

Latin. Only those involved in legal and military matters had to use some Latin in order to deal with the Romans. Consequently, there may not have been many people in Palestine who spoke much Latin. However, the knowledge of a few words probably helped in some dealings.

Three languages were written above Jesus on the cross where He died: Hebrew, Latin and Greek (John 19:20). ∎

TEACHING METHODS ▫ Easily the most predominant teaching method of formal education was rote memory. Any learning which did not include recitation was often viewed with suspicion.

This Dead Sea Scrolls parchment is from Isaiah, the same book Jesus read from in the synagogue. This parchment is written in Hebrew.

CGI

Students were expected to give evidence that they had learned by reciting long portions of Scriptures word perfect. This explains why Jesus and others were so familiar with what the Scriptures said.

Some studies were made easier because of rhythmic meter. Much of the Scriptures are written in double or triple rhythms making learning more enjoyable. ∎

SUBJECTS TAUGHT □ While the Scriptures were basic to a Jewish education, they were far from the sole subjects taught in Israel. Reading, writing, music, mathematics, engineering, law, and languages were only a few of the subjects available at one type of school or another. The large structures, buildings, roads and aqueducts in Israel are evidence to a diversified education.

These subjects were important to Jewish life and thought; however, some disciplines apparently were not. Throughout centuries of archaeological research, no significant art work has been found. The prohibition of Ex. 20:4 prevented Jews from working with life forms and images. Even the image of an eagle provoked the Jews to distraction.

Any attempts to study science were restricted by the limitation of their theology. They were not free to investigate areas which their tradition already had denounced. Some rabbis cautioned against challenging the unknown. The Jews did venture into astronomy. However, their knowledge was limited to the current trends and an understandable disdain for astrology.

Their concepts of nature, however, seem quite advanced. They enjoyed animals and gave themselves to considerable observations. The Jews made lists to distinguish between different varieties.

Romans and Greeks may have had a more open approach to general education than the Jews. It is safe to assume that much of their knowledge and curiosity spilled over into the Jewish community. ∎

BOYS AND GIRLS □ The general tendency was to academically educate boys and not girls. Yet, there were many women in Israel who had good

The Jewish educational system was enriched by the infusion of subjects other than Scripture and by other cultural influences. This Roman aqueduct, near Caesarea, is evidence of diversified educational and engineering expertise.
TW

educations and served in capacities where they could use it.

Deborah (Judg. 4), Huldah (2 Kings 22:14–20) and Anna (Luke 2:36) are each examples of knowledgeable prophetesses who played significant roles. Mary, the mother of Jesus, as a young woman showed herself to be extremely well-versed in the Scriptures. Her hymn recorded in Luke 1:46–55 is comprised almost entirely of Old Testament quotations.

The amount of education a girl received may have depended on her circumstances, her temperament and the attitude of her parents. Normally her education was limited to the home and centered on domestic responsibilities.

No matter how much education the boy received, he was expected to learn a trade. This would protect him from becoming heavy with theories and light on practical experience. Early tradition required a rabbi to support himself, as Paul did with tentmaking, by some means other than teaching the law.   ■

JESUS AS A TEACHER □ As mentioned earlier, two titles often applied to Christ are rabbi and master, which would indicate respect for Him as a teacher. Probably more people saw Him in this role than as the messiah, for they debated His messianic claims. The masses readily acknowledged His ability to teach and communicate.

One key factor in Jesus' teaching role was His authoritative manner unlike that of the scribes (Matt. 7:28, 29). It is possible that many considered the scribes as petty and meddling, while they saw Jesus as concerned with important issues based on the concerns of God. He may have been perceived as knowledgeable, confident and caring, which would have contrasted with the local religious nit-picking.

Whatever His precise qualities, Jesus and the religious leaders were noticeably different. Not only did He differ from the scribes, but He transcended all men, for some remarked that "no man ever spoke like this man" (John 7:46, RSV).

Jesus used a wide variety of teaching methods. One leading characteristic was His ability as a storyteller, which is exemplified by His parables. Jesus allowed the impact of an interesting story to clarify His message.

Another strength of His teaching was His use of object lessons. His points were rich with nature illustrations, things that He picked up or pointed to. Christ's discussion of sheep and shepherds is a prime example of objects and a lifestyle that contained lessons. His cursing of the fig tree and taking a coin from a fish's mouth were memorable.

At times Jesus lectured, at other times He asked questions or provoked questions from His audience. He also taught by experience. He asked His disciples to do things, and they became the wiser for being involved.

Not everyone appreciated the teaching of Jesus nor did everyone understand Him. In some cases He felt that His listeners were not ready or willing to comprehend (Matt. 11:15; Mark 8:17, 18).   ■

Jesus' teaching style frequently included assembling crowds on the sloping shores of the Sea of Galilee and speaking to them either from the shore or from a small boat anchored just out in the water. This grassy slope on a prominent hill overlooking the Sea of Galilee just south of Capernaum is believed by many to be the spot where Jesus preached the "Sermon on the Mount" (Matt. 5) and where He chose His apostles (Luke 6:12, 13).   TW

CHAPTER 11

OLD AGE

The people of Israel put a great deal of faith in the wisdom and experience of the elderly. Tradition was important and they trusted their elders to keep them from wandering too far from the proven paths. This attitude gave the nation strength and stability, though sometimes it made Israel rigid and reluctant to accept anything new.

Early in their history when Moses found it impossible to govern the people by himself, he selected others to help according to the wisdom of his older father-in-law, Jethro (Ex. 18). Jews frequently gleaned guidance from the elderly.

Respect for age was written into the heart of the law. Those who paid sufficient honor to their parents were promised many years on earth (Ex. 20:12). Even after they had married and no longer had to obey their parents, they were still expected to pay them respect.

When the Bible describes a society which has fallen under judgment, it says that boys will become the officials and young people will turn against the elderly (Isa. 3:4, 5). A society that disregards its elders has run amuck.

ELDERS □ The term elder became a title of dignity in both the Old and New Testaments, for an elder was looked to for knowledge and leadership. The 70 people Moses appointed as judges in Israel were elders and they were the ones who received the outpouring of the Spirit (Num. 11:25).

When Israel settled in Canaan, each city appointed elders to help govern their new territories.

After the monarchy was established, the elders functioned as a legislative body. Throughout Israel's turbulent history, the elders were a cohesive force. Through the turmoil of the Exile and return the nation survived, because the elders frequently took control.

When Jesus ministered in Israel, the elders were operating as a body called the Sanhedrin. They ruled from Jerusalem over religious matters and held power in many areas of civil government.

The formation of the church began with respect for elders. Seasoned men were expected to be wise in spiritual matters and help keep the church on a steady course. The word *presbyteros*, from which we derive presbyter and Presbyterian, means elders or eldership. Peter, as an elder, encouraged young men to submit themselves to older men in the churches.

There is no doubt that respect for elders continued in the church, but that is not to suggest that there was a blind following of aged men. The key factor was wisdom, not years. The Bible does caution that a wise young man is better than an old fool (Eccles. 4:13). In this spirit Paul admonished the relatively young Timothy to stand his ground and not let the older believers belittle him (1 Tim. 4:12). Nonetheless, that halo of reasonable respect was not to be violated. Young, energetic Christians were not to speak rudely to the elderly (1 Tim. 5:1).

While the primary meaning of elder had reference to age, its significance began to change. Elder also designated a leader and as an office did not necessarily require old age.   ■

HOW OLD WAS OLD? □ Longevity in biblical times under-

went drastic changes. The first patriarchs lived an amazingly long time. Before the Flood, Adam died at 930 years of age; Mahalaleh at 895; Methuselah at 969; Noah at 950.

We do not have a record of averages, but we do know that the figures dropped dramatically after the Flood: Arphaxad died at 403 years; Peleg at 209; Reu at 207; Nahor at 119.

By the time of the monarchy ages were comparable to modern times. King David died at 70. This seemed the acceptable age for a full life. However, if a person reached 80, he was assumed to possess unusual strength (Ps. 90:10). The Babylonians felt the same way, considering the age of 70 average, 80 very old and 90 extremely unusual.

The age of 70 was an expected lifetime during New Testament times. Some men such as John may have exceeded it considerably; it is probable that he lived longer than the other disciples and may have reached 90.   ■

THE HOARY HEAD □ It probably was not threatening to most

Jews to have one's hair turn white. Some were youth conscious, and went to extremes to hide wrinkles, gray hair and bulging mid-riffs, but most accepted aging as a mark of dignity. The Bible depicts gray hair as a crown of splendor (Prov. 20:29). Eliphaz supported his argument by insisting that the gray haired and aged were on his side (Job 15:10).   ■

INFIRMITIES □ Much like modern old age, long life took its toll

on the Jewish body. The physical machine began to run down as the decades ran up. It was not uncommon for an older person to begin losing his teeth. One's back began to lose its rigidity and develop a marked stoop. Hearing often became faint. Fears grew and one avoided heights. Frequently he had trouble seeing, lost drive and had trouble sleeping (Eccles. 12:1–7).

Barzillai is a good example of an old man caught in the diffi-culties of aging. At 80 years of age, he could no longer taste what

he ate or drank. Barzillai also had trouble hearing the songs men
and women sang (2 Sam. 19:35).   ■

DISAPPOINTMENT □ One of the saddest stories concerning
an old man is about the 98-year-old Eli (1 Sam. 4). A high priest
and judge, Eli had failed to correct and control his sons, Hophni
and Phineas. Eventually the Philistines defeated the Jews, stole the
ark, and killed his two sons. When Eli was told of the tragedy, he
fell backwards off his chair, broke his neck and died.

The Bible paints many pictures of the elderly who had their
hearts broken with disappointment. However, there is also an
abundance of happy stories. Jewish life was replete with both sides
of reality.   ■

RETIREMENT □ A Jewish adult worked hard to reach independence before he was too old to work. Many did not accomplish
this and were dependent on charitable gifts or the good attitude of
their children. Israel had an excellent program of sharing with the
poor, but naturally most tried to avoid being objects of charity.

A major principle of personal financial planning, laid down in
the Scriptures, was that parents should lay up goods for the children and not the children for the parents (2 Cor. 12:14). However,
this did not always work out. When, for whatever reasons, the
parents failed to secure their own retirement, the children were
morally obligated to support them.

This was in marked contrast to the evil trickery of some of the
Pharisees. Some of the religious leaders of Israel wriggled out of
supporting their own mothers by merely declaring "*corban*" (Mark
7:11–13). This meant that they had given or even promised gifts to
the temple and thus expected the temple to care for their mothers.

The church became involved in helping the elderly, especially
widows. However, clear standards were given to prevent abuses
whenever possible. If an elderly widow had relatives who could
support her, they were obligated to do so. Should they refuse to
support a needy relative, they were considered as infidels or worse
(1 Tim. 5:3–8). The churches also spelled out restrictions concerning
the elderly themselves in order to prevent abuses by those who
simply were too lazy to work.   ■

CHAPTER 12

VOCATIONS

The Bible holds physical labor in high regard. Idleness and avoidance of work are condemned. Jews felt this so strongly that they considered work ordained by God. They therefore turned pots, plowed fields and baked bread to the glory of God.

It is unlikely that every laborer always felt so noble about his work, but such an attitude was in his consciousness. Man was created to work, not to be at leisure, and work was both expected and accepted.

From the beginning man's purpose was to use God's resources and make something useful of them (Gen. 1:28; 2:15). The concept

Hard work was expected and accepted in a land where sparse, rocky soil and little rainfall made agriculture difficult. Here men gather wheat near the oaks of Mamre, Abraham's ancient home near Hebron, just to the west of the Dead Sea.   TW

of work being honorable carried over into the New Testament as Paul told his readers to work for their masters "heartily" (Col. 3:22, 23, KJV).

This does not suggest that every Israelite and first-century Christian was a feverish worker. Many people avoided responsibility. Others resorted to fraud rather than honest labor. However, it does mean that many people were conscientious hard workers who accepted their tasks willingly.

ORGANIZED LABOR □ By the time of Jesus, society was both rural and urban. Jeremias estimates the population of Jerusalem at 25,000 plus; Palestine was home to at least half a million and some historians claim much larger numbers. City life necessitated many workers with a variety of skills.

In such a sophisticated society the common needs of the working man made it necessary to organize into guilds. By the time of Christ workers' guilds were accepted, widespread and regulated. They were not the exact prototype of our modern labor unions; however, there are many similarities. While some people worked alone in isolated areas and only rarely had contact with others, the rule was to perform labor and handle merchandise in connection with groups.

As early as the 24th century B.C., in Sumer, labor guilds were organized to meet specific needs. People who belonged to guilds found it easier to purchase materials and were able to learn skills from each other and share work. They also protected their jobs by restricting access to their trade. Though the original purpose of organization was not to create a bargaining base, later they did use their collective strength.

In many cases members of a guild lived in the same area. Often this may have been the result of a supply of raw materials. For instance, there was a great deal of ore at Edom, so metal workers settled there; dyers may have lived near Thyatira because they needed shellfish to make dye; the Tyropoeon Valley was occupied by dairies and was called the "valley of the cheese mongers." Not only did they center in cities, but guilds also dominated neighborhoods. During the time of Christ fullers lived in one part of town, fish

Ornamental metalworking is still a large industry in the Middle East. This plate is being hand-crafted in a small shop on a side street in Cairo, Egypt. TW

salesmen in another, bakers in yet a third. There is evidence of guilds for chariot builders, potters, musicians, fowlers, butchers, carpenters, metalworkers, sculptors, priests, houseboatman, etc.

Men were proud to belong to a guild. Often when one referred to himself as "Malchiah the goldsmith's son," or the son of a gate-keeper, he was making reference to his membership in a guild (Neh. 3:31, KJV; Ezra 2:42). There was a prophets' guild (1 Kings 20:35), probably comprised of a professional class of court prophets. When Amos said he was not the son of a prophet, he meant that he was not a member of the guild (Amos 7:14), and it is likely that none of the writing prophets were. The guild prophets were gen-erally the opponents of true prophets (1 Kings 22:6-28).

In many cases "son of a silversmith" meant the person's father was a silversmith and he was a member of the silversmiths' guild. Frequently a son learned his father's trade and joined the related guild.

This raises some interesting questions about Jesus and His oc-cupation. We do know that His foster father Joseph was a carpenter (Matt. 13:55) and that Jesus became a carpenter (Mark 6:3), but we do not know if Jesus belonged to a carpenters' guild. Yet, we do know that it is possible, for many workers did belong.

Guilds were so common during this time that the Roman gov-ernment licensed them because the emperor wanted to make sure they did not become political forces.

There were many practical benefits of belonging to a guild be-sides the ones already mentioned. Some offered insurance against stolen tools and equipment. Others could provide funeral plots. A form of unemployment insurance was available. In a few areas members were so concentrated that their guild made up the entire congregation at the synagogue.

Along with the fraternal benefits came jealousy. Some workers were jealous of other guilds and at times the members of one guild kept the members of another from securing a job in their territory.

We have little recorded information about organized strikes, but they did occur. Often they were sit-down strikes by a group disgusted with working conditions. There are records of strikes over money: In early Babylonia, stonecutters refused to work until the king paid them; the bakers of showbread for the temple went on strike during the first century and refused to let anyone else bake their secret recipe. In comparison to the number of workers and guilds, there were few strikes. The tremendous amount of unemployed at the time of Christ may have discouraged most strikes.

At times there were attempts to break the guilds. Temple of-ficials in one instance brought in independent artisans but even-tually were forced to rehire original workers and double their sal-aries. The proliferation of guilds does not suggest that they had exclusive rights. Many people away from the population centers were carpenters or silversmiths without joining a guild. ∎

THE SANCTITY OF WORK □ Most who heard and followed Christ were of the working class. For them the gospel upheld the dignity of labor, the fairness of wages and the danger of idleness. Jesus and the disciples easily identified with these needs. Referring to ancient Jewish culture, Jesus insisted that honest work deserved a reasonable wage (Luke 10:7) as did Paul (1 Cor. 9:7; 1 Tim. 5:18). God has always been concerned that man not overwork, and thus instituted the observance of the Sabbath (Ex. 20:8, 9). James depicts God as the friend of the laborer. He wrote that when an employer holds back a worker's wages, the cries of the cheated are heard by a caring heavenly Father (James 5:4).

The Bible does not view work as merely a necessary part of this life. In it we are told to do the best job possible for our employer, even if we are slaves under a harsh master (1 Pet. 2:18); under no circumstances can we justify stealing from our employer (Titus 2:10); the church is to provide help for those who have lost their jobs; however, if the person simply refuses to work, he is not to be given food (2 Thess. 3:10).

Jesus was a member of the working class and identified easily with them. Many of His stories used illustrations from labor and employer-employee relationships (Matt. 6:28; 9:37; 20:1; etc.). Some of the same problems that concerned workers of that day also concerned Jesus Christ and His leading apostles (Peter, Paul and James). ■

OCCUPATIONS, TRADES AND CRAFTS □ We read of a great many skilled and semiskilled laborers in Bible history. Briefly we will describe some of the occupations which are significant in the Bible accounts. A few jobs (fisherman, tax collector, etc.) are discussed more fully in other chapters.

Bakers. Bread was the most common food eaten in Israel and usually was baked at home. However, much of society was urbanized after Solomon's time and bakers were called for. The early bakers worked for kings, pharaohs (Gen. 40:2) and the wealthy, but later the common people also used their services.

Later bakers had shops and were so plentiful that a "baker's street" existed in Jeremiah's time (37:21). Today many bakeries are located near the Damascus Gate in Jerusalem. Similar shops existed during the time of Christ.

Bankers. The need to exchange currency and the demand for credit caused banking to blossom by the first century B.C. Most exchange "banks" resembled our modern fair concession booths, being little more than tables. However, some banking institutions were developing which paid interest on money deposited (Luke 19:23). Debt has always been an uncomfortable situation and many bankers were disliked. Under Roman law a debtor who could not pay could be jailed (Matt. 18:25).

In ancient times monies and valuables were usually buried

This vendor of freshly-baked bread propels his pushcart along a busy street in Jerusalem near the Damascus Gate.   TW

for safekeeping, and charging interest on money loaned to the poor was outlawed by God (Ex. 22:25). By the time John's Revelation was written, historians tell us Laodicea was a banking center; John declares the believers there are suffering spiritually because of their abundant wealth (3:17).

The most famous confrontation between exchange bankers and Jesus occurred in the temple (John 2:14; Matt. 21:12). This seems to have taken place twice during His ministry. There was a need to exchange coins to temple currency, but the bankers apparently charged an unfair amount.

One would probably be struck by the similarity between banking practices of the first century and now. Savings accounts were available; mortgages were possible; emergency loans were made, with interest rates (usually 12 or 13%) sometimes soaring to nearly 50%; letters of credit were issued; international loans were made; and safe deposits were in use.

Beggars. Owing to the large number of illnesses, injuries and birth defects, and the high rate of unemployment in Jerusalem, begging had become a sizable profession. Some people knew no other job during their lifetimes. Religious pilgrimages to the temple made the city a good place to collect alms. Giving to the poor was an ancient Jewish tradition and when a celebration was at hand, most felt particularly generous. Income from begging was good

Begging is a sizable profession in Palestine. This beggar sits near the Church of the
Annunciation in Nazareth.   TW

The Pool of Siloam, in the lower Tyropoeon Valley at the southernmost part of the City of David, is the site of Jesus' healing of the blind man in John 9:1–11. TW

enough that some charlatans feigned lameness in order to arouse sympathy and thus earn more.

Because of the high number of beggars in the temple area, laws were written that dictated what they could do and where they could go. Some men drifted from one religious celebration to another, hoping to receive alms at weddings and funerals.

Jesus crossed the paths of many beggars and used others as teaching illustrations. In the story of the rich man, Lazarus was a beggar covered with sores (Luke 16:20). Blind Bartimaeus (Mark 10:46) and the lame man at the Gate Beautiful (Acts 3:2) are well-known New Testament beggars. Few caused as great a commotion as the blind man Jesus healed at Siloam (John 9).

Building trades. During the time that the Herodians ruled Israel, workers in the building trades prospered. The Herod family rebuilt the temple and the palace, built a magnificent tomb, a theater and

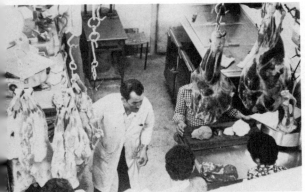

a hippodrome. These and many other projects provided a great deal of employment.

Butchers. This group had their own guild and had a butcher's street

Open-air butcher shops and meat-markets are a common sight along the crowded streets of the Old City of Jerusalem. TW

named after them. Many Jews were butchers.

Carpenters. This occupation takes on special significance because both Jesus (Mark 6:3) and Joseph (Matt. 13:55) worked at it. Carpenters were not usually house builders because homes were not made of wood, but they did have wooden trim and fixtures. Jesus likely spent His time fashioning ox yokes, stools, plows, cabinets, carts and lattice windows. On occasion carpenters also made artificial teeth!

The tools Jesus handled were the axe, hatchet, saw, knives, plane and square. Hammers and bronze nails were in use at the time . It was also possible that He worked with a bow-drill.

Eunuchs. During the time of Jesus there was a fair number of eunuchs who worked as staff members in palaces to guard harems. Some eunuchs had actually been castrated but others merely held the title.

The making of bricks was in biblical times, as it is now, an honorable occupation and part of the building trade.   BAS

We cannot be sure which type Philip led to faith in the Messiah (Acts 8:26ff.).

Often eunuchs had considerable influence in the royal courts. There are many eunuchs who appear in Old Testament history (2 Kings 20:18; Jer. 41:16). Daniel and his colleagues may have been official eunuchs (Dan. 1:19).

Jesus said that some people would volunteer to forego marriage in order to serve the kingdom of God (Matt. 19:12), in effect making themselves eunuchs.

Gardeners. There were several different types of gardens, including some for orchards, some for vegetables and some for beauty. Ahab was willing to kill Naboth for a garden (1 Kings 21). Solomon loved gardens and may have worked in them himself (Eccles. 2:5). Adam was a gardener by God's decree (Gen. 2:15).

A lovely garden, attractively planted with trees, shrubs and scented herbs, surrounds The Garden Tomb, a peaceful enclosure in the southeast sector of Jerusalem which is generally accepted by Protestant groups as the family vault of Joseph of Arimathea, the wealthy Jew who gave his own garden and mausoleum for Jesus' burial.   TW

The only direct mention of a gardener in the New Testament is in John 20:15. Joseph's tomb was located in a manicured garden that required the services of a professional gardener.

Heralds. Royal courts had heralds whose job it was to make public announcements for the king. This was done often in the Old Testament (2 Kings 18:18, 37; 2 Sam. 8:16; 1 Kings 4:3). When Paul wanted to explain sharing the gospel, he told his readers to announce it as a royal herald would (1 Tim. 2:7; 2 Tim. 1:11, NIV). He thus emphasized the importance of the gospel and those who declare it.

Innkeepers. Originally travelers took their chances by either camping outdoors or securing a place in a private home. As life became more sophisticated and travel increased, the need for commercial inns became apparent. Rahab the harlot may have been the keeper in one of these inns (Josh. 2:1). Later these inns became *caravanserais* which provided care for animals as well as people.

All populated areas had inns by the time of

Agriculture is a major industry in the Galilee region today. Here wagonloads of picked avocados await shipping at a kibbutz in Galilee.
CD

Christ. His parents were turned away from one (Luke 2:7), for during holidays and festivals it was hard to find room in these establishments. The huge crowds made many stay outside the city in neighboring towns or sleep on the ground in tents.

•   According to Scripture some innkeepers were caring and dependable (Luke 10:34). However, the facilities probably provided only the bare necessities.

Lawyers. (See *Scribes* in index.)

Merchants. The number of merchants and peddlers during New Testament times was considerable. Some grew or made what they sold; others bought large quantities of goods and resold them as retailers.

While the nations had always engaged in trade, two historical shifts caused the number of Israelite merchants to increase sharply during this time. The first was the prosperity and urbanization under Solo-

This Turkish caravanserai is located on the Haifa side of the Old Town section of Akko, on the Mediterranean Sea. These caravanserai, several of which are located near the harbor, include warehouse facilities for the goods brought in by camel train, as well as accommodations for the drivers and merchants. Akko was one of the main ports for the flourishing caravan trade.   TW

mon. The second was the Babylonian exile. While in exile they had little land to cultivate and were forced to trade and sell for a living. After their return to Israel, many returned to their agricultural vocations, but changing times and a growing population led to a sharp increase of merchants.

There were different kinds of retail merchants. One was the shopkeeper. Their stores stood next to each other in shopping districts. A few merchants owned stores in three or four cities. In Jerusalem these stores were called *sugs* and were located on narrow streets.

A second type of merchant was the peddler, or hawker. They set up tables or stands for the day and dismantled them at night.

The third variety was a traveling merchant. These men carried

their wares from town to town and often tried to be in Jerusalem at times of high traffic such as Passover.

Good roads and safe travel were essential to prosperous trade. Both King Herod and the Roman Empire worked to provide these.

Consumers had many of the same concerns as we have today. Honest weights, good products and fair prices were major issues. It is believed that generally a merchant's profit margin was 20% to 30%, though it sometimes climbed to 100%.

This fur merchant is typical of the hundreds of retail merchants whose tiny shops line the streets of the old city of Jerusalem. The shops are called *sugs*.   TW

Josephus tells us that the Jews of his time had a distaste for being merchants. However, the economic realities caused many to take up this trade (Matt. 22:5), and we read of many of them in the Scriptures. Lydia was a merchant who dealt in purple cloth (Acts 16:14). In Jesus' story of the ten virgins (Matt. 25:9), the women are told to go to the merchants of oil and buy some. When Jesus overturned

The peddler, or hawker, set up a table or stand for the day and was gone at night. Candied-fruit-on-a-stick is peddled here by a traveling peddler in Jaffa.   TW

the moneychangers' booths in the temple, He also chased out those who sold doves (Mark 11:15).

Metalworkers. This skilled trade spread throughout Israel and flourished during the time of Solomon. Craftsmen skillfully worked with gold, silver, iron, lead, copper, tin or other metals. Their work adorned buildings and their jewelry was worn by many. They also created pagan images. At Ephesus the metalsmiths prospered so much making statues of Diana that they revolted when the preaching of the gospel threatened their business (Acts 19:24).

Philosophers. Certain Greeks and Romans made their living by divulging their knowledge and wisdom. They exacted fees from individuals or governments who sought their services. Leaders such as Nero and Aurelius often employed them.

These people represented a wide spectrum of thought. Those who agreed with one considered the philosopher a tremendous intellectual. Those who disagreed looked on him as comical.

Because of their divergent views which contradicted Scripture, Paul warned the church at Colosse to avoid them (Col. 2:8). In turn, the Stoic and Epicurean philosophers viewed Paul's approach to life as absurd (Acts 17:18). The apostle seems to have fared well when addressing them at Areopagus (Acts 17:32–34).

Mail couriers. A large volume of letter writing resulted from a high rate of literacy. The need to transport this correspondence called for a postal system.

As early as the 6th century B.C. the Persians used mounted couriers, a type of pony express. Good horses and messengers were stationed a day's journey apart to move official mail.

The Romans had a similar system complete with inns to house couriers. However, to date we have no evidence that these systems were available to the private sector. As far as we know all personal correspondence was delivered by friends or merchants. Paul evidently sent a great deal of mail this way.

Potters. Pottery was in use even before recorded history. In many cases pottery was preferred over leather or baskets because it lasted longer, held liquids better and offered protection from animals and insects.

This rocky knoll below the Propylaea in Athens is known as the Areopagus, or Mars' Hill. It was from this natural pulpit the Apostle Paul preached the sermon found in Acts 17:22ff.   TW

After the invention of the potter's wheel and the development of kiln firing, it became possible to produce pottery which was both functional and aesthetic as well.   TW

The earliest pottery was shaped without equipment, but after the invention of the turning wheel a potter could work faster and create a more uniform, symmetrical product (Jer. 18:1–6). Potters made not only bowls and jars, but also toys and dolls.

After a product was shaped it was fired in a kiln. The "Tower of the Ovens" (Neh. 3:11) may be a place where kilns were used. Some residents of Jerusalem objected to the making of pottery there because of the smoke from the kilns.

In New Testament times pottery was used for water jars (John 2:6), oil vials (Matt. 25:1–13), and lamps (Matt. 25:1–8).

The abundance of pottery in Israel resulted in a proportionate abundance of broken pottery. Job's terrible sea monster had an underside like broken pottery (Job 41:30).

Archaeological finds have shown that shards of broken pottery were used as a writing medium. In ancient Israel most writing was etched on pieces of broken pottery. Generally, papyrus and leather were too costly to be widely used. Personal letters, legal documents and maps were printed on clay tablets or pottery. Writing began as a series of pictures but soon gave way to refined letters. If the document was official a seal might be impressed into the clay. Today the writings found on this pottery and clay are of tremendous help to modern archaeologists.

Sailors. The Jews were not fond of the sea, but as the nation became wealthier, they needed to venture out for more commerce, supplies and artisans. The Phoenicians, who were experienced seamen, carried out most of the seafaring projects. Many sailors were present in the coastal cities of Israel. Their life was difficult and

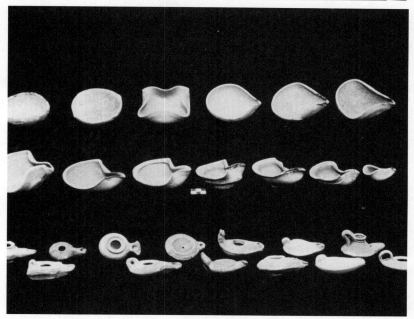

This assemblage of lamps details the development of oil lamps in Palestine for more than 3,000 years, from Early Bronze Age into Byzantine and Arab times. At top is the Bronze Age sequence, beginning with a simple saucer with several string wicks hung over the lip. Indentations for wicks were later added, then grew into four spouts, but this was later discontinued in favor of a single spout, first with a slight pinch and then triangular in shape. In the Iron Age (middle row) the pinch of the spout is more severe, and a rim-flange is developing. A base is added in the late Iron Age, but drops away in the Persian period when the pinch is pressed all the way to the bottom of the lamp. Finally, during the Maccabean times, the sides are brought completely together to form a "slipper" lamp. Hellenistic, Roman and later lamps in the bottom row are mould-made rather than products of the potter's wheel. The splayed nozzle (left of center bottom) is typical of the Herodian period. To the right are lamps of the Islamic/Arab period.   DM

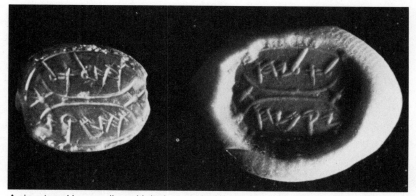

A signet seal in carnelian with its impression stamped in clay. From an archaeological find at Gezer and dated about 700 B.C., this is the first occurrence of the name "Elijah" on the Judean seal.
                                                                                                              DM

some were gone from home three years at a time. The most extensive description of sailors in the New Testament is found in the account of Paul's voyage to Rome (Acts 27, 28).

Tanners. Leather played a large part in daily life, being used in shoes, containers, tents, clothing, armor and writing parchments. Because the tanner dealt in dead animals, he was both needed and disliked. He was forced to live outside the city because lime and other substances used in the tanning process had a terrible odor, and because he needed a ready source of water.

Simon the Tanner lived by the seashore at Joppa (Acts 10:6) and was generally avoided. The visit to his house by Peter is a key event since the apostle steps over old laws of uncleanness into a new era in which God declares all things clean.   ■

CHAPTER 13

SLAVERY

Slavery was a subject with which the people of Bible times were all too familiar. For thousands of years slavery was an integral part of life. Israel's economy and, to much greater extent, Greece and Rome's were dependent on this cheap form of labor.

The average person in the first century frequently saw slaves at work, and being bought and sold. He also saw prisoners of war being marched through the streets on their way to becoming slaves.

Despite biblical laws to prevent brutality, cruelties occurred; families were separated and homelands were left behind forever. Yet there were silver linings in this terrible trade. A Jew who found himself hopelessly in debt could choose slavery as an alternative to imprisonment or other punishment. Many slaves went on to prosper, finding freedom and positions of prominence.

It is not fair to compare slavery in Bible times with slavery in the United States before the Civil War. In the U.S. slaves were forbidden by law to receive an education or acquire property, and they could rarely gain on their own the means to buy their freedom. Jewish law, on the other hand, offered hope for slaves.

It is important to understand ancient slavery because many of our biblical terms were adapted from that practice. When writers such as Paul and Peter sought to explain Christ's sacrifice for us, they resorted to the vivid imagery of slavery. While Jesus Christ could not always guarantee physical freedom, He provided the means for spiritual liberty, both now and for eternity.

ACQUIRING SLAVES □ Under Jewish law there were several ways to obtain slaves. The laws protected Jewish slaves with well-defined boundaries; however, these statutes did not guard foreign slaves under Jewish masters.

Selling oneself. If a person could no longer support himself and volunteered himself as a slave (Lev. 25:39), he was to be treated as a hired hand and at the year of Jubilee be released. Should this person marry during his six years of slavery, he had the option to remain with his master. If he did, it appears he belonged to his master for the rest of his life (Ex. 21:5, 6). The servant then had his ear pierced as a sign that he was a slave. Neighboring nations had similar laws. This law offered a measure of security to those who faced economic collapse.

Victims of debt. When in this predicament, some people sold themselves as in the previous section, but others were forced into servitude. This practice increased under the monarchy. When a thief was unable to repay what he had stolen, he could be sold as payment (Ex. 22:12). Some sons and daughters were sold into slavery because of poverty during Nehemiah's time (Neh. 5:1–5). This showed that a righteous leader was needed. The widow faced the imminent danger of having her children taken away into slavery if she could not pay her debts (2 Kings 4:1). This practice may not have had biblical sanction, but it was done.

Purchase of foreigners. A sizable slave trade was carried on between Israel and other nations. For the most part foreigners were brought into Israel. Rarely were Jewish slaves sold to foreigners because a strong law condemned a person to death for selling a Jewish slave (Deut. 24:7). These foreign slaves were not guaranteed freedom and could be left as an inheritance from generation to generation (Lev. 25:46).

Captives from war. The Jews were well accustomed to the ugly results of war. Often their people were carried off into slavery. The young girl serving Namaan's wife was a prisoner taken from Israel (2 Kings 5:2) during a raid by the army of Aram (Syria). The people of Israel engaged in the same practice and collected many servants from the battles they won. After capturing Midian the army brought captives and spoils to Moses and Aaron (Num. 31:11, 12). Some argue that this was the humane thing to do since the alternative was to kill them. Others, however, do not feel such an end justifies the means.

The laws of Israel addressed some aspects of taking captives as slaves. For instance, if a man married a captured slave, she then had to be treated as a free woman (Deut. 21:10–14). She could not be sold back into slavery.

On at least one occasion the Jews captured fellow Jews and tried to make them slaves, such as when the armies of Israel defeated Judah and Jerusalem. Obed, a prophet, interceded when Israel planned to turn the population into slaves (2 Chron. 28:10). ∎

SOLOMON'S SLAVES □ Much of the glory that belonged to Israel was built by foreign slaves, conquered people who had been distributed among government leaders and the king. Solomon did not make slaves of his own people but did use foreigners (1 Kings 9:21). Some of these slaves labored in the southern mines. Others may have been trained as sailors for the Jewish navy.

Government slaves were used by Israel from the time of David until the time of Ezra and Nehemiah. However, private ownership began when they entered the land and conquered the Canaanites (Josh. 16:10). ∎

PROTECTION FOR JEWISH SLAVES □ A master could not do anything he pleased with his Jewish slave. The Bible spells out a number of guarantees of humane treatment which did not necessarily apply to non-Jewish slaves.

These are found in Ex. 21:1–11; Lev. 25:39–55; Deut. 15.

1. He had to be freed after six years.

2. If he married while in slavery, he was free to stay forever with the master.

3. If he married a wife provided by the master and they had children, he could not take the wife and children with him when he left.

4. If a master accepted someone's daughter as a slave, he could not sell her to foreigners.

5. If she married the master's son, she became his daughter.

6. A slave wife who was deprived of food, clothing and affection could go free.

7. The poor man who sold himself as a slave was to be treated as a hired servant and not as a slave.

8. The master could not treat a Jewish slave ruthlessly.

9. Slaves could be redeemed by relatives.

10. A freed slave was to be given supplies so he could renew his life.

Most of what we know about the treatment of slaves in Old Testament times we learn from the Bible itself. ∎

MARKING A SLAVE □ During a slave's six years of service, he could not be marked as a slave. However, if he chose to remain a slave for life, he would lean against a doorpost and have his ear pierced to indicate his status (Ex. 21:6; Deut. 15:17). The marking was made by using a carpenter's awl just as a hole was made in wood or leather.

A number of other markings were used in ancient times and some may have been used to designate slavery. Tatoos were placed on people's hands and marks on their foreheads (Ezek. 9:4). Five hundred years before Christ, slaves in the Jewish community bore the names of their master on their wrists. ∎

INJURIES TO SLAVES □ If a Jewish slave was injured by his master, he could insist on certain penalties or compensation, as exemplified in Ex. 21:20ff.

1. Should a slave die from a beating, the master would be punished. If the slave revived in a few days, the master was blameless.

2. If a man hit a slave and the slave's eye was knocked out, the slave could go free.

3. If the slave's tooth was knocked out, the slave could go free.

4. Should a bull gore another man's slave, the owner of the bull must pay 30 shekels of silver to the master of the slave. ∎

A SLAVE'S PROPERTY □ It was possible for a slave in Israel to accumulate land and wealth for himself. Provision was made whereby a slave could acquire enough to pay for his own release (Lev. 25:49). Saul's father's slave claimed to own a fourth of a silver shekel (1 Sam. 9:8). Aiba, Saul's slave, owned 20 slaves himself (2 Sam. 9:10).   ■

MEANS OF FREEDOM □ Jewish law provided several ways to set slaves free. Not all of these regulations applied to Jews who held foreign slaves. We also assume that not everyone kept these laws to the letter.

1. Neither a Jewish slave nor his wife could be kept longer than six years (Ex. 21:2–4).

2. Any slave who was permanently injured by his owner had to be released (Ex. 21:26, 27).

3. If a slave escaped his master, a new owner could not take him in and return him to his former master (Deut. 23:15, 16). If he chose to leave and live elsewhere, he was permitted to do so.

4. If a male slave gave his daughter to a master under the condition that the master would later give her in marriage to one of his sons, failure to keep that promise automatically freed the daughter (Ex. 21:7–10).

5. A slave's uncle, cousin or blood relative could pay to have him released or if the slave had accumulated some prosperity, he could redeem himself (Lev. 25:47–49). This biblical concept of redemption can be applied to several areas of life. Land could be redeemed or recovered by a kinsman redeemer. In the spiritual sense of the term Jesus became our redeemer (Gal. 3:13). The price Jesus paid as our kinsman redeemer was His blood on the cross (Eph. 1:7, 8). The concept of redemption includes more than slavery, but a slave-owning culture easily understood the terminology. Christ bought us, redeemed us, from sin, evil, guilt and the curse of the law.   ■

NEW TESTAMENT SLAVERY □ In order to better appreciate the writings of men such as Paul, we need to understand how greatly slavery permeated his society. Our concept of the word "servant," which usually refers to slave, is inadequate to convey the emotional and social impact. Too often we think of a household servant, an office worker or a member of a construction crew. When Paul used the word "servant," he often meant "slave" (The primary meaning of *doulos* is slave, with an emphasis on bondage).

Deissman's explanation (p. 320) of the Delphi transactions may provide background for some of Paul's thinking. There an owner would bring his slave to the temple and sell him to a god. The price for the slave was paid out of the treasury after the amount was supplied by the slave. In other words, the slave paid for his own redemption. Consequently, the god then owned the slave and the person was in effect free. It is possible that Paul's discussions of spiritual slavery and freedom are partly based on this widespread practice.

Paul pictures the believer as one who has been set free by Christ (Gal. 5:1). Many of his references to spiritual freedom have their foundations in slavery because Christians have been bought with a price (1 Cor. 6:20; 7:23). Some members of the early congregations were slaves (1 Cor 7:21) who would have clearly understood the concept of redemption. ■

JERUSALEM □ A very active slave trade existed in Jerusalem during the time of Christ. The city had a slave market complete with an auction block. Jewish slaves were sold in the city during this era. Gentile slaves were imported from Syria where Tyre was a slave center. Most of the slaves in that area probably worked in the city rather than rural areas.

Slaves were one of the major reasons for serious unemployment during that time. Because slavery offered relatively cheap labor, the free man had to accept starvation wages to compete for jobs.

Many Old Testament principles were still operative around the first century. A Jewish thief could be forced into slavery to pay for his crime. Often a Gentile slave became circumcised if the master was a Jew. Herod the Great owned a large community of slaves.

A Gentile slave was worth up to 100 times as much as a Jewish slave because he remained property for life, while a Jewish servant served a maximum of only six years. Consequently, there were far more Gentile slaves than Jewish ones.

Josephus reminds us that the Jewish laws concerning slaves were not necessarily obeyed. Herod readily sold Jewish slaves outside the nation's boundaries—a practice which the Bible forbade. Jews may not have been eager to acquire Jewish slaves, for the law demanded that they be treated well and eventually released. This explains the ancient saying, "Whoever buys a Jewish slave buys a master." ■

THE ROMAN EMPIRE □ Slavery was extremely common throughout the empire; millions, possibly half the total population at times, were slaves. The treatment of slaves varied from ruthless to genuine affection. Some slaves worked in large gangs for wealthy landowners and they were treated quite differently, much more harshly, than those considered members of the master's household. Some slaves were murdered; however, many others were freed and rose to prominent positions in government.

Many Jews, as Roman slaves, were transported and freed in another part of the world, in a foreign culture. Often these freed slaves succeeded financially and socially.

Indications are that most Roman slaves ate well, dressed adequately and were treated as well as the working class, sometimes better. Their living quarters were respectable and frequently in the master's house. The Roman Empire prospered tremendously through the use of slaves.

The newly formed church contained masters, slaves and freed slaves who had become Christians. Their relationships thus faced drastic changes. They now were expected to fellowship, have communion, pray and sing together.

Therefore the biblical writers addressed the subjects of slavery and inter-relationships. Peter urged slaves to submit to their master, even if that owner is harsh and beats his slaves (1 Pet. 2:18–25). Paul demanded respect between the believing slave and his believing master (1 Tim. 6:1, 2). His letter to Philemon encouraged a Christian master to accept the return of the runaway slave, Onesimus.

During the early centuries of the church, slaves and ex-slaves held leadership positions in the congregation. Many slaves who had found little hope in this life embraced Jesus Christ for eternity and even died for their faith. There is no evidence that any of the original disciples either had been slaves or ever owned slaves. Later, Christians came from both categories.   ■

ATTITUDE OF THE NEW TESTAMENT □ In an era when slavery had almost overwhelming acceptance, we have no record of the apostles or other early Christians speaking out against the practice. However, many things occurred which are not recorded in the Bible (John 20:30, 31).

Paul maintained that if a slave was offered his freedom, he was certainly at liberty to take it (1 Cor. 7:20, 21). He treated slavery as a situation in which God could use a believer. Physical freedom was preferable, but Paul did not desire to lead a movement to free the slaves.

The apostle's first-century position should not be interpreted as what he would have said during the 19th century in the United States concerning civil rights. Rather, this passage affords us a view of what the small, fledgling church had to say in its state of affairs. Given another time, possibly Paul would have encouraged otherwise.

Normally we conclude that practical Christianity would have made slavery impossible, for in Christ there is neither bond nor free (Gal. 3:28; Col. 3:11). Christian masters were exhorted to view their Christian slaves as brothers (Philem. 16). Through the years millions of slaves have found Christianity an island of hope and accepted it gladly.

Jesus told His disciples that He no longer called them His servants (*doulos*, slaves), for they were now His friends (John 15:15). Paul presented a similar theme as he compared our former state as slavery to fear; under Jesus Christ we have become sons of God (Rom. 8:15–17).   ■

CHAPTER 14

POVERTY

Poverty was evident throughout Israel. The general population lived barely above the subsistence level, but a noticeable percentage sank below it into stark poverty. Enough people were poor to attract the attention of writers and charitable Jews alike.

In the biblical context, poverty existed in Israel because of disobedience to God's laws. If people had taken good care of themselves and provided for those who could not, there would have been no poverty among the Jews. Obedience to God would have resulted in abundance for everyone (Deut. 15:4, 5).

Nevertheless, the ideal frequently broke down as the poor increased in numbers. Under Jacob, Joshua, the monarchy, exile, the Greeks and Romans, poverty became a recurring and ugly matter. The prophetic writings are replete with outrage over the way orphans and widows were mistreated.

Across the centuries the voice of God revealed a constant interest in the poor. While the Scriptures reprimanded those who were too lazy to work, they also offered compassion for the ones unable to provide for themselves and their families.

Compassion for the poor was an important element of the messianic hope. Jesus openly identified himself as the anointed of God by reading from the prophet, who had written that God's Messiah would come preaching to the poor (Luke 4:18; Isa. 61:1, 2). When John the Baptist sent men for assurance that Jesus was sent from God, Jesus told them to tell him the gospel was being preached to the poor (Matt. 11:5).

The comfort Jesus offered to the poor was not merely spiritual. He taught a system which told people not to be content to invite the rich to dine. Rather, Christian love demands that a person summon the poor and handicapped (Luke 14:12–14).

PROVISIONS FROM THE OLD TESTAMENT LAWS □

The law reflected God's personal concern for the poor. Those who assisted the needy walked in His approval; those who oppressed the poor risked His swift judgment. These principles are evident in the guidelines which God provided:

1. Every third year the produce was to be tithed and distributed to the poor (Deut. 14:28, 29).

2. Every seven years all debts were cancelled to allow the individuals to start again (Deut. 15:1, 4).

3. The poor could feed themselves from the grain fields and the vineyards (Lev. 19:9, 10). Farmers were not to harvest the edges of their fields and they were prohibited from going over their fields a second time. The gleanings and edges were available for the poor to gather.

4. Any Jew who became a slave had to be released after six years of service (Deut. 15:12–18).

5. Interest could not be exacted from the needy (Ex. 22:25).

These laws were instituted to insure that the prosperity of God's people would be shared. Unfortunately the prophets bear witness to the neglect of these humane provisions.   ∎

WHAT CAUSED POVERTY? □ Several major factors contributed to the large number of poor people in Israel. Naturally, there were many personal variables. However, in order to understand the total picture, we need to consider a few of the obstacles they faced.

Taxes. The tax structure became a burden to many families, farms and small businesses. Throughout Israel's history, government building projects and military expenses placed a crushing burden on the common people. It was the excessive taxation placed on the people by Solomon that led to the division of the Kingdom.

Near Bethlehem lie the fields of Boaz where Ruth gleaned and met her lover.   TW

Under the Romans, tax collectors worked overtime to meet the levies imposed by Rome to pay for transportation, commerce, imports and whatever else the empire could produce. Add to these the taxes levied by Herod and the temple and the squeeze became painful.

Unemployment. When a nation's economy is built with slaves, the working class has to suffer. Cheap slave labor reduced the value of the laborer.

Slaves did not affect the economy in rural areas, but in cities they created an imbalance. Because people were cheap, one wealthy man owned a slave merely for the purpose of leading his horse. Consequently, it was important to learn a trade in hope of securing a good income.

Physical handicaps. There were few attempts and fewer means to rehabilitate the handicapped. Often a caring family tried to meet the needs of someone who could not work but it was a meager living at best.

With little hope for a better life, beggars dotted the streets looking for gifts to help buy food. Many of these had been crippled or blind from birth.

Prospects were worst for the fathers who became maimed as adults. Their blindness, illness or the loss of a limb could devastate the entire family.

Death of a father. Whether by accident, sickness or war, the loss of a father usually led to poverty, especially if the children were young.

Drought and famine. Nature could easily destroy a season's crops. Too little rain, too many insects, too much rain at the wrong time and other natural hazards could quickly destroy a family's livelihood.

Even today, many unemployed in Israel resort to begging, such as this woman and her child in Nazareth.   TW

Four months of normal drought (Ps. 32:4) in some areas left the farmers in a precarious position if the rest of the year's rain failed. The added impact of a hot east wind was often devastating.

Usury. The law forbade charging interest to a poor person (Ex. 22:25). Despite this warning many creditors were ruthless in the interest they charged and in the methods they used to collect. This remained a problem throughout Jewish history, and biblical writers repeatedly protested its excesses.

If a creditor kept the law, he was not left powerless to regain the amount he loaned. Debtors were required to offer a pledge, collateral, which would be defaulted if the loan was not repaid. However, rules governed collection of the pledge. The creditor could not enter the debtor's home, but with witnesses present would receive the item at the door (Deut. 24:10, 11). Nothing necessary to daily living could be accepted as a pledge (Deut. 24:6). Later Amos condemned the behavior of the Jews because they accepted clothing as a pledge for debts (Amos 2:8).

By the time of Christ Jewish law was not strictly followed, and many of the Greek and Roman concepts of justice had been adopted by the Jews. We do not know the extent of the usury practiced by Jews, but in neighboring nations, interest rates as high as 50% were common. Some broke the laws with enthusiasm and even humor. One teacher in the Talmud ventures, "If Moses had known how much you can gain by lending money at interest, he would never have thought of forbidding it."

The story Jesus told of the hapless debtor depicts the creditor as throwing the delinquent servant in jail (Matt. 18:34) after threatening even worse consequences—selling his family and goods (v. 25). Deissman has demonstrated that not only was it possible to imprison people for debt but there are ancient papyri which state it. Among Greeks and Romans this was an accepted legal custom.

The penalty of imprisonment or of slavery could be enforced by the creditor himself. One must assume that such powers left a debtor in serious jeopardy. Once a powerful figure seized an individual it could be confusing and difficult to free him.

In this first century context of debts and repayments, the gospel offered the gift of forgiveness. Christ's use of the word "debt" in the Sermon on the Mount refers to sin, but it is the word meaning to owe something (Matt. 6:12). They were well aware of the pressures presented by debt and the pain of being unable to pay. ∎

VOLUNTARILY POOR □ Not everyone considered riches the gauge for a successful life. Many were content to spend uncomplicated lives in pastures, on farms or tending tiny businesses. Others were extremely generous with their goods and distributed them freely to those in need. This attitude is especially evident in the lives of men such as Barnabas who sold his land in order to share it (Acts 4:36, 37). Societies such as the Essenes volunteered to share common goods and monies. This was similar to the attitude of Jesus Christ who took on the form of a servant for us.   ∎

ORPHANS □ There is enough discussion of orphans to know that there was a sizable number of them in Israel. Both Testaments seem equally concerned with the heartbreaking problem.

In the Jewish economy an orphan did not have to be a child without parents. If the child was without a father he was often deemed an orphan. This explains the frequent mention of widows and orphans. In most cases a father was the family's sole source of material security. If he no longer was alive, the family unit faced financial difficulties.

As in most societies the father exposed himself to the greatest physical risks and consequently was more likely to die early. If the deceased father left property, the majority of the inheritance went to the eldest son. Therefore, a younger daughter might have difficulty surviving well.

Sometimes daughters without fathers were easy prey for the cults which required prostitutes. It was not convenient for a female of any age to find acceptable employment in Israel, for she was trained to be a mother and a homemaker. If this prospect did not materialize, she was expected to remain within the protection of her father or brothers. When that system fell apart, she was often thrust into a precarious situation.

One solution to the orphan problem was the willingness of friends and relatives to aid them or incorporate them into their families (Job 29:12; 31:18). Another was to make food available to any orphans to gather and eat.

Despite the generous attitude of many Jews, orphans were often exploited, robbed and even murdered (Job 24:3, 9; Ps. 94:6; Isa. 10:2). However, neither God nor the prophets took lightly the abuse of orphans. In a list of grievous sins the mistreatment of orphans is included as a sign of a decadent society (Ezek. 22:7). God warns anyone who would abuse or deprive an orphan that He will send a sword and make the offender's children orphans and his wife a widow (Ex. 22:22–24).

Care for orphans was a clear standard of Christianity. James insisted that pure religion took care of orphans (James 1:27).

Orphans were included in the provisions made for the poor. Every three years all the tithes of that year's produce were to be stored in order to feed orphans and others who had no income (Deut. 14:28, 29).   ∎

GOD'S ROLE IN POVERTY □ Generally God was not blamed for poverty. Instead, people tended to give Him credit for successes and only occasionally the blame for originating hardship. Most Jews were more prone to place the responsibility on their own shoulders and those of others. Both laziness and oppression were leading culprits. When nature brought despair the victim was hard pressed to decide whether God was a primary or secondary cause. While they saw much of life as the judgment of God, they recognized other factors.   ▪

WAS JESUS POOR? □ Poverty is a relative term. At times Jesus appears to be a person of few possessions, yet other clues suggest that He lived above the poverty level. We can survey some of the evidence and weigh it.

His family. Joseph was a carpenter and would have had the advantage of a fairly skilled trade. Nevertheless, he was the father of six or more children. The offering which Joseph and Mary sacrificed at the temple was that of a poor couple (Luke 2:24). Only if they could not afford a lamb were they to offer doves or pigeons (Lev. 12:8).

This traditional view of their poverty, however, leaves some unanswered questions. Possibly they were short of resources since they were away from home when Jesus was born. The magi did visit the family, bearing expensive gifts, but this was probably after the family had returned to Bethlehem from the ceremony at Jerusalem.

Their choice of a sacrifice suggests economic stress, but that fact alone is not conclusive.

His house. Jesus lived in a home which is described as His (Matt. 13:57). However, He did say that "the Son of man has no place to lay his head," so it is questionable that He was the owner. The "his" probably refers to His family's ownership.

His lifestyle. There is no suggestion that Jesus had totally denied the possessions of this life. He was not an ascetic as was John the Baptist. Jesus did not identify himself with any of the groups that practiced voluntary poverty.

His ministry. The extensive demands of Jesus' ministry were bound to affect His ability to earn money as a carpenter. We cannot be sure how this sacrifice changed His income level. It is probable that during the last years of His life, Jesus depended on others for support.   ▪

JESUS' ATTITUDE TOWARD THE POOR □ There is a great compassion in the statements of Christ concerning the poor. He made no derogatory remarks and did not cast the blame at their feet.

He acknowledged the fact that life consists of more than just helping the poor (Mark 14:7), but this does not change poverty's significance. Briefly we can outline Christ's views on the subject as follows:

1. His concern for the poor was part of His credentials as the true Messiah (Luke 4:18).

2. We should invite the poor instead of the rich to our feasts (Luke 14:13).

3. After Christ had dinner with Zacchaeus, the tax collector demonstrated his repentance by giving half his goods to the poor (Luke 19:8).

4. Jesus chose the relative poverty of this life for our gain (2 Cor. 8:9; Phil. 2:5ff.). ∎

POVERTY IN THE EARLY CHURCH □ A sizable number of the first Christians were poor. If they were not poor when they became Christians, poverty often followed. There are several reasons for so many poor Christians.

1. Many of the poor and physically handicapped were attracted by the love of Jesus Christ.

2. Some of the first Christians no doubt lost their jobs because they became Christians.

3. Christians were hunted and persecuted and thus could not hold jobs.

4. Some new converts may have been forced to leave their families because they were no longer accepted.

5. Christians gave extravagantly of their goods to support those who had none. This dramatically reduced the resources of many believers.

6. A few foolishly gave up their jobs and refused to work because they believed Jesus would come back any day. The apostle Paul suggested these people be allowed to go hungry. If this tactic failed, the person was to be avoided (2 Thess. 3:6–15). Paul's remedy was blunt: if they refused to work, they would not eat. ∎

ASSISTANCE FOR THE POOR □ *Help from the early church.* The first believers were acutely aware of economic hardships and made immediate provisions to share their goods. Some relief was offered organizationally and others were helped through private initiative.

Help for widows. One of the church's first functions was to care for the widows who had embraced the Christian faith. This program raised difficulties because of oversights and possible prejudices. The apostles addressed the problem by establishing a group to take leadership of this distribution (Acts 6:1–6).

Sharing of possessions. Members of the early church voluntarily donated their goods to be distributed among Christians in need. It became a widespread practice to share with others (Acts 4:32). They did not merely give of their excess or their tithes. Christians sold homes and farms and gave the proceeds to the apostles for distribution. The magnitude of their gifts speaks of both their dedication and the depth of need among the believers.

Goods were probably distributed on a local level. At times the believers met daily (Acts 2:46) and possibly shared their resources with whichever people needed them on that day. Such open-hearted generosity may have created the need for which Paul took a collection on their behalf.

Wide distribution. Not only were local assemblies concerned with the people they knew, but there was remarkable compassion for those in distant communities. When Jerusalem suffered from famine (Acts 11:28), the Christians at Antioch responded by sending supplies.

This was not an isolated case. Years later more goods were brought to Jerusalem by the hands of the missionary Paul (Acts 24:17). ∎

ASSISTANCE IN JERUSALEM □ Historians tell us there were many programs in first-century Jerusalem to assist the poor. This city held more than the average number of needy. Pilgrimages brought an overwhelming supply of poor people. Some came to worship, others sought to take advantage of the generous spirit of religious pilgrims. A healthy array of charities were in position to give them assistance. These methods were born out of a basic Jewish obligation to help the poor. We are told of a chamber of secrets or sins where people quietly left gifts. The needy could then slip in just as quietly and claim the goods. If this is not the chamber Jesus had in mind when He spoke of giving secretly, it certainly reflects the spirit He commended (Matt. 6:4). Religious groups also, such as the Essenes, provided food and clothing to the destitute.

Jeremiah tells us the Jews had two special systems called the "poor bowl" and the "poor basket." The poor bowl consisted of foods needed for the Passover—bread, beans and fruit. It was made available daily. The poor basket offered clothing and food on a weekly basis.

Rulers of the time were known for occasional acts of human kindness. Even men who were given to violence, and even insanity, at times bubbled over with charity. Josephus tells us of Herod the Great's almost heroic sacrifices while distributing supplies to famine-stricken subjects. The king used some of the gold and silver ornaments from his luxurious palace to finance the relief program in 23 B.C.

The Roman Empire suffered several harsh famines during the reign of Claudius (A.D. 41–54). Josephus reports that during this time a severe famine in Palestine (44–48) was partially relieved by imported grain from Egypt. This may correspond to the terrible famine recorded in Acts (11:27). The generous aid of Queen Helena of Adiabene made this assistance available.

Beyond all the programs, systems and public efforts was the steady flow of personal contributions. Many Jews counted it an integral aspect of their faith to help the needy.

CHAPTER 15

AGRICULTURE

Because the Israelites depended greatly on agriculture, much of their theology centered around agricultural concepts. They considered themselves in partnership with God, each farmer doing his best to care for his crop but knowing that its final success or failure was in God's hands. He looked at rain and sunshine as direct gifts from God. Storms and drought were interpreted as the displeasure of the Creator. Many of the significant festivals Israel observed focused on agricultural themes. The Jew returned 20% of his crop as an offering to God. He observed religious laws to protect his land and allow it to resuscitate.

The Jewish involvement with the land was reflected in the teachings of Jesus Christ. His imagery and illustrations gave His listeners vivid pictures, such as a sower, pouch at his side, flinging seed across a newly plowed field. He frequently used metaphors about rich ripe grapes and fruitful vines.

This Bedouin shepherdess tends her goats near the Red Sea much as was done in the days of the ancient Israelites.   JJ

Palestinian Jews lived close to the land that God had given them. We may assume the devout Jew worked it with a sense of God's nearness.

WATER AND IRRIGATION □ Having sufficient water has

always been a problem in Palestine. The difficulty is not necessarily the amount of rain received, but in its lack of uniformity. Annual rainfalls differ radically from nearly none at the Dead Sea, to a meager eight inches annually in eastern Jordan, to a lush 40 inches in upper Galilee. It is impossible to know the rainfall over the past several thousand years. However, during the past 100 years Jerusalem has averaged 25 inches of rain annually. This compares with the average rainfall in the state of Nebraska.

Uneven rainfall is only part of the problem. Much of the rain comes in heavy downpours, and the ensuing quick runoff is thus easily lost. Consequently, there was a need for creative methods by which to retain as much water as possible.

Two annual rainy seasons were crucial in Israel. October and May have been vital throughout recorded history; the Bible refers to them as the "autumn" and the "spring" rains (Deut. 11:14). Jews

considered adequate rain during these times as a sign of God's approval. Centuries after Deuteronomy was written, Joel acknowledged the two rainy seasons (2:23), as did other prophets (Jer. 3:3; Hos. 6:3; Zech. 10:1).

The first rains in October were crucial because they prepared the ground for planting. After three or four months of drought, moisture was essential for proper germination. May rains were necessary because they allowed the

Gibeon, a town about eight miles northwest of Jerusalem, has a spectacular water system and cistern. Cut entirely from solid rock, it includes this 82-foot-deep pool, which has a circular stairway of 79 steps. This cistern was probably dug about 1100 B.C. by removing 3000 tons of limestone to provide access to fresh water.   CD

crops to finish ripening just before harvest. This type of climate is quite similar to that of Southern California.

Israel received water from other sources such as springs, rivers, wells and dew. In some years dew could be a deciding factor in a Jew's prosperity. Heavy dews came in August and September, and at the end of a dry summer could aid both people and crops.

Whatever other water supplies were available, the unpredictable rain was still the determining factor for most farmers. One of the most successful means of storing rainwater was the cistern. Not only did farmers and village dwellers build them, but entire cities used cisterns to supplement their water supplies.

Cisterns were large pits hewn out of rock often in a bell shape. An opening at the top allowed rain in as did drains. Water would be brought up later through the same opening with pitchers.

King Uzziah had many cisterns built 800 years before Christ (2 Chron. 26:10) to allow for construction of defensive sites in areas without natural water sources other than rainfall. Many of his subjects in the more hospitable hill country where rainfall was more predictable were farmers or herdsmen.

A huge cistern has been found at Gibeon. Built under the city, it has a large staircase leading to the bottom of an immense pit from

Two miles south of Bethlehem, off the road to Hebron, are located three lovely large reservoirs surrounded by pine trees and palms. Called Solomon's Pools, they today collect rainwater and spring water which is pumped to supply the Old City of Jerusalem.
                                                                                    TW

which a tunnel leads deeper underground to the cistern itself. It is estimated that 3,000 tons of limestone were removed to make the container. This may be the "pool of Gibeon" by which Joab and David's men sat (2 Sam. 2:13). Jeremiah found an empty cistern an uncomfortable slimy prison (38:6). The cisterns of the fortress Masada, large enough to sustain over 900 Zealots for three years, were fed by an intricate system of drain pipes that covered the mountain.

In other areas pools were constructed to capture water from springs or other sources. Several of these pools are mentioned in the New Testament. The pool in Jerusalem, called Bethesda, was considered a source of supernatural healing (John 5:2ff.). A blind man was healed after washing his eyes at the pool of Siloam (John 9:7–11). Pools were probably sizable since the New Testament word means "a place of diving." Some of these pools have survived to this day and play a significant role in Jerusalem's water supply.

From the natural and constructed water supplies, some Jews created irrigation systems. Usually they were run by gravity. Ditches carried water to rows of plants or trees. Other irrigation systems may have included oxen or men carrying water on their shoulders. Some of these irrigation methods were being practiced during the time of Christ. Irrigation was generally not commercially feasible for the average farmer who depended on the rainfall (cf. Deut. 11:8–14). Irrigation was primarily used for gardens of the wealthy.

The land has changed over the centuries. Some parts have not needed irrigation (Deut. 11:10, NIV), but other sections have needed it continuously—but have seldom received it. ∎

THE FERTILE CRESCENT □ Israel is located at the southern tip of a rich portion of land. Shaped like a quarter moon or a boomerang, the Fertile Crescent runs north from Palestine and curves to the southeast through Mesopotamia to the Persian Gulf. The southern boundary of that curve skirts the northern edge of the Arabian Desert, while to the north it is bounded by a series of mountain ranges. Gaza marks the southwestern end of the Fertile Crescent.

The area of Mesopotamia (modern Iraq) receives enough rainfall to support several crops, but, like Palestine, its sequence of rainfall is marginal for successful agriculture. With a combination of adequate rainfall and irrigation, farmers were able to produce crops in normal years. Sometimes it is bombarded with too much rain which can erode its topsoil, while in other years rain is too sparse to produce crops and the residents turn to sheepherding to survive. The Egyptians called it the land where the Nile falls from the sky.

Only 40 miles wide in Israel, the Crescent served as a much traveled lane across which merchants and armies moved to and from Egypt. ∎

This method of terrace farming, shown here in Samaria, prevents water from escaping and resists soil erosion.   CD

TERRACING □ Because of the steep hills that roll across much of Israel, the Jews had to become creative farmers. They planted patches wherever there were open spaces, much as people do in areas of Kentucky. Whenever practical, though, they turned to terrace farming.

Terraces are level rows on hillsides constructed by building short stone walls. These prevented water from escaping and eroding the soil. In areas with adequate rainfall vineyards have prospered on these terraced hills.

Bethlehem, when Christ was born, was near terraced farmland. Moses would have seen terracing in his lifetime.

Possibly 60% of the hills west of Jerusalem are terraced for agriculture. Most of these terraces are of ancient origin. The people who built these terraces as early as 800 B.C. performed no small feat by transforming a rolling hill into a farm.

Terraces around Jerusalem may have been necessitated by a population burst during the time of Hezekiah. Archaeologists Edelstein and Gibson believe some of these units were built by the government as well as individual farmers.   ∎

STONY FIELDS □ Many farmers in Israel are plagued with an abundance of stones in their fields. Most of the stones are limestone, marble, basalt, flint, granite or brimstone. Geological disruptions and erosion have caused the stones to break off from the substratum and surface.

The Jews have shown their innovative spirit by using the stones for many practical purposes. Nevertheless, the stones remain a headache for farmers. In some areas this handicap has been overcome by planting vineyards, where rocks are not so great an obstacle to cultivation.

In the story told by Jesus, the sower's seed landed on a rocky place and could not survive (Matt. 13:5; Luke 8:6). Some soil covered the rock substratum, but not enough to hold water necessary to support the plant. A plant would spring up quickly because of the warmth of the shallow soil but it could not be sustained.   ∎

PLANTING □ There were two important steps to putting a successful crop into the ground. Although equipment and methods differed somewhat according to time, place and conditions, the basic functions remained the same.

Breaking the ground. The best groundbreaking a Jewish farmer could do was to harness two oxen and hitch them to a plow of wood or iron. The Bible forbids yoking two different types of animals together (Deut. 22:10). However, some mixed teams of oxen and donkeys are used to plow in the Near East to this day. Several different types of animals could be used under the law; however, they were not to be mixed.

The apostle Paul used this concept as an illustration to warn Christians against being unequally yoked with non-Christians (2 Cor. 6:14). He again applied the concept when he deemed his Christian friends as yokefellows who walked in accord (Phil. 4:3).

Jesus also used this picture because so many of His followers knew it well. He told His audience to take up His yoke and they would find it easy (Matt. 11:28–30). Jesus offered no oppressive burden of picky laws such as the Pharisees demanded.

Yokes were made of heavy wood and designed to accommodate one or two animals. A length of rope dropped from the wooden bar and wrapped around the animal's neck. One long stick ran from the middle of the bar between the two animals to the plow which it pulled.

The bottom of the plow was usually made of iron. Metal was used as far back as the time of David and plows were used before Moses. The first plow must have been revolutionary, bringing about as much change as tractors did thousands of years later. These plows did not make the neat rows of modern equipment, but they were effective in turning the topsoil. In some cases the seed may have been sown before the soil was turned, contrary to the method we know.

The metal plow blade is what gives the words of Isaiah special meaning. He prophesied of the day when swords would be beaten into plowshares (2:4).

Jesus used the metaphor of the plow to call His disciples to follow without wavering (Luke 9:62). We might be cautious about comparing this illustration

The best plowing a Jewish farmer could do was to harness two oxen and hitch them to a wooden plow. Teams of oxen and asses are used to plow in the Near East to this day.   BAS to current farming. The Jews may not have had as neat, straight furrows as we imagine. The analogy concerns the dedication to the task, not the appearance of the furrows. Jesus could have been showing His sense of humor by picturing the man going far afield while looking back—accuracy depended on the forward look.

Those who had no plows used simple tools similar to hoes with metal ends. Some of these were mattocks with a combination of a blade on one side and a pick on the other. These tools could break the soil for gardens or other small patches of ground.

Hoes and plowshares both would become dull with use and had to be resharpened. During the time of the Judges and David's early career, there were no blacksmiths in Israel; the farmers had to take their tools to the Philistines, who held a monopoly on iron working, to have them sharpened (1 Sam. 13:20).

Good land in Israel was red when plowed and purplish red under a clear sky. The worker would often pray, "Lord, my task is the red, the green is thine; we plough, but it is Thou that dost give the crop" (Daniel-Rops, p. 233).

A perusal of the Scriptures will show many colorful references to the plow. When Samson accused the Philistines of finding by trickery the solution of his riddle, the strongman claimed they had plowed with his heifer (Judg. 14:18). When the prophet Micah predicted doom for Israel, he told them Zion would be plowed like a field (3:12). The psalmist, when bewailing his plight, moaned, "Men have plowed my back; and made their furrows long" (129:3).

A plowman carried a goad or an oxgoad to prod his animals along. It was a long stick, five to seven feet long, with a sharp end. Shamgar used such a goad to dispatch 600 Philistines (Judg. 3:31). The writer of Ecclesiastes considers the words of the wise as helpful goads which prod the listless (12:11). When Jesus called Paul on the road to Damascus, He alluded to this instrument. Evidently, God had been prodding at Paul, trying to get him to follow Jesus Christ. Until that hour Paul successfully resisted (Acts. 26:14).

Sowing. After the ground was sufficiently prepared, the farmer would plant seeds by scattering them. In typical fashion he carried seed in a basket or small pouch by his side and with his free hand would dip in and toss the seed across the turned soil. Seeders attached to plows were used in neighboring countries, but there is no record of sowing in Israel except by hand broadcasting.

Once the seeds were scattered, the farmer went over the field again with his plow or he dragged branches across it. This operation was necessary to cover and protect the seeds from birds or strong winds.

This method of planting extends back at least as far as Isaac (Gen. 26:12), who, we are told, scattered seed and received one hundredfold in return.

Jesus gave us a parable which provides an excellent picture of

The biblical sower, pouch at his side, sending seed flying across a newly-plowed field, is one of the dominant agricultural images throughout Scripture.   BAS

sowing and the hazards that might await the seed (Matt. 13:3–8; Mark 4:3–8; Luke 8:5–8). Seed could be trampled on ill-defined roadways and pathways that often cut across fields, unhindered by fences. Other seeds were lost to birds, shallow soil and choking thorns. The seeds which did prosper reproduced a hundredfold as did Isaac's.

The practice of seed-sowing was so common that the term found its way frequently into daily conversation. Thus the Bible text refers often to sowing.   ■

FERTILIZER □ Some observers doubt that fertilizer was widely used in Israel, but it is certain that at times the Jews treated the soil. During the time of Isaiah farmers would mix straw with manure for the purpose of making fertilizer (25:10). The Jews, like the Egyptians, used to mix salt into manure to create a fertilizer. Weak salts were good for little else (Luke 14:34). Farmers fertilized their vineyards by digging around the base of the plants and applying manure (Luke 13:8).

The major fertilizer for grain crops may have come from the limestone occurring naturally in the ground. Wight suggests that the rainfalls dissolved the lime and mixed it into the soil.   ■

TYPES OF CROPS □ Israel's land yielded a wide variety of crops including grains, vegetables, flax and fruits. We will delay our discussion of fruits (dates, figs, grapes and olives) until later.

Grains. The two most significant grains were barley and wheat. The Israelite's diet was heavily dependent on bread as a staple of his meals.

Winter wheat was planted after the autumn rains and harvested in May or June. Galilee and the Jordan Valley were key areas for growing wheat.

Wheat, one of the most significant grains mentioned in the Scriptures, is grown in abundance throughout Galilee and the Jordan Valley. This wheat, set against newly-plowed ground of a farming kibbutz near Tiberias, is planted after the autumn rains and is harvested in May or June.   TW

Barley was considered a lower quality grain but was planted on poor soil and usually harvested a month earlier than wheat.

Inferior grains such as spelt or fitches were sown around the borders of wheat or barley.

When we see the term "corn" in the King James Bible, we must ignore our modern concept. The word actually meant grain. The Pharisees criticized the disciples for eating grain in the field on the Sabbath (Matt. 12:1). Grain was used as a sacrificial offering to God (Lev. 2:1).

Vegetables. Beans were a common vegetable raised by Jews, but were not treated as a valuable food. Generally poorer people ate them as a cheap cereal in bread and other foods. This was not exactly the same as the beans to which we are accustomed. They were important to the diet because of their protein content, since poorer people had little opportunity to eat meat. Beans were often raised in small garden plots near the houses.

Lentils are small peas or beans which can be boiled into a red stew. Esau gave up his inheritance for a bowl of red stew made of lentils (Gen. 25:29–34). They were raised in fields throughout Israel for many centuries (2 Sam. 23:11). Daniel asked his captors to give him a vegetable diet rather than the usual royal fare of meat (Dan. 1:12). Some believe this was the pulse made from lentils, but the word may have had a broader meaning than peas or beans.

Garlic was a food which the Jews learned to love in Egypt (Num. 11:5). This was also true of the large onions, lush melons, and leeks which were a long-stemmed variety of onion.

Cucumbers were plentiful in Israel for centuries (Isa. 1:8).

Many types of vegetables were available, but they may have been used with less frequency than the above. Red and green peppers, pumpkins, lettuce and eggplant were but a few of the possibilities. Herbs and spices also were grown in abundance. Gourds were grown as well, but scholars disagree whether a gourd is a fruit or a vegetable so we have listed it among the fruit.

Flax. The flax plant was a familiar sight in Israel. Raised primarily to make fabric and wicks, flax played a large part in Jewish life and a crop failure was considered a catastrophe (Hos. 2:9).

Harvested stalks of the plant were treated until they could be pulled apart, combed and spun to make thread. Today, oil is crushed from the plant as it possibly was in ancient Israel.

The use of flax spans biblical history. When God sent hail to coerce Egypt, the flax plant was in bloom and consequently destroyed (Ex. 9:31) along with the barley. The excellent woman of Proverbs 31 could select flax well and work with it (v. 13). When the flax was first harvested, it was laid on the roof to dry out. Rahab took the spies at Jericho up to her roof and hid them among the drying flax (Josh. 2:6).   ■

DESTRUCTION OF CROPS □ A number of natural factors can spell disaster to the farmer's crops. Therefore his was, and is, a precarious occupation.

Hot winds from the deserts could scorch crops. Called *siroccos,* similar to the Santa Ana winds in Southern California, they came in the early fall and could last from 3 days to an entire week. Temperatures might increase by 20 degrees while the humidity would drop dramatically. Even the skies looked awesome with a yellow tint from the blowing dust. The prophet Isaiah was acquainted with this possible terror (27:8), and possibly so was Jesus Christ (Luke 12:55). Ezekiel knew how the east wind could devastate a young vine (17:10).

Insects were another problem which threatened farmers. None were more damaging than the locusts (1 Kings 8:37). A sudden swarm could totally devastate a field as the farmer watched, defenseless. A sudden, strong wind that might drive them off was one of his few hopes (Ex. 10:19).

As in most farm areas drought was always a fearsome possibility. A terrible drought during the reign of Herod (24–25 B.C.) resulted in famine in Israel. Elijah's prayer during Ahab's reign prevented rainfall for three years (1 Kings 17:1; 18:1). The disciples responded to a serious famine in Judea by carrying supplies for aid. Agabus had predicted the widespread hunger (Acts 11:28) which occurred during the reign of Claudius.

Fungi sometimes ruined crops. Mildew was the one most likely to spread in the area (1 Kings 8:37) when there was too much dampness.

Animals, especially large ones such as donkeys, goats, etc., could cause considerable damage to crops. Farms have been found with high stone walls to keep animals out. The walls referred to in the story of Balaam (Num. 22:24) may have been built for this purpose.

Probably no animal has done as much damage to vegetation as the goat. It totally destroys a plant, not only eating the leaves and twigs but when possible pulling the plant up by the roots. This not only removes the vegetation but greatly speeds up soil erosion.

■

THE HARVEST □ The Gezer Calendar gives us a good description of the harvest times as they occurred in the 10th century B.C. This was the general cycle:

> Flax: March–April
> Barley: April–May
> Wheat: May–June
> Figs and Grapes: August–September
> Olives: September–November

Grain was harvested with a sickle. The worker grabbed the stalks with one hand, and with his sickle in the other sliced it near the ground. The ancient sickle had a cutting edge made of flint but later iron was used. As he cut the stalks, the worker would pile them in the field. The stalks were then tied into sheaves and later hauled away and stored (Gen. 37:7). Sometimes grain was cut closer to the grain head, leaving most of the stalk in the field.

Women often harvested. We find Ruth in Bethlehem just at

Grain harvesters cut the stalks, tie them into sheaves, and later haul them off for storage. This family harvests wheat near Bethlehem.   TW

Piles of grain lie near this open-air threshing floor near Bethlehem.　　　TW

the time of the barley harvest (Ruth 1:22). She worked hard in the field as she followed the women harvesters (2:7). She was engaging herself in Israel's welfare program ordained by Moses. Anything left in the field was free for the poor to harvest and keep. The farmer was discouraged from reaping his entire crop because it would deprive the needy of food (Deut. 24:19–21).

Jesus painted a word picture of the harvester and applied it to the kingdom of God (Mark 4:26–29). The book of Revelation also makes use of the harvest imagery (Rev. 14:14–20). When Jesus stood at the well in Samaria (John 4:35), it was probably December, for He told His disciples it was four months until harvest. Most likely He was referring to the April barley harvest. However, He said the fields were already white for harvest. At this point He had switched from grain to people. People, not grain, were ready to be reaped.　■

THRESHING □ After the grain was gathered, it was taken to a threshing floor where the kernels could be separated from the straw. A threshing floor was a hard-surfaced area either near one's house or at a public place. King David built an altar to God on the threshing floor of Araunah the Jebusite (2 Sam. 24:18).

Three ways of threshing were common among the Jews. The most primitive method was merely beating the stalks with a stick to loosen the grain. Gideon was beating out the grain when the angel of the Lord appeared to him (Judg. 6:11).

This farmer is threshing with a horse pulling a wooden sledge over the grain.　　　RI

A second method was tramping the grain under an animal's feet. If this plan was followed, the owner could not forbid the ox from eating the grain as it worked (Deut. 25:4).

A third method was to pull a sledge over the grain. Built of wood, the sledge dragged stones or other rough objects across the grain. A donkey or ox pulled while the driver rode atop the sledge (2 Sam. 24:22). Some of the sledges were equipped with wheels to ease the ride (Isa. 28:28). ■

WINNOWING □ The purpose of winnowing was to separate the grain from the chaff. Since the grain was heavier, this could be accomplished by tossing the mixture into the air when a wind was blowing. The wind would carry the chaff away but the grain would fall back to the ground.

Either a six-pronged pitchfork or a scoop.shovel was used to winnow. John the Baptist pictured Jesus as one who carried a winnowing fork (Luke 3:17; Matt. 3:12), in order to separate grain and chaff—believers and unbelievers.

Others sifted their grain through a sieve. Some used the sieve as the final step of processing their grain. Amos said God would test Israel as if in a sieve (9:9). ■

STORAGE □ Once the farmer completed the harvest, he could keep the grain to feed his family, sell the grain, or store it for sale at a later date. Sometimes Israel was prosperous enough to sell its crops. Solomon seems to have delivered over 100,000 bushels of wheat to Hiram, king of Tyre (1 Kings 5:11).

This farmer employs his winnowing fork to separate wheat from chaff. The location is near Gibeon, about eight miles northwest of Jerusalem. TW

These huge grain storage bins atop the ancient Hebrew fortress of Masada are typical of ancient storage facilities for large quantities of grain. These were excavated during 1963–65 under the leadership of Yigael Yadin of Hebrew University.   TW

This ancient grain silo from King Solomon's time is at Megiddo on the southern side of the Jezreel Valley.   RN

Grain was usually stored in clay jars of varying sizes for a farmer's personal use.

However, archaeologists have discovered large underground silos 25 feet wide and over 20 feet deep. Dry cisterns were probably also used. Solomon designated entire cities to hold grain (1 Kings 9:19) as had David (1 Chron. 27:25). The Egyptians used forced labor to maintain store cities long before this (Ex. 1:11). These were similar to the large grain complexes on the Great Plains of the U.S. Jesus was critical of the self-sufficient man who enlarged the storage facilities for his added grain (Luke 12:18).

Some of the grain storage methods were excellent. Ancient bins have been unearthed with the contents still dry and intact.   ■

MILLING □ Before grain could be used to bake bread, the kernels had to be broken down and ground into flour by rubbing them together between two stones. Milling was practiced across Israel by wives in their homes and by commercial millers. Two types of millstones were used and both kinds have been unearthed. Generally the rocks were coarse to provide greater friction.

The first type of millstone was the saddle variety. One hollowed stone held the grain while a rounded stone was rubbed into it. The "saddle" stone was 1½ to 3 feet long.

A second type was larger and heavier. It was made of two round, flat stones, possibly two feet across, made from limestone. A wooden upright handle turned the top stone. A hole in the top stone allowed grain to be poured in. Some millstones were so large that an animal or strong man was required to turn them. The defeated Samson performed this job in a Philistine prison (Judg. 16:21).

Jesus spoke of a day when two women would be grinding at a millstone and one would be taken while the second would remain (Matt. 24:41). He also warned that those who caused children to sin would be better off if a huge millstone were hung around their necks and they were tossed into the sea (Matt. 18:6). Abimelech met a shocking death when a woman dropped a millstone on his unsuspecting head (Judg. 9:53).   ■

FRUIT □ For variety, taste and health, fruit played a vital role in Israel's diet. Trees and bushes could grow on poor soil, stretch their roots through rocky ground, resist torrid winds and sun and, with proper care, still produce acceptably. Once established, a tree might yield for hundreds of years.

Healthy fruit trees were the pride of Israel. Typical of people in the Mid-East, Jews carved figures of beautiful ripe crops. An abundance of fruit reassured them of God's blessing on their nation.   ■

GRAPES □ The grapevine goes far back into history. Noah probably kept a vineyard (Gen. 9:20). When Israel was on the verge of invading Canaan, their spies brought back such a large cluster of grapes that two men were required to carry it (Num. 13:23, 24).

Israel's climate and the grapevine seemed made for each other. The highlands of Ephraim were superb for vines (Isa. 28:1).

Planting and maintaining a good vineyard were hard work. A large space was cleared of rocks, and often stone walls were built to serve as protective boundaries. Vines were spaced eight to ten feet apart, allowing plenty of room for the twisting vines to stretch out. The farmer often propped up the vine on stones, sticks or possibly a trellis. Since it remained close to the ground, the plant could benefit from the dew during the warm summer. Breezes from the sea helped provide dew for almost a third of the nights during the hot season. The farmer needed to tend the vines and possibly twice a year weeded the area for maximum growth. He also trained the vines to prevent them from spreading too far.

Farmers were not allowed to eat the fruit of any tree or vine for the first three years (Lev. 19:23). As with grain, when grapes were harvested some had to be left for the poor (Lev. 19:10). Consequently, harvesters were not to pick over the vines a second time.

In most cases the September harvest was done by the family that owned the vines. However, larger operations had hired hands or slaves to help (Matt. 20:1). Barclay tells us that men gathered early in the morning at the marketplace waiting to be hired. If they owned tools they brought them. Hired men were from the poor class of people.

Some men rented out their vineyards. Each year at harvest, the tenants paid rental fees. Jesus told a story of tenants who refused to pay and eventually killed the landowner's son. In the story Jesus gave a brief description of the structure of a vineyard (Mark 12:1–12).

The abundance of grapes in Israel was a mixed blessing. Not only did it provide the benefit of good drink, grape honey and raisins, but it presented serious problems of drunkenness from overindulgence.   ∎

WATCHTOWERS IN VINEYARDS □ There were two uses of watchtowers in ancient Israel—large ones built to safeguard cities against attack and smaller versions built in vineyards to ward off thieves and animals.

Often watchtowers were constructed of stone, and sometimes they were quite elaborate, being up to two stories high with sleeping facilities and food storage on the ground level. Not every watchtower was built of stone. A few were mere sheds or huts made of branches to provide shade (Job 27:18). The towers were not always occupied but nonetheless served to discourage raiders.

King Uzziah built towers both to protect cities and to guard his crops (2 Chron. 26:10). On at least one occasion God promised to watch over Israel as a careful keeper of the vineyard (Isa. 27:3).

Foxes could do measurable damage to a vineyard. It is not certain if they enjoyed digging around the vines or had a particular palate for grapes (Song of Sol. 2:15).   ∎

PRUNING □ Drastic pruning of the vines guaranteed maximum

yields. Twigs that would not yield were removed, usually with a pruning hook or a sharp knife. We assume a pruning hook was a metal blade with a curved wooden handle. Evidently the pruning was done after the blossom was finished and the flower was becoming a grape (Isa. 18:5). A vineyard that was not pruned was considered abandoned or useless (Isa. 5:6). However, under the Levitical law a farmer was to leave the vineyard unpruned every seventh year (Lev. 25:3, 4).

Jesus told His followers that His Father, as a careful gardener, prunes off the branches that bear no fruit (John 15:1, 2). The ultimate promise to end wars says that when the people beat their swords into plowshares, they will also reshape their spears into pruning hooks (Mic. 4:3).

Scholars disagree on whether the Jews used trellises for their vines or if this practice was introduced later. The wording of Micah indicates vines were elevated to keep them off the ground (4:4). ■

OLIVES □ Olive trees, olives and olive oil played a significant role

in Israel's daily life. The trees are plentiful throughout the countryside and in the past were probably found in far greater numbers. The Israelites found them flourishing when they arrived in Canaan and the trees continued to prosper during the life of Christ. Later, invading armies under the Turks discouraged their cultivation.

This stone watchtower, located in the central hill country of Israel, may well be the kind of tower King Uzziah built to protect his cities and to guard his crops (2 Chron. 26:10).   RI

162 TODAY'S HANDBOOK OF BIBLE TIMES AND CUSTOMS

The person who grows olives must be patient, for the tree does not produce fruit for its first 15 years. However, once it starts the olive tree will bear for hundreds of years.

An olive is green as it grows and then turns black at maturity. The leaves of the tree are ash grey. The fruit is harvested in the fall by beating the branches with a stick (Deut. 24:20). As with other crops, some olives had to be left on the branches for the poor. A particularly sturdy tree, it can thrive in great heat with a minimum of water.

Olives were eaten either raw or cooked, but this was not their main use. Far more were pressed into oil to meet many personal and religious needs. Olive oil

Gethsemane comes from the Hebrew *gat-shemen*, or oil press, referring to the oil extracted from the fruit of the olive trees with which the hill was covered. There are eight ancient olive trees in the Garden of Gethsemane, which many believe are descended from cuttings of olive trees alive in the garden when Jesus prayed there before His crucifixion.   TW

The Mount of Olives, a limestone ridge east of Jerusalem and separated from the city by the Kidron Valley, received its name because of the olive trees on its slopes. The large building at the foot of the Mount of Olives is the Church of All Nations.   TW

was used to cook, to fuel lamps, as a cosmetic, as a medicine and as a sacrifice. The very concept of Messiah means "anointed one." Anointing was done with olive oil.

The New Testament tells us of areas around Jerusalem that received their names because of the olive trees. The Mount of Olives was named because of the groves. Though it is a limestone hill, it can still support olive trees. In the latter days of His ministry Jesus retired to this mount (Luke 21:37) each evening after teaching. Gethsemane, meaning oil press, was a garden located near the Mount of Olives (Mark 14:32, etc.). From these names we can picture a grove of olive trees adjoining an area for pressing olives into oil. A stone fence would have marked off the area.

Olive oil was so plentiful around Jerusalem that it was one of the few products regularly exported. Solomon gave Hiram, king of Tyre, over 100,000 gallons of pressed olive oil (1 Kings 5:11).

To make olive oil the olives were crushed with bare feet or a stone. The mash was poured into sieve-like baskets which allowed the oil to drain into jars. Later the top layer of oil was skimmed off and used as the "pure" oil. This was also called vinegar oil, which could be burned in the temple. The remainder was saved for general purposes.

Despite the tree's ruggedness the olive crop did have some natural enemies. One was the locust which was capable of stripping a tree's leaves (Amos 4:9). Another was an early, killing frost.

In poetry the Jews used the healthy, hardy olive tree as a simile or metaphor for beauty and the assurance of God's blessing. Jeremiah wrote that God once called Israel a "thriving olive tree with fruit beautiful in form" (11:16).

The apostle Paul used an illustration of grafted olive branches to demonstrate how the Gentiles as well as the Jews are recipients of God's grace (Rom. 11:17). Consequently, Herculean efforts have been made to explain how the Jews grafted wild olive branches into regular olive trees. It might be better to let our imaginations rest and assume that no such practice took place in Israel (cf. Lenski, Barclay, Deissman). Maybe at some remote time this was done, but it is highly unlikely. As Paul himself says, this was "contrary to nature" (v. 24). It is an important point since not every biblical allusion to

Olives were crushed in presses such as this one, located in front of the Church of the Multiplication at Tabgha.   TW

This sycamore-fig tree, located just outside the modern city of Jericho, is pointed out to tourists as typical of the sycamore tree in which Jesus encountered Zacchaeus in Luke 19:1–10.   TW

nature and daily life requires an exact parallel in history. ■

FIGS □ Philip found Nathanael sitting under the large leaves of a sprawling fig tree (John 1:48) and told him Jesus was the Messiah. The picture is typical because of the many fig trees in Israel and because of their thick, shady foliage. These are the same leaves which made clothing for Adam and Eve (Gen. 3:7). Figs still grow in Israel on both tended and wild trees.

Often a fig tree yields two annual crops. The first comes in May or June, while a second harvest ripens around September. Usually the spring crop yields before the leaves are fully formed (Song of Sol. 2:13).

An expression that signified peace and happiness depicted a man sitting under the leafy shade of his own fig tree. The family that owned a fig tree was indeed blessed because that tree would continue to produce for hundreds of years with a minimum of care. As with many of the trees in Israel, the fig is able to survive in poor soil even under dry conditions.

Related to the regular fig tree is the sycamore-fig. It does not produce as good a fig and is generally considered an inferior tree. It is this tree that Zacchaeus climbed to get a better view of Christ (Luke 19:4). Amos had a job tending sycamore-figs as well as tending sheep (Amos 7:14). Under kings David and Solomon sycamore-figs flourished in Israel along the foothills (1 Chron. 27:28; 1 Kings 10:27).

Jesus told the story of a man who had a fig tree that gave no fruit for three years (Luke 13:6–8). He decided to give it one more chance by digging around the roots and applying fertilizer. If that did not work, he would cut it down.

The area from which Jesus sent His disciples to find a colt (Mark

11:1) was evidently a place of many fig trees. Bethphage, the nearby town, means "house of figs." ■

Nuts □ The Jews included a variety of nuts in their diet.

Almonds were produced from a tree that normally blossomed early in Israel. Almonds were included in the presents Jacob sent to Egypt (Gen. 43:11). When Aaron's staff sprouted, it produced almonds (Num. 17:8). Almonds were regularly used in desserts, and bitter almonds were used to make some cosmetics.

Pistachios were another nut in the Israelite diet. In a list of the cities given to the tribe of Gad is a town named Betonim, which probably means pistachio. It may have received its name from the abundance of pistachio trees raised in that area. We do know that pistachios were grown in Israel and that they were part of the presents delivered to Joseph (Gen. 43:11).

Walnuts, according to the historian Josephus, were grown near the Sea of Galilee. The Song of Solomon speaks of going down to a grove of nut trees (6:11), which could refer

These green almonds, which are sold from the streets of Jericho, are produced from a tree and are mentioned frequently in Scripture.   CD

A healthy date palm, like this one near Bethlehem, might produce dates for more than 200 years.
CD

A palm tree sheltered a mourning Jew in this coin, made after Titus conquered Judea, A.D. 70. TW

to any type of nut or it could be translated walnut garden. ∎

DATES □ There are few references to dates in the Bible, but palm trees, some of which produce dates, are frequently mentioned. Therefore it is safe to assume that many dates were eaten in one form or another. Several of the passages which mention honey may be referring to date honey and not the bee variety.

Palm trees are well suited for the region. Most often growing in groves, they provide excellent shade as well as tasty fruit. Their leaves are frequently nearly ten feet long. A healthy palm tree can produce dates for over 200 years.

Resourceful Jews used almost every part of the tree for dyes, sugars, oil, wax, camel feed, beads and a strong intoxicant called *arrak*.

Some cities were famous for their palm tree groves. Palmyra, ancient Tadmor (2 Chron. 8:4), probably gained its name because of its palm tree; Jericho was called the city of palms (Judg. 1:16).

The palm tree has sometimes been a special symbol of Israel. After Titus conquered Judea in A.D. 70, a coin was minted showing a Jew mourning beside a palm tree. Palm trees were carved on the doors and walls of Solomon's temple (they were also carved on synagogues later).

Towering as high as 90 feet, one special palm tree served as the place of Deborah's court (Judg. 4:5). On Jesus' triumphal entry into Jerusalem, the crowd used palm branches to greet Him (John 12:13). ∎

POMEGRANATES □ Pomegranates are a succulent fruit filled with juice and seeds, and round like an orange. Pomegranates usually grow on short shrubs, though some plants develop into fair-sized trees. Saul stayed under a large one near Gibeah (1 Sam. 14:2). Their flowers range from white to scarlet to yellow. They are plentiful in Israel and have long been considered a sign of the nation's prosperity.

The Jews were pleased to know there would be pomegranates in their new land. Moses assured them they were part of God's blessing (Deut. 8:8) and the spies brought them back as evidence of the fertile country (Num. 13:23).

The pomegranate be-
came part of Israel's religious symbolism. Replicas
of blue, purple and scarlet
were sewn around the hem
of the priest's robe (Ex.
28:33). They were also
carved on the pillars of Solomon's temple (1 Kings
7:20).

The author of the Song
of Solomon often uses
pomegranates to describe
the physical loveliness of
the Shulamite woman (4:3;
4:13; 6:7). ■

APPLES □ The question
of apples in ancient Israel
remains unanswered. It is
true that apples grow there
today; it is also true that the
Romans enjoyed them.
However, most authorities
doubt that this is the accurate translation of the
Hebrew word which oc-
curs several times in the
Old Testament. Several believe the apricot fits the
picture better. ■

This graceful palm tree, located near Jericho, gives
ample evidence why this oasis in the arid Judean
wilderness is referred to as the "City of Palms" in
Deut. 34:3 and 2 Chron. 28:15.   TW

It would be hard to overestimate the number of sheep in Israel. Flocks of sheep literally
dot every hillside, traverse every road, and their bleating can be heard almost every-
where throughout Palestine.   TW

LIVESTOCK FARMING □ The person who chose to raise live-

stock did not select an easy life. Animals required continuous care and if not watched carefully could be lost, stolen, injured or killed. For most farmers the loss of an animal meant a painful setback.

Livestock raising was at the backbone of Israel's life for many centuries. The people's clothing, food and religious sacrifices were tremendously dependent on the success of their livestock. When a Jew tried to visualize God's love and care for man, he pictured a shepherd and his animals; it was one of his favorite metaphors. The image made it easier for the Jew and early Christian to have his faith in God.   ■

SHEEP □ It would be hard to exaggerate the number of sheep in

Israel. When Moses defeated the Midianites, he received over 600,000 sheep (Num. 31:32). When Solomon dedicated the temple, he sacrificed 120,000 sheep and goats (1 Kings 8:63). During Asa's reform 7,000 sheep and goats were sacrificed (2 Chron. 15:11).

We have no definite figures on how many sheep grazed in Israel, but some of the numbers just listed give us an idea of the massiveness. They may also help us appreciate why the terms permeate the Bible and its lifestyle. The word sheep appears over 500 times.

The breed of sheep mentioned most often is distinguished by its broad tail, which weighs 10 to 15 pounds and is considered prime

The personality of the sheep makes it very dependent upon the shepherd for its care and well-being. This shepherd watches his flock near Bethlehem.   CD

eating. If a sheep was prone to stray too freely, the shepherd might tie one leg of the animal to its tail. Most sheep are white but they can be brown, black or spotted. During the summer some sheep may acquire a reddish hue.

The disposition of sheep is somewhere between meek and dull. Many farmers would rather work with any other animal. The animals' lack of aggression makes them easy prey for predators, thieves or even hazardous environments. Their vulnerability makes them extremely dependent on shepherds for their well-being. Wild mountain sheep are much wiser and more self-sufficient. Because of its dependency, a sheep is a tender and affectionate animal. This accounts for the close relationship many shepherds have with their sheep.

A sheep's dependence on a shepherd is a major theme in the New Testament. Jesus saw people as sheep, tired and aimless from wandering without a leader (Matt. 9:36). They would soon fall to the ground helplessly. When a sheep is lost, a shepherd dares not wait for it to come home. The shepherd must go to retrieve the easily confused animal (Matt. 18:12, 13).

When Jesus spoke of believers as sheep, He emphasized their need for help and His willingness to meet their needs (John 10:15). His analogy of sheep to describe us does not mean we are *exactly* like sheep. We can easily strain the issue by taking the comparison too far. Jesus may have had this in mind when He insisted that

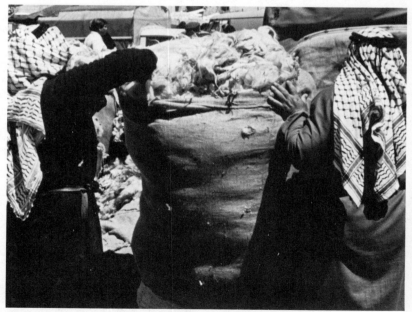

Wool, for sale here at the open-air market in Beer-sheba, is stuffed into huge burlap bags for transport to market after shearing.   TW

people are much more valuable then sheep (Matt. 12:12). It is unwise to base our theology on how a shepherd carried a lamb or whether sheep were led or driven.   ■

SHEEP PRODUCTS □ Much of the early economy of Israel was based on sheep and their by-products. Clothing, food, milk, sacrifices, tents and barter were heavily dependent on the large and small flocks which were scattered throughout the nation.   ■

SHEEPFOLD □ Sheep had several enemies. Robbers, wolves, lions or rough weather could each be dangerous if precautions were not taken.

Through the centuries shepherds built retaining areas to hold sheep, goats and cattle during high risk times such as at night. Often several shepherds shared the same facility.

A sheepfold or sheepcote was often well built, consisting of high stone walls, possibly with thorny branches scattered on top. The gate would be guarded by a shepherd. Some writers believe there was no gate except the shepherd himself because Jesus referred to himself as the gate (John 10:7–9); however, this was probably a figure of speech rather than a physical fact. A few excellent commentators (e.g. Barclay) believe the shepherd acted as the literal door when the sheep were in sheepfolds far from the village, and some assert this is still done.

In the morning it was easy for each shepherd to collect his sheep from the intermingled flocks. Sheep recognized their shepherd's voice and followed him. In fact, the shepherd had each sheep named (John 10:3–5). This is still true in the Near East. If a stranger calls for the sheep, they will reject him on the basis of his voice.   ■

SHEEP GATE □ The Bible tells us the pool of Bethesda was near the Sheep Gate in Jerusalem (John 5:2). It is one of the gates built by Nehemiah (Neh. 3:1) and probably served as the sheep market in that city.   ■

SHEEPSHEARING □
This was a happy time for the family that cared for sheep. Part of the Festival of Shearing, the family

This clay tablet of the old Akkadian Period (ca. 2200 B.C.) is written in cuneiform writing and Akkadian-Assyro-Babylonian language. It appears to be a receipt for wool by three individuals.   EHLE knew it would have wool or the good products the wool could be traded for.

Two types of people might do the shearing: the owners of the sheep or professional sheepshearers who worked for a king or a large farm. Jehu had 42 men killed at a shearing house, Beth Eked (2 Kings 10:14). A man from Maon had 3,000 sheep sheared at Carmel (1 Sam. 25:2), which would require many men. Shearing was done following the lambing season in the spring. Isaiah pictured a sheep as silent, even possibly powerless, before its shearers (Isa. 53:7; Acts 8:32). The first wool sheared each year was to be presented as an offering to God (Deut. 18:4).   ∎

SHEPHERDS □ Because of David's experience and Jesus' illustrations there are many biblical references to God as a shepherd. Since much of the population was familiar with this way of life, such imagery made an effective teaching tool. The shepherd was one of Israel's earliest concepts of God. When Jacob was dying, he testified that God had been his shepherd (Gen. 48:15).

Human shepherds, however, were not always respected. Some Jews considered them the backbone of the nation, but others viewed shepherds as dirty, unprincipled and lacking ambition. Village shepherds may have been held in higher esteem than the nomad variety.

The major function of a shepherd was care. The docile sheep, much like a zoo animal, could not fend for themselves. They had to be led to water and pasture. When attacked, a lamb had to be defended. When lost, it normally had to be found. At evening the shepherd would stand by the entrance to the fold and account for each sheep as it passed under his staff or hand (Ezek. 20:37; Jer. 33:13). For Isaiah, the concept provided the picture of the shepherd as a tender person who cares lovingly for each animal (Isa. 40:11). A sheep without a shepherd was in great danger (Num. 27:17; Mark 6:34).

The shepherd's life was a harsh one which called on him to combat the threats of rough weather year round. It also demanded bravery, for many of the dangers to the sheep's life were likewise dangers to the shepherd. Wolves, lions, bears, panthers and

The sling, an excellent weapon which allows shepherds to hurl a stone over 90 miles an hour and strike a target with pinpoint accuracy, was also the weapon with which David killed the giant Goliath.   RI

To entertain themselves, shepherd boys often played a small hand-flute.   TW

thieves were not easily deterred.

Ancient shepherds such as Jacob worked under these threats (Gen. 31:39). David gives a graphic account of his fights with a lion and a bear to rescue his sheep (1 Sam. 17:34, 35). The future king chased the predator, clubbed it and freed the sheep. When the animal turned on David, the youth grabbed it by the hair and killed it. Because of the prevalent danger, there were probably many heroic stories about shepherds.

To meet such dangers a shepherd may have carried one or more effective weapons. The most well-known of these was the sling, which allowed the shepherd to hurl a stone over 90 miles an hour and strike his target with pinpoint accuracy. It is still used by some as a superior hunting device. David's expertise with the weapon gave him a clear advantage over the gigantic Goliath.

The shepherd might also carry a wooden club. His club was made all the more effective by studding it with stones or pieces of metal.

A staff or stick was commonly carried, even by those who were not shepherds. Anyone on a journey might carry one to help him walk or to repel animals. The disciples used staffs when they traveled. However, Jesus told them not to carry a staff in one instance (Matt. 10:10; Luke 9:3), but take a staff in another (Mark 6:8). A reasonable explanation is that the disciples were not to carry a new staff or a spare one. This could be possible, but a better understanding may rest beneath the surface of the Aramaic.

A shepherd needed versatility with his staff, so consequently it had a curve at one end. This gave him the ability to reach out for lambs and pull them with the curve of the staff. The staff can cause injury to an attacker, but most often it is pictured as a comfort and welcomed sight (Ps. 23:4).

To sustain himself during the day a shepherd would carry a leather bag filled with food. His meal may have consisted of raisins, bread, cheese and olives. He often entertained himself by playing a flute, or a harp which was similar to our guitar. David probably spent many hours on the hillsides playing songs about God, mankind and nature.

Jesus described himself as the "good shepherd" (John 10:11, 14) and as the gate of the sheepfold (John 10:7). His willingness to lay down His life for His sheep (John 10:15) may not have been fully appreciated at the time, but was later. Jesus is described as the Chief Shepherd by His close friend, Peter (1 Pet. 5:4), as he addresses church leaders whom he labels shepherds. We do not yet know if this term, "chief shepherd," was used among shepherds themselves. When several shepherds worked together, one seems to have taken charge; but we have no record of him holding a title. Deissman, however, has found the term written in Greek. ■

GOATS □ Goats, like sheep, played a major role in daily life for many centuries in Israel. They came in a variety of colors including black, brown, white and spotted (Gen. 30:32). White, hornless goats were difficult to spot and separate when mixed with the sheep, as they sometimes were. Some object to this idea, insisting the two were never mixed. Generally this is true, but sometimes they did graze together and the shepherd had to divide them (Matt. 25:32, 33).

In ancient Israel goats probably made up a larger part of a shepherd's flock than did sheep. There are accounts of huge herds exceeding 7,000 goats (2 Chron. 17:11). Over the centuries their numbers diminished in favor of more sheep.

The goat was an economic boon in Israel. The Jews ate goat meat, though they probably preferred lamb. They drank goat milk, ate goat butter and cooked with its by-product, *semn.* Goat hair was combed and woven into many useful products: coats, tents, carpets. Goatskins were sewn together and used for bottles

Goats, shown here grazing near the site of ancient Shiloh, were a very important part of life in ancient Israel. The Jews ate goat meat, drank its milk, ate its butter, cooked with the by-product, *semn,* used goatskins for bottles, sometimes wore the goatskins, and used goat hair for a variety of uses, including coats, tents and carpets.   RI

(Matt. 9:17). When believers were persecuted, they wandered about wearing goatskins because they were poor (Heb. 11:37).

Goats were used for sacrifices (Lev. 4:23) and accepted as a clean animal. ■

DAIRYMEN □ The Jewish palate enjoyed milk, cheese and butter. Since many people could not produce their own, they were dependent on farmers who did. Milking animals, especially goats, on a large scale goes back many centuries. Ancient Ur of the Chaldees knew of such a trade during the time of Abraham. Some dairymen brought their products to the city and sold them directly. Others sold them through markets run by others. Jerusalem had an area called the "valley of the cheese makers."

David had his famous battle with Goliath because he delivered ten cheeses to the commander (1 Sam. 17:18). ■

OXEN AND CATTLE □ Cattle are specifically named several times in the Bible, but generally the word refers to the domestic ox. This animal played a large role in Israel's economy, especially as a work animal, though most farmers could afford only the less-expensive donkey.

Oxen had other uses besides work but none as important. Some of the wealthy ate oxen (1 Sam. 14:31–34), but it would have been an expensive meal for the average person. A king might roast one for a wedding banquet (Matt. 22:4). Solomon is reported to have served 10 or 20 a day in his palace (1 Kings 4:22, 23). The Jews also used oxen as sacrifices (Lev. 3:1). Other religions, such as the worshipers of Zeus (Acts 14:13), also offered up oxen.

However, a farmer prosperous enough to own an ox was not quick to butcher his. There were too many jobs on the farm that required a strong animal. Oxen were expected to pull plows, drag threshing sleds, drive waterwheels and pull carts. A farmer without an ox was not as likely to make his business prosper. Those who had more than one ox were considered people of great wealth.

The thoughtful farmer took good care of his oxen and made certain they had sufficient water and feed. The death of an ox was equivalent to the modern loss of a tractor. Jesus believed people should be treated at least as well as oxen (Luke 13:15). Christ was also concerned that the sick could not be healed on the Sabbath but an ox could be rescued from a ditch (Luke 14:1–5). Paul believed pastors should fare no worse than the four-legged beast (1 Tim. 5:18). ■

DONKEYS □ Most farmers had only a donkey to carry out the bulk of the work. Only the poorest of families had none. Though not ideal work animals, donkeys were nevertheless more cooperative than most mules. They were frequently used to till the soil (Isa. 30:24).

Strolling along the streets of the Old City of Jerusalem, the modern traveler frequently sees a beast of burden waiting for its next assignment. TW

The donkey is still used throughout Palestine to perform a variety of heavy jobs. This man and his modern donkey-cart move jauntily through the modern town of Akko (Acre) near Haifa.   TW

Donkeys can differ considerably in color. Gray or brown are the most frequent varieties, but a reddish shade may also have been common. White donkeys were quite rare animals (Judg. 5:10).

The donkey rose to its highest role when Jesus rode one, symbolizing that He was the King of Peace (Matt. 21:1–7; John 12:14). This was a fulfillment of the prophecy of Zechariah (9:9).   ■

MULES □ Because they are hybrids, mules were not supposed to be bred in Israel (Lev. 19:19). Mules are sterile and can be produced only by crossing a male donkey and a female horse. The offspring of a female donkey and a male horse is called a hinny. If mules were not bred in Israel, they certainly were imported. The advantage of a mule is its strength and larger size, blended with the durability of a donkey. Mules were especially good for carrying heavy burdens.   ■

HORSES □ There were many reasons to raise horses, but few of them were agriculturally related. Most of the horses in Israel were used for military purposes. Consequently most were owned by the king and the state.

The Egyptians owned horses but Israel was to shun them (Deut. 17:16). The major fear of horses was that they would lead a king to love war and leisure (1 Sam. 8:11). Solomon was unimpressed by the statute and stocked his army with at least 12,000 horses (1 Kings 10:26). (Some translations raise the count to 40,000 horses due to 1 Kings 4:26.) The king paid 150 shekels per horse and imported them from Egypt. At one point in Israel's history, statues of horses (or possibly real horses) were in the temple as part of the worship of the sun god (2 Kings 23:11).

We don't know how common mounted couriers were in Israel. However, Persia may have had several, similar in some respects to our pony express (Esther 8:10). Horses were not raised for food because the Jews were prohibited from eating horse meat (Lev. 11:4).

The horse appears to be of limited value for the farmer, though some were used to pull carts and plows. There was some profit in breeding horses for other purposes, though. Horses were not as useful as donkeys for rugged work because the latter could exist on less water and poorer quality of food. ■

CAMELS □ While important to nomads, camels played a smaller role among farmers. Camels were excellent for transporting heavy loads. Their specialized feet, eyes, nostrils, and food-storing hump

This watering trough atop Tel Megiddo, on the southern edge of the Plain of Esdraelon, signifies the military importance of Megiddo during Solomon's time. It was one of his "chariot cities" (1 Kings 10:26), and excavations have revealed facilities to care for 450 horses and 150 chariots.   TW

The camel is superbly engineered to cope with the hot, harsh environment of the desert nomad. The camel conserves water well and supplies transportation, milk, clothing and companionship on a long caravan journey.   TW

This mother camel and her young wait to be sold at a camel market in Beer-sheba. The single-hump dromedary camel was counted among the prized possessions of rich men like Abraham and Job.   TW

and water-storing stomachs make them ideal for desert living.

Camels offered many benefits. Besides the obvious ones listed, camels also supplied milk, fuel (dung chips) and leather. Several societies ate camel meat, but it was forbidden in the Jewish diet (Lev. 11:4).

By New Testament times most Jews used animals more practical than camels, when possible, for camels are notorious for their foul tempers and need for a large area to pasture. Job must have been a prosperous landowner to care for 3,000 camels (Job 1:3), among his other animals.   ■

PASTORAL NOMADS □ From the earliest days of the patriarchs, there have been several types of nomads roaming in the area of Israel. It is difficult to make general statements that apply to all nomads. We cannot look at present-day nomads and assume that ancient Jews dressed, lived or practiced religion in the same way. While change did not come rapidly in the Near East, it did come, and comes more quickly today than in ancient times.

The nomads we are concerned with were the type who kept herds or flocks and moved from area to area for grazing. They lived a rugged life in tents. Some Jews lived as nomads as early as Jabal (Gen. 4:20). Abraham also lived a nomadic life but only after living in a sophisticated city.

In ancient Israel nomads and settlers did not always co-exist well. Much like the early West in the United States, differences in lifestyle resulted in distrust, thievery and war.

Israel gave up the nomadic life for the security of Egypt only to renew it after the Exodus. When the Jews invaded Canaan, they began to return to city life. Some of the continuing conflict faced by Israel came from roaming nomads such as the Midianites and Amalekites (Judg. 6:5).

Many of the nomadic Jews tended donkeys from pasture to pasture. Others tended sheep (Ex. 3:1) and horses. Some recent discoveries indicate nomads cared for camels as early as the time of Joshua. The pastoral nomad lived off the animals he grazed. Clothing, utensils, food, fuel and tents were produced from the herd or flock. Often nomads were not totally aimless. They followed familiar routes, depending on the season and pasture supply. Nomads often traveled as extended families in several tents, with one man establishing himself as the leader. Some groups acquired considerable wealth and sizable herds or flocks. ∎

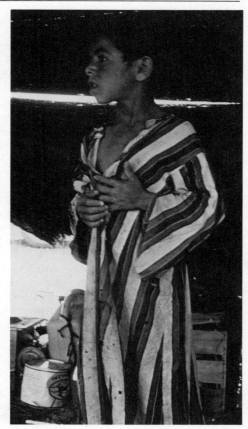

This Bedouin boy, whose family lives as pastoral nomads in a goat-hair tent, moves with his extended family from place to place, depending on the season and the supply of pasture for the livestock.   TW

POULTRY □ There is no doubt that Jews raised chickens, but use of the broad term "fowl" makes it difficult to know exactly what was raised and how widespread the practice was. Ducks, geese and pigeons were also available. We do know that chickens were raised within the city

Domesticated fowl such as ducks and geese are raised commercially in some of the kibbutzim and collective farms in the northern agricultural areas of Israel.   TW

limits of Jerusalem during the time of Christ. Some laws restricted their location because there was concern over their habit of scratching. Officials did not want the ground dug up so insisted they be confined and provided scratching areas. Chickens could be bought at the local meat markets.

Eggs were collected from several sources, including wild fowl or reptiles (Deut. 22:6) and were a normal part of the diet by New Testament times (Luke 11:12). Jesus used imagery of the chicken in His teaching (Matt. 23:37), and a rooster played a sad role in Peter's life (John 18:27).   ■

SWINE □ The Jews had strict laws and strong feelings against eating pork, as did several of the nations around them. Nevertheless, some farmers did raise and sell swine. We must not assume that because there was a law against something that it was not done. Swine were well known to the Jews and some proverbs were written about them (Prov. 11:22). Some of the pigs were wild (Ps. 80:13), but others were bred and raised in captivity. At Gadara a herd of the latter type rushed to their death in the Sea of Galilee (Matt. 8:30ff.). The swine's owners went into town to protest. When the prodigal son became destitute, he found a job caring for pigs (Luke 15:11ff.). This was in a far country, but is evidence of how low he had sunk.   ■

BUTCHERING □ Farmers probably did their own butchering, but so many people lived in the city that there were many butchers by trade. By the time of Christ a butchers' guild and a butcher's street existed in Jerusalem. A meat market existed in Corinth as it did in most cities. Great controversy arose over whether Christians should buy meat there after it had been offered to idols (1 Cor. 10:25). Later a butchers' guild in Rome put pressure on Christians because the spread of their religion caused a decline in the need for sacrificial animals.   ■

DOGS □ Most of the dogs in Israel were wild and unwanted. The very term is normally used in contempt. Notable exceptions were watchdogs and sheep dogs. Shepherds as early as Job's time used dogs to protect their flocks (Job 30:1). Other nations may have appreciated dogs more since many dog faces are carved in pottery and some religions sacrificed them. They were used by royalty and other elite in hunting. Except for shepherds who probably cared about their dogs, there probably was not as much affection for dogs in Israel's society as there is in ours.

It would be enlightening to know the tone in Jesus' voice when He commanded not to give that which is holy to dogs (Matt. 7:6). Jesus does use an affectionate term for dog in Matt. 15:26. The Greek word means "little dog" and suggests the status of a pet (Lenski, p. 598; Robertson, p. 125).   ■

CHAPTER 16

THE ROMAN OCCUPATION

The small nation of Israel was frequently a victim of the major powers which marched across its territory. Too often an empire would settle among the Jews, take control and stay for centuries. Assyrians, Babylonians, Persians, Greeks and Romans occupied, exploited and mistreated Israel and its people. Thousands were conquered, restrained and assimilated into the enemy culture. However, many others fought to maintain their independence and identity, causing a great deal of bloodshed.

Despite difficult odds, the Jewish people did maintain their identity.

The Jews possessed too many distinctives to be homogenized with other cultures. Some of these marks were cultural, others spiritual. Their traditions were deep and strong, tied irrevocably to their faith in God. This was their key to survival. They were convinced they could not abandon their past. Foreign occupation has always been a terrible trauma, but the Jews' need for purity was fanatical. Though they had been invaded and the strong arm of force resided over them, they were determined to persevere, and still do.

In spite of the negative aspects, the Roman Empire may have been good for Israel's economy. Its presence brought commerce, transportation, leisure, military security, education and other opportunities.

The one thing Rome did not provide was the thing most important to the Jew: his freedom. This lack placed the two peoples on a collision course.

ROMAN CAPTIVITY □ The expanding Roman Empire devoured Judea in 63 B.C. Josephus tells us that in October, on the Day of Atonement, they captured the temple. Suspicious of such a dramatic story, other historians disagree and place its fall in August.

Israel was not unaccustomed to occupation by a foreign power. Previously they had been subjugated for 250 years by the Greeks. In recent years there had been much bloodshed as the Jews tried to oust their invaders. The conflict was so severe that many Jews welcomed the Roman invasion.

Pompey led the Roman forces into Jerusalem and angered many Jews by his ruthless tactics. Large numbers of priests were murdered as they carried out their duties, and Pompey himself had the audacity to enter the sacred Holy of Holies. The Jews were outraged.

Fifteen years later Julius Caesar forced Pompey out of a shared leadership role. Pompey escaped to Egypt seeking refuge, only to be assassinated there. The Jews received the news joyfully, viewing the murder as an act of God. Julius Caesar then assumed his position as the most powerful figure in Rome. These early atrocities and insensitivities against the Jews set in motion hostility and friction which continued until A.D. 70 when Rome crushed Jerusalem.

The Israel into which Jesus was born was under the oppressive rule of a pagan power. Many of the Jewish authorities retained their positions by seeking to please their captors. Often offices were acquired and maintained by bribery and extortion. These conditions were important factors in the life, ministry, and death of Jesus Christ.   ■

ROMAN EMPERORS □ During the life of Christ and the early years of the church, five men reigned successively as emperors of Rome. A brief look at each will help us understand the times.

1. *Augustus Caesar (29 B.C. to A.D. 14).* Under his leadership Egypt was defeated along with Antony and Cleopatra in 31 B.C. It was his decree to enroll all the world for tax purposes which sent Joseph and Mary to Bethlehem (Luke 2:1). Augustus levied no great hardship on the Jews and generally allowed the people of Judea to govern themselves through the Sanhedrin.

2. *Tiberius (A.D. 14–37).* This man would have been emperor during the ministry of Jesus Christ. When Jesus asked whose face was on the coin (Matt. 22:17–21), it was Tiberius' profile. An insecure man, Tiberius may have suffered mental illness late in life. An unpopular emperor, he was noted as a libertine of excessive sexual appetite in an age of excess.

3. *Gaius (A.D. 37–41).* Better known as Caligula, this emperor was most likely insane. Imagining himself divine, he expected others to recognize him accordingly. He even ordered that a statue of himself be placed in the Holy of Holies in Jerusalem. However, one official cunningly delayed the project and thus prevented terrible bloodshed in Israel. Fortunately, Gaius died before the decree could be fulfilled.

4. *Claudius (A.D. 41–54).* During his first years of rule, Claudius displayed some benevolence toward the Jews. Later, however, he seemed to grow suspicious and began to restrict their movements. The Bible tells us some Jews moved to Corinth because they were commanded by Claudius to leave Rome (Acts 18:1, 2). Historical records show Claudius prohibited the Jews from gathering and thus, in effect, forced them to abandon Rome.

The terrible famine which Agabus predicted would cast its horror across the world came during the reign of Claudius (Acts 11:28).

5. *Nero (A.D. 54–68).* Though the early years of Nero's reign,

under Seneca's counsel, were laudable, there is little to commend this madman who had his own mother murdered. His persecution of Christians is as famous as it was gruesome. Nero had many Christians arrested, tortured and even burned alive, partly to divert attention from his political problems (e.g. the burning of Rome) and partly to amuse himself.

Paradoxically, it was to Nero's justice that Paul appealed (Acts 25:10–12); when Festus told Paul that to Caesar he would go, Nero was that Caesar. And when Paul called for obedience to the government because all authority comes from God (Rom. 13:1–7), it was Nero's government that was in power. Under Nero the apostle Paul was executed, as was Peter.   ■

EMPEROR WORSHIP □ A Roman emperor was usually considered a god. A much misunderstood concept, its fulfillment depended greatly on the emperor as well as the opinion of the population. There were three ways that an emperor might be worshiped.

First, the people supposedly worshiped spontaneously. Once the precedent had been set, the acceptable thing was to join in and worship him. Resistance could be dangerous.

Second, an emperor could be declared a deity after he died and worshiped thereafter. This was done by a vote of the Senate and happened occasionally.

Third, an emperor might appoint himself as a god while he was still alive. This was considered unacceptable and subjected

This ancient Roman figurine was used as a household god (Gen. 31:19). Under King Josiah's reform (640–609 B.C.) use of these images among Hebrews was officially outlawed (2 Kings 23:24).
EHLE

him to much antagonism—even murder.

Emperor worship left the Jews and early Christians in an awkward position. They could have no part in elevating men as gods, and their disdain for the practice was noticed by government officials. Romans had no trouble adding new deities into their theological arena.

Christian theology blatantly contradicted Roman religion; they conflicted most severely as schools of thought rather than as practices of worship. The converted Jews knew they could not approach God as the pagans addressed their deities. But of more importance, could they think the same way the Romans thought? Consequently, the heated issues concerned philosophies such as Hedonism, Epicureanism, Stoicism, and Cynicism rather than actual worship procedures. The dichotomy rested in values, and their consequent priorities and attitudes, instead of sacramental debates.

Efforts to impose images on coins and flags met direct conflict from Jews. Yet, with Paul the issues were of a cerebral nature (Acts 17). Sacrifices, circumcision, holy days, and temples were no longer of paramount importance to Christians. ■

SIGNIFICANT LOCAL RULERS □ *Pilate.* The appointment of men such as Pilate (A.D. 26–36) to govern the Jews was a particularly hard pill to swallow. His powers not only undermined Jewish law but also affected their religious practice. For the average Jew it was cruel enough to have opportunistic, and sometimes maniac, Herods reigning; the added misery of Roman governors was nearly intolerable.

Pilate had final authority over affairs at the temple. If he did not approve of activities there, he could disband or cancel them. He kept the vestments of the high priest in his possession. When Pilate visited Jerusalem for holidays, he brought them along and loaned them to the Jews. This served as a constant reminder that the Jews were not totally free to worship God as they deemed necessary.

The governor did not live in Jerusalem but only visited from his residence at Caesarea. A cornerstone has been found in that city which bears the name of Emperor Tiberius and Pilate.

His callous attitude toward the Jews revealed itself in several acts which aggravated them and eventually weakened his position. His most famous mistake concerned the banners he displayed in Jerusalem early in his appointment. These banners, bearing the image of Emperor Tiberius, were a terrible shock to the Jews who believed images were an insult to God. Governors before him were aware of this sensitive issue and avoided displaying them. Evidently Pilate was either ignorant, which is unlikely, or attempting to show his power. Whichever the case it was a dreadful error, and Pilate was forced to withdraw them. A week later the banners were returned to their places, minus the images.

Another act of Pilate incited huge riots in the streets of Jerusalem. Since he had control over the temple funds, Pilate boldly confiscated a sizable amount to build an aqueduct. The Jews were predictably outraged. Luke tells us Pilate ordered some Galileans killed while they were sacrificing in the temple (13:1, 2). Reportedly, Roman guards dressed in robes slipped in behind the Galileans as they worshiped, drew clubs from their sleeves and beat them to death. Not only were the deaths reprehensible, but to kill them during worship was horrendous.

The tensions created by these tactics weakened Pilate's position, and citizens' complaints were being carried to Rome. Consequently, at the trial of Jesus Christ, Pilate was forced to treat the Jews carefully. This probably accounts for his attempt to transfer the case to King

This fragment of a Roman inscription was unearthed at Caesarea. It is the first archaeological evidence of Pontius Pilate, under whose rule (A.D. 26–36) Jesus' crucifixion took place. It also mentions Emperor Tiberius.   TW

Herod (Luke 23:6–7) and his willingness to condemn an innocent man. Pilate's past errors had boxed him into a hopeless political situation. His fears were well founded, as later history tells us Pilate was recalled to Rome after mounting complaints by the Jews.

Felix. During the ministry of Paul a new governor represented Rome. Antonius Felix had moved to Caesarea to take up residence in the Praetorium, a lavish palace built by Herod the Great. From there Felix ruled the area, including Judea.

There is little good to say about Felix, either by Scripture or other historical accounts. A ruthless man, he resorted to murder whenever it served his purposes or tightened his control. Tacitus describes him unglamorously as exercising "the power of a king and the mind of a slave." Because of his character and barbaric mentality, the region was in almost continuous upheaval and revolt.

His encounter with Paul does nothing to alter this sordid picture. While feigning an interest in the gospel, his devious mind fished for ways to extract a bribe from Paul (Acts 24:26). Felix toyed with Paul's future for two years without resolving the predicament. Finally Nero relieved him of his responsibility as governor. Therefore, instead of reaching a decision concerning Paul, Felix left him in prison in order to please the Jews (Acts 24:27).

Festus. After Felix's regime, Festus was a welcome relief. He made sincere attempts to correct the deteriorating situation which he inherited. Festus arrested many common criminals and partially restored a sense of order.

It was the mental alertness of Festus which prevented the Jews from killing Paul; they had recommended he be sent to Jerusalem for trial, but were plotting to murder the apostle as he traveled (Acts 25:3).

When Festus asked Paul about the charges against him, the prisoner appealed to Caesar. After wisely consulting his council, Festus agreed to send Paul to Rome (Acts 25:12).   ∎

TAX COLLECTORS □ An empire as large as Rome's required huge sums to finance its many functions as well as its multiplied dreams. Highways, amphitheaters, harbors and armies all cost money. Even with the use of inexpensive slave labor, they were a financial burden.

To fill its ravenous coffers, the Romans devised a franchise system for tax collection which, by the time of Christ, had been in operation for 200 years and served the empire well. It did not, however, always serve the local citizen with equal benefit. Oppressive taxation was intolerable, and doubly so when the taxes were being levied by a foreign power.

The Jews of the first century appear to have had a valid complaint about high taxes. In addition to the Roman taxes, King Herod demanded revenues to feed his lavish appetite for buildings to enhance his comfort and glory. The temple also demanded taxes to support its operation. Under the best conditions these taxes would have been heavy, but they became all the more burdensome because of the franchise system. This method allowed a tax collector to purchase an area of jurisdiction from the Roman censor. His contract, which had a duration of several years, specified a quota which the collector was to fulfill each year and give to the government. The purchaser of the franchise in turn made a profit by collecting more than required for his quota. How much more he collected depended on his conscience and ingenuity. He was also free to sublet his area to others (for a fee) who collected for him. Resultantly, the taxes collected from the average citizen were outrageous. These unscrupulous men frequently charged far beyond a fair amount and were not averse to receiving a bribe for the purpose of alleviating the tax burden of a rich man and shifting it to the poor. Tax collectors were commonly despised by the general public. It would have been difficult to accept a member of their nationality exacting taxes for an occupying force. It would have been similar to a French tax collector working for the Nazis in occupied France.

Considering their reputation, it is startling that Jesus would become involved with tax collectors, thus leaving himself wide open to criticism, suspicion and hostility. It is interesting that Jesus not only ministered to tax collectors but also took the initiative in seeking them out. For instance, Matthew, a booth attendant who collected taxes from those who used the highways, was approached by Jesus and called to become a follower (Matt. 9:9). Matthew responded by serving a feast at his home and inviting his tax collector friends to attend (Matt. 9:10). In another instance, Zacchaeus, a chief tax collector, was viewing Jesus from a tree when the Messiah announced He was coming to Zacchaeus' house. As a result of this encounter the wealthy tax collector gave half his goods to the poor and reimbursed fourfold anyone he had cheated (Luke 19:1–10). Jesus received strong rebuke for pursuing such unseemly relationships (Luke 7:34). ■

CITIZENSHIP □ The number of people who could claim Roman citizenship was on the increase during the life of Paul. Over four million claimed the rights and privileges it guaranteed. Rather than a mere title, Roman citizenship endowed a person with several practical advantages, including a trial. If under trial for a capital crime, he could, after a verdict, appeal to Caesar. It was then his right to be delivered to the emperor for a personal trial (Acts 16:37; 25:11).

A Roman citizen could not be beaten. Since Paul was beaten, we surmise there either were exceptions to this rule (i.e., those under Jewish authority) or Paul was beaten illegally. Also, citizens, though they could be executed, could not be crucified. Any violation of these protections might result in the harshest of punishments.

Most people became citizens by being born into that state. Paul was one who fit that category. We are not told if his father or grandfather had acquired the privilege, but we do know it was inherited (Acts 22:28). Others gained their citizenship by purchase (Acts 22:28). Some emperors actually had membership drives in which they attempted to make more people feel they were part of the empire.

It may be out of Paul's understanding of Roman citizenship that he made reference to spiritual citizenship in God's kingdom. He assured believers that they are "fellow citizens with God's people" (Eph. 2:19). ■

HEROD'S REIGN (37–4 B.C.) □ This infamous king of Israel was placed on the throne by the Romans and bowed to their whims. Previously, Herod, while reigning as king of Galilee, had proven a

David's Tower, an outstanding Jerusalem landmark, was part of Herod's great palace. It was rebuilt in 1537 by a Turkish sultan.   LB

valuable ally to the coalition of Cassius and Brutus who murdered Julius Caesar on March 15, 44 B.C. Herod raised money for Cassius and moved against Judea when it revolted. After Antony defeated Cassius, he distrusted Herod and brought charges against him. Herod proved a survivor and emerged as a tetrarch of Judea. Later Antony, Octavius and the Roman Senate bestowed the title of King of Judea on Herod, but his throne did not come easily. Herod then had to fight to gain the throne and finally ousted his opposition in 37 B.C.

Because of the Roman involvement and his questionable Jewish lineage, many Jews did not trust him. Others, however, were drawn to his lifestyle and flamboyant changes, and thus supported him. ∎

THE CHRISTIAN ATTITUDE TOWARD THE EMPIRE

□ From the beginning Jesus made no attempt to put himself or His ministry in opposition to Rome. Some of His followers may have expected Jesus to declare war on the occupation forces, but He would have none of it. Many seemed disappointed that He would not violently establish the kingdom of Israel. There were a number of movements afoot (Zealots) who strongly advocated violence.

On occasion Jesus' enemies tried to corner Him by making Him choose sides in this issue. In one such instance, spies were sent to find grounds for accusations they could make against Christ. Consequently, they asked if Jews should pay taxes to Caesar (Luke 20:20–26). He replied that Caesar's likeness was on the coin so they should give to Caesar what belonged to him.

Christianity and the Roman Empire were diametrically opposed in matters of religion, its values and practices. Nevertheless, Paul describes government as ordained by God, its officers as ministers of God and its laws to be obeyed (Rom. 13:1–7). The once volatile Peter echoed this viewpoint, insisting that kings and governors were instituted by God (1 Pet. 2:13, 14).

Even in the face of death, Jesus affirmed the fact that Rome maintained its power by the authority of God (John 19:11). He did not hold Rome responsible for His mistreatment but those who handed Him over.

However, we do see serious clashes between the apostles and Jewish officials over the question of preaching the gospel. When ordered to cease preaching, the early Christians flatly refused (Acts 4:19–20).
                                                                    ■

THE ROMAN ATTITUDE TOWARD CHRISTIANITY
□ At first the empire saw Christians as little more than a nuisance. This may explain why Nero faced little resistance in persecuting them. Although Roman law protected the Christians' freedom, there was no one of consequence to defend this sect of Judaism, leaving them extremely vulnerable. Any insane emperor would find them easy victims.

Specifically, Romans had several reasons for disregarding Christianity.

First, the Christians were foreign and Jewish. Why take seriously something that is different?

Second, the Christian refusal to worship more than one god led to accusations of atheism. The polytheistic could not imagine a religion so exclusive as to have only one god.

Third, because of its foreignness and exclusiveness, Christianity fell victim to gossip. Rumors of cannibalism and offensive sexual practices were widespread and readily believed by suspicious nonbelievers.

Fourth, although there was no basis for the opinion, the church's loyalty to the empire and the emperor was highly suspect. References to a kingdom and a returning king did much to antagonize Roman authorities.

Nevertheless, the empire did at times show benevolence to the fledgling church. Paul's life was saved more than once by Romans who cared about fairness. The apostle would have been murdered during a shipwreck had not a centurion defended him (Acts 27:42–43). Earlier Paul's life had been rescued in a similar manner. At that time the Romans called out 470 men to guard the missionary (Acts 23:23). The New Testament accounts are generally kind to Roman centurions. Yet, the distrust of and even dislike for such an odd sect left the Christians virtually defenseless when Nero went shopping for a scapegoat.
                                                                    ■

THE CLASH BETWEEN JESUS AND ROME □ It probably
never occurred to the Romans that a carpenter from Galilee was a threat to their power. Jesus had no ambition to physically dislodge the iron grip of the empire. However, several of Jesus' followers may have entertained visions of violent revolt (i.e., Judas, Simon and maybe Peter).

The bust of Vespasian, emperor of Rome, appears on this bronze Judea Capta coin, a sestertius struck in Rome in A.D. 71 to commemorate the Roman victory over Judea.   BAS

The supposed clash was also born in the imaginations of Caiaphas and the Sanhedrin. It was they who suggested to Pilate and the Roman officials that Jesus wanted to overthrow the government. Pilate was incredulous from the beginning (John 18:33), and if, in fact, Jesus claimed to be king of the Jews, that was of little concern to the Romans. After all, a king without a kingdom was no threat to the Roman Empire.

Uneasy with the situation and feeling he could not ignore the issue, Pilate tried to turn it into a nervous joke. He asked the crowd if they wanted him to release the "king of the Jews" (John 18:39). The crowd insisted Jesus be executed, but Pilate later ridiculed them by saying, "Here is your king" (John 19:14). To complete his mockery, Pilate had written on the cross, "Jesus of Nazareth, the King of the Jews" (John 19:19).

From atop the fortress Masada, the visitor can look down on remains of one of the siege camps of the Roman general Silva who finally conquered the fortress in A.D. 73.   TW

This was not a confrontation with the government which Jesus sought. The enemies plotting His execution manipulated the issue to their particular advantage. ■

THE FALL OF ISRAEL □ The rebel fires which flamed high during the time of Pilate and rose again during the governorship of Felix were not to die easily. Pockets of resistance began to appear frequently enough to greatly concern King Herod Agrippa II and the Roman government. Unfortunately the Jews' bickering among themselves only made their efforts more difficult, thus making their hope for freedom even more improbable.

In A.D. 67 and 68, Vespasian, at the command of Nero, recaptured Galilee and Samaria and marched on Jerusalem. The death of Nero sent Vespasian back to Rome to become emperor. After he took firm control of the empire, he sent his son Titus to complete the conquering of Jerusalem. In A.D. 70 Jerusalem fell, though at some outposts such as Masada patriots fought on for three more years.

Israel did not begin recovery from this disastrous war until it became a nation again in 1948. ■

CHAPTER 17

TRAVEL AND COMMUNICATION

It took a determined effort to travel within a country or to another nation, but many people were willing to face the risk, expense and hardship. Time was not as crucial during biblical times, and it was relatively easy to set aside a month and journey off to see the wonders of the world or to plead one's case to a high Roman official.

Not everyone, of course, was able to travel. Many, such as Jesus, ventured little more than 100 miles from home in their lifetimes. Yet most had done some traveling. The very fact of religious pilgrimage necessitated that those living outside Jerusalem eventually had to travel.

Mobility had deep social ramifications. Because of travel, there was a great influx of ideas into Israel. The average Jew may have distrusted the outside world, but he could not ignore it. His friends and relatives had seen the far-off cities, witnessed the pagan religious practices and encountered foreign values. He had much more to consider than mere Jewish traditions. Sometimes this exposure severely threatened his way of thinking. It also widened his opportunities.

Whatever its difficulties, the relative ease of travel was a miraculous gift to the young church. The gospel arrived at a time when its message could be transported rapidly to the four corners of the earth. In fact, one of the accusations against the apostles was that they had caused upheaval throughout the world (Acts 17:6). Soon, converts and full-fledged churches were standing boldly and telling the Good News with others in the distant corners of the known world. Rome had built a magnificent system of transportation. Christians quickly utilized it in dramatic fashion.

HIGHWAYS AND ROADS □ If travel was to become a common experience, an excellent system of roads was esssential. The first century was thus a golden time for travel. The Roman network of main roads comprised over 50,000 miles with almost a quarter million more miles of second-class arteries. Rome's roads were not only well graded and leveled, normally they were solidly constructed with a top layer of stone for paving.

Roman roads were built in a complex fashion. First the roadway was excavated and a large amount of sand poured in as a base. Stones were then set in a layer of cement. Then crushed stones were placed in more cement. After that an even layer of stone slabs

The quality and care with which Roman roads were constructed can be seen in this road, still in use near Emmaeus. The Roman network of outstanding roads reached out for over 50,000 miles in biblical times.   BAS

or blocks was placed on top. To protect against erosion, gutters were constructed on both sides of the road.

These roads were built so durably that several of the highways have become famous and are in use even today. One such remarkable road is the Appian Way which runs southeast from Rome to Capua. Called the "queen of roads," it was built three hundred years before early Christians traveled on it to hear Paul (Acts 28:15), and the road still survives. Built under the direction of several emperors, the 18-foot-wide highway eventually stretched 360 miles (approximately the distance from Los Angeles to San Francisco).

Some construction details of the Roman roads may be seen in this example from Christ's time, currently being excavated in Jerusalem. In addition to the even layer of stone slabs as a finish surface, a curb may be seen at the left. JJ

Such quality construction assured not only access to faraway areas at relatively good speed, but also safe travel in bad weather. Storms could still impede the journey, but hazards such as mud and flooding were less likely. The builders, undaunted by streams and rivers, used their superb engineering skills to construct sturdy bridges.

Many older and less traveled roads were little more than glorified paths that developed their configuration by constant use. These roads were undependable during bad weather and sometimes allowed only slow travel during the good. Some roads would be smooth and easily maneuvered, but others had huge ruts from wheels, or deep paths from cattle tracks.

There were two especially rapid routes on which to travel north and south through Israel. One was the "King's Highway" (Num. 20:17), running from Damascus to the Gulf of Aqaba. At least 4,000 years old, it was traveled by Moses as he led the Jews toward Canaan (Num. 21:22). A second major thoroughfare was the Via Maris, stretching along the lower Mediterranean coast from Megiddo to Egypt.

Another famous roadway was the one from Jericho to Jerusalem. The Jericho road played a significant role in several Bible stories, including the story of the Good Samaritan (Luke 10:25–37). Jesus had often traveled this small twisting road and was well aware of its reputation as an alley for thieves. Some called it "the red and bloody way."

The Romans stationed guards along the road.

The concept of roads blended well with Christian theology. Many referred to this faith as "the Way," patterned after Jesus' description of himself as "the way" (John 14:6), which alluded to a pathway or a road. The term is found several times in the book of Acts (19:9, 23; 22:4; 24:14, 22; also 16:17 and 18:25). The early believers seemed to picture life as a journey and Jesus as the way to travel through this world.

Tel Megiddo, rising from the southern edge of the Plain of Esdraelon, covers about 13 acres and includes ruins from about 20 cities built upon one another. At Megiddo the Via Maris forks with the western route continuing along the Mediterranean coast and the eastern route going overland. TW

WATER ROUTES □ An average citizen could, and a large number did, take long journeys across the many narrow or wide waterways. For centuries, sailors had braved the strong winds which swept across the Mediterranean Sea. When the winds failed, their vessels were propelled by wooden oars.

The best time to travel the sea was in the summer, but surprises could arise even then. Winters were extremely risky and normally only dire emergency would tempt a crew to venture out.

Paul's journey across the Mediterranean on his way to Rome is a dramatic account of a stormy voyage (Acts 27, 28). Previously the ship had been hit by a hurricane force wind near Crete called a "northeaster" or *Euraquilo* (Acts 27:14). More exactly it was an east-by-northeast wind which would suddenly sweep down from Mount Ida. Paul's experience points up the sometimes hazardous conditions which travelers faced on the sea.

The trip began in Caesarea, meandered across the Mediterranean (including wide open sea), wrecked at Malta and eventually delivered Paul to Rome.

Another famous biblical sea disaster involved the stubborn prophet, Jonah. In order to avoid the call of God, Jonah boarded a ship in Joppa and sailed for Tarshish (Jon. 1:3). Joppa is modern Jaffa, located just south of Tel Aviv. Speculation persists about the location of Tarshish, although we do know it was a port in the Mediterranean. It may have been as far away as Italy or even Spain. The desperateness of Jonah's act implies that Tarshish was a great distance away. Jonah's voyage ended in apparent horror as first the cargo and then the prophet himself were tossed overboard to save the ship from breaking up in the storm. As we know, God spared Jonah for His purposes.

Since slaves were plentiful and inexpensive, ships frequently were constructed to use many oarsmen. As many as 40 or 50 were used to propel larger vessels.

The peace of Rome played a notable part on the seas. Especially under Augustus, pirates were hounded, captured and virtually eliminated. This assurance of safe travel had a profound effect on the travel of early believers and therefore the spread of the gospel. It does not seem the Jews felt drawn to the open water. Fishing in the Sea of Galilee was a common vocation, but the Mediterranean was an area they avoided. Nevertheless there was a need to ship merchandise for export and import. In most cases the Jews seemed satisfied to send materials and goods on Greek and Roman vessels.

The time needed to travel by sea could vary widely. Dependent on sails, labor and favorable weather, schedules were not viewed very seriously. A traveler might sail briskly from Alexandria to Rome in 10 days. However, the return voyage could be 60 days.

Cargo was the main incentive for the commercial seafarer. Most ships were designed to carry cargo and included passengers only for extra income. Generally, passengers had to bring their own food and care for their own needs.

The burgeoning shipping industry called for an increase in suitable harbors around the Mediterranean. In response harbors were fortified to resist storms and in some areas man-made harbors were constructed.

Pagan sailors believed that certain deities watched over and protected them. The most common sea gods for the Romans were Castor and Pollux, referred to by Luke as the Twin Brothers in some translations (Acts 28:11). It was believed they would look down from the stars and help those who were in peril. Sparks, from electrical charges, appearing on the masts of ships during lightning storms were supposedly a sign that the Twin Brothers were present and giving aid. The Twins were taken quite seriously. Temples were built in their honor throughout the Roman Empire. To gain the favor of these gods, vessels frequently had a figurehead of each god mounted on the prow.   ∎

TIMES AND DISTANCES □ The time duration of a journey depended greatly on the mode of travel, weather and physical condition of the traveler. Safety was also a factor but less so under the Romans during the time of Christ.

Those who moved on foot probably averaged 15 to 20 miles a day. The actual distance between Jerusalem and Jericho is 15 miles, but the road is narrow, winding and steep. Jerusalem to the Sea of Galilee is nearly 80 miles. Bethlehem to Galilee is a little more than 80 miles. Except for His trip to Egypt as a child, Jesus may have never traveled more than 85 miles from home. Paul, however, journeyed extensively around the Mediterranean Sea.   ∎

ANIMAL TRANSPORTATION □ Much of the travel in Israel was accomplished by wagons, carts, chariots, and beasts of burden.

The camel, often called "the ship of the desert," was used to haul heavy loads. They were comparable to a modern truck in load-bearing capacity.   TW

The horse, used extensively by the Romans, is still widely used throughout Palestine. Here a lone Arab horseman gallops through the ancient red-rock city of Petra in Jordan.   TW

The animals offered greatly varying degrees of comfort and cooperation.

Camels. People occasionally rode these tall "ships of the desert," but their greater value lay in their ability to haul heavy loads. They are seldom mentioned in the New Testament, but there are enough references to confirm their use. Camels could be compared to our trucks. Camels are reported to travel as much as 25 miles a day carrying half a ton.

The debate continues over whether Jerusalem actually had a gate (referred to as an "eye of a needle") through which no fully loaded camel could enter (Matt. 19:24). Christ's reference is probably only a figure of speech, an example of His humorous use of hyperbole.

Donkeys. These sturdy, lightweight animals functioned much as a modern pickup truck would. Many biblical stories mention them, including the Good Samaritan (Luke 10:34) and Christ's triumphal entry into Jerusalem (Mark 11:1–11). Easy to care for and fairly pleasant in disposition, donkeys were a common choice for travel. In Jesus' time these were in use among the common people, but in early Israelite history they were the steeds of the wealthy.

Horses. The Romans used horses extensively, especially to equip their mobile armies. Though too expensive for the average person, many horses were ridden by government officials.

Elephants. These would have been a rare sight in Israel, but elephants were in use in some areas. Transportation, however, was not their best function. The elephants' more practical role resembled that of army tanks. They were utilized several times during the Intertestamental period and on one occasion Lyoias used 32 of them as he fought the Jews (163 B.C.). ∎

SHIPPING GOODS □ Both building and commerce necessitated the movement of large amounts of material across great distances, as in the case of Solomon building the temple. Therefore many caravans of pack animals and heavily-laden ships wended their way from city to city and country to country.

The Jews mainly exported agricultural goods and imported other needed materials, including gold, silver, ivory, wood, iron, marble, spices, cloth, silk, pearls and bronze (Rev. 18:11–13).   ■

THE MOVEMENT OF ARMIES □ As in modern times thousands of young men were able to see much of the world while serving in the army. In Old Testament days the armies of Egypt, Babylon, Persia and Israel, as well as other nations, saw considerable travel.

By the time of Christ, Roman armies were stationed throughout the empire. Centurions and the men who served under them were getting a taste of foreign culture and bringing a foreign culture with them. The Romans also had a sizable naval fleet which toured the empire.   ■

THE ROMAN PEACE □ A major contribution to the ease of travel was the relative peace guaranteed by the Roman Empire. The armies could not totally eradicate the menace of robbers and pirates, but they suppressed most dangerous elements. The Romans also practically eliminated the threat of foreign armies disrupting commerce. Both security and intimidation were attributes of the Roman presence.

The Roman emperor most responsible for the peace was Augustus Caesar (27 B.C.–A.D. 14). He brought the fighting to an end and called the empire to rest. This was providential timing since it granted soon-to-be-born Christianity open roads and free communication to spread the gospel rapidly.   ■

TOURIST TRADE □ Because traveling conditions in the first century may seem primitive to us, it is surprising how many people set out to see the sights. Maps have been found similar to our tourist maps, showing distances from one town to another, indicating where inns were located and noting what services were offered.

Travel was not restricted to nearby wonders. Though transportation was slow, it was possible to see the marvels of Africa, Spain, Egypt, Germany, Scandinavia and even China.   ■

PERSONAL REASONS TO TRAVEL □ Other than business, war and tourism, there were several reasons why a person would venture out into the world on the excellent roads and ships available.

Visit relatives. Because of increased mobility and far-flung business enterprises, large numbers had moved away from their original family units. On special occasions they traveled to see loved ones.

Religious pilgrimages. The Jews felt an especially strong desire to return to the temple in Jerusalem and celebrate the religious holidays. As many as a quarter million pilgrims traveled to Jerusalem to worship at one time. On the day of Pentecost we find Jews who had traveled from North Africa and throughout Asia Minor (Acts 2:9, 10), as well as Rome and the Arab countries. Other religions also encouraged pilgrimages to their holy places.

Athletics. Contests had become so popular that both spectators and participants were willing to travel great distances. The Corinthian games helped account for the large numbers of visitors to that city. Some athletes followed a circuit which took them to several places during the season.

Academics. Certain areas were noted as centers for learning. A distinguished school, scholar or group of teachers would attract students from miles away. Tarsus and Athens were known for prestigious education. The fabulous library in Alexandria would have been another center. The pursuit of knowledge was honored and encouraged as a worthy activity.

Medical treatment. Cities frequently held claim to special cures and their reputations drew thousands of the afflicted. In some cases a famous doctor resided in the locality. Other places, such as Capernaum, boasted hot springs which offered cures of miracle proportions.   ■

BUSINESS TRAVEL □ The business world had an international flavor. While some workers, craftsmen and executives stayed in

Capernaum, on the northwest shore of the Sea of Galilee, probably had about 10,000 inhabitants in Jesus' day and was the headquarters for most of His public ministry. Today the city is no more; all that remains are excavated ruins, including a picturesque limestone synagogue.   TW

their towns all their lives, others crossed many borders to increase their reputations and fortunes. During the time of Solomon, craftsmen were imported from Tyre as stonemasons (1 Kings 5:18). In the time of Christ, the demands for building were growing. Shrines, temples and other magnificent buildings required craftsmen to make long journeys and to stay for long periods.   ■

POSTAL SYSTEM □ In order to stimulate trade and to govern a far-flung empire, some form of communication system had to be maintained. The first postal system apparently was founded by Darius I (522–486 B.C.) of Persia. Government postal systems, basically courier services for official matters, continued for centuries with little or no such service for private citizens. Nevertheless, a great deal of personal correspondence was handled by travelers who agreed to carry letters for friends. Early letters to the churches and private Christians moved with a fair amount of ease. Not only could they depend on regular traffic, but much missionary activity kept Christians moving on the roads and seas. The Romans, as the Persians before, set up mounted courier stations similar to our pony express. Many of these stations also served as inns; however, their main purpose was to supply food and fresh mounts for Roman couriers.   ■

INNS □ Israel was noted for its open-armed hospitality. Travelers frequently stayed in the homes of friends, relatives or even strangers. However, the history of public inns goes back for centuries before Christ.

Inns supplied a night's lodging and meals for a price. Many of them were legitimate establishments, but others also offered the services of prostitutes. During the time of Christ this was true, especially at Roman inns. In this regard the exact role of Rahab is difficult to define (Josh. 2:1). Was she an innkeeper as well as a prostitute? It is possible that she was both (Heb. 11:31).

Inns ranged from simple accommodations (sometimes an extension of a home) to the large *khan* or caravanserie. These were full-service facilities, like our modern motels or even truck stops. Often found at well-traveled intersections, they offered care for animals as well as food, beds, baths and other travelers' needs. Even large caravans might stop to spend the night at one of these.

Instead of havens of rest, some of the inns were brothels or actually dens for thieves. Occasionally a weary traveler was robbed or murdered in the very lodge where he sought safety.

The precise nature of the inn in Bethlehem where Mary and Joseph sought shelter is uncertain (Luke 2:7). The inn on the road to Jericho in which the Good Samaritan hired services may have been a large edifice because the road was heavily traveled (Luke 10:34, 35). Today an inn, the Khan Hathrur, exists on this road; tradition says it stands on the same site where the inn of the story was.   ■

CHAPTER 18

RELIGIOUS AND POLITICAL GROUPS

When Jesus began His ministry, many diverse, self-seeking groups were in place and none was willing to give way to His leadership. Opposed to change, they were threatened by an outsider making claims that He had a kingdom and that He had come from God.

Political and religious structures had become rigid in an effort to survive. Jews were frequently slaughtered, and those in leadership roles were prone to be exterminated first. They did not take lightly to anyone who might enter the scene and cause chaos.

Those in power served for various reasons. Some were corrupt, either seeking wealth and security, or the power and prestige that went with their office and title, or both.

Some Jewish leaders held tenaciously to their positions because they genuinely wanted what was best for the Jews and Israel. They even craved to serve God. However, their sights had become so narrow that they could not accept Jesus as the Messiah. Wanting what was good, they rejected what was best.

To the Jews, Jesus' great sin was that He was "other." If He were right, they felt He should have been one of them. How could He have been sent from God and not identify with their causes? They had paid terribly to attain their position; they would not now surrender their titles to follow someone else.

Jesus arrived without acceptable credentials. He fit into none of the pigeonholes already established. Without an established identity, He had little hope of winning over those who already "belonged." Although Jesus convinced some organizational people, most scarcely gave Him hearing.

ZEALOTS □ A few religious groups were deeply entrenched in their beliefs and were willing to both kill and die for them. The Zealots fit this category. Their name comes from the Hebrew words for "zeal" and "jealous." They refused to tolerate the foreign societies which polluted their religion and controlled their government. Zealots willingly risked their lives in combat to serve their God and restore their nation.

Historically the term "zealot" was used in two senses: to describe an official party or to explain the attitude of a person, whether or not he was part of the group.

The Zealot party came into prominence during the time of Christ. As a resistance movement they caused great frustration for the Roman government. Their movement was crushed in A.D. 70 when Rome invaded Jerusalem and decimated Israel. Today the Zealots are best remembered for their final stand at Masada, which ended in May, A.D. 73.

Despite their terrible losses to the Romans, pockets of Zealots were found later, still defiantly resisting foreign, Gentile influence.

The influence of two groups can be seen in the Zealots. The first is the militant and often respected Maccabean movement which had met such horrid bloodshed. The second is the Pharisees. Force was not espoused by the Pharisees; consequently, most would have rejected the Zealot's philosophy. However, the political-religious sentiments of the two groups were similar, and it is possible that a few Pharisees broke rank and became closet Zealots.

The Zealots, rather than being one official political-military organization, were most likely many little groups scattered around the country who called themselves Zealots and took up the cause in their own way.

The most famous Zealot in the New Testament is Simon, who became one of the original 12 disciples (Luke 6:15; Acts 1:13). It is assumed that he was a *former* member of the group, for he could not in good conscience belong to both simultaneously. However, it would be safe to say that the disciples did envision some form of removal of the Roman government. Several of the disciples may initially have followed Christ, because they considered a messianic

Masada, an immense brown crag about 2½ miles from the Dead Sea, means "fortress" in Hebrew and was the site where 960 Jewish patriots, under the leadership of Eliezer Ben Yair, chose to commit suicide in A.D. 73 rather than be captured by the Romans.   TW

movement a resistance movement. Many of them came from Galilee which was noted for its rebellious residents, whom the Roman government viewed as troublemakers (Luke 13:1).

The apostle Paul exhibited some characteristics of a Zealot; however, it does not appear he belonged to the party. Paul was a Pharisee and he was willing to kill for his Jewish faith—the persecution of the early church was passionate and ruthless (Acts 8:1–3). Although this does not demonstrate that Paul was an official member of the Zealot party, it does show he was an advocate of that spirit. Several times in describing his desire to persecute the church, Paul uses the word "zeal" (Gal. 1:13, 14; Phil. 3:5, 6).

Paul takes care to denounce unbiblical "zeal" because it is often held by people who have no true knowledge of God (Rom. 10:1–4). Those same Jews who were zealous for God tried to murder the apostle because of his Christian faith (Acts 23:12–14). ■

ESSENES □ The Essenes felt just as strongly as the Zealots about the adulteration of their religion. As purists they longed for the "good old days" which they imagined to be better and truer to God's laws.

Although of kindred spirit to the Zealots, they drastically disagreed concerning their methods. The Essenes believed that withdrawal and seclusion, not violent confrontation, were the best relief from an oppressive, pagan society.

This group is not directly mentioned in the Bible, but their influence may have been felt by men such as John the Baptist. We have no evidence that he lived with such a group, but his lifestyle would have lent itself to that thinking and surroundings. They had tremendous impact on the 20th-century church when the Dead Sea scrolls, produced by an Essene community, were discovered in Qumran.

One of their reasons for retreating to an austere desert life (though some lived in the city) was to escape worldly contamina-

tion and cleanse themselves. By striving for holiness they hoped to prepare a society which would welcome the Messiah, to fulfill the scriptures of Isa. 40:3–5 and thus hasten the presence of the Messiah.

Cave Number 4 at Qumran contained more of the Dead Sea Scrolls than any other cave. They were discovered in 1948 by a young Bedouin goatherder, Muhammad Adh-Dhib.   TW

The concept of Messiah was important in the minds of many Jews during the first century.

The Essenes did not welcome an outsider readily. Only after observing him closely for a year did they consider accepting someone as a novice. Once a person gained membership, he was expected to sell his property and donate the proceeds to the group. He had to promise to love everyone in the community and hate those outside. If he failed the rigors of this highly regimented life, he could be banished without friends or compensation.

The group at Qumran remained intact over 200 years, from about 200 B.C. through the time of Christ. Other Essene communities existed, but the one at Qumran is the best documented. ■

MESSIANIC MOVEMENTS □ Jesus was not the first or last person who claimed to be God's anointed. The Jews were longing for a deliverer to restore the days of glory their ancestors had known under David and Solomon. Since then they had suffered a thousand years of division, exile, and occupation. Many were holding firmly to the promises of the Scripture and looking eagerly for the Messiah.

However, the culture was replete with a variety of theories concerning His arrival, His appearance, and His actions. Some felt that they had to prepare the way with either a call for a return to holiness, military action, or both. Others insisted that nothing could be done until after the Messiah revealed himself. It is noteworthy

Qumran, at the northwest corner of the Dead Sea, is the site of ruins from a monastic sect called Essenes who copied the Sacred Scriptures on large parchments during the first century A.D. Above and to the left of these ruins of the Essenes' living quarters can be seen the Dead Sea.   TW

that these same diverse opinions exist among some Jews and Christians today.

This is a recurring theme in the ministry of Jesus. Not only was messiahship an important subject to Him, but it was vital to those He met. When Andrew went to find his brother Peter, the first thing he told him was, "We have found the Messiah" (John 1:41). The woman at the well asserted she knew the Messiah was coming (John 4:25). Jews at the Feast of Dedication asked Jesus bluntly if He was the Messiah (John 10:24).

Messianic hope may never have been at a higher pitch than when Jesus was on earth. At least once the crowds were ready to take Him by force and make Him their king (John 6:15). Such anticipation of the Messiah left many Jews wide open to deception. Many self-appointed prophets declared themselves to be the Messiah and frequently attracted large followings. Whoever promised the deliverance of Israel (Luke 1:68) guaranteed himself a hearing.

History records a few of the early false Messiahs. Theudas attracted a large following and asked them to join him as he parted the Jordan as Joshua had done. The Jordan did not part but Theudas' crowds did.

An Egyptian claiming to have messianic identity called for a huge meeting at the Mount of Olives. He had advertised that those in attendance could see the walls of Jerusalem collapse at his command. The walls stood firm. This is probably the same Egyptian that Luke mentions (Acts 21:38); he says the man had a following of 4,000, but Josephus claims it reached 30,000.

Even in the final days of Jerusalem, as the Roman soldiers prepared to set the torch to the temple, 6,000 people gathered under another prophet's leadership. They fully expected deliverance into heaven at that very hour.

When Jesus arrived, His claim to messiahship was not a new or absurd concept. The hour was right and expectation was high. Jesus was aware of the public mood and therefore warned His followers against the claims of false messiahs to come (Matt. 24:23, 24).   ■

HASIDIM □ This was not an official party but an attitude held by many Jews some centuries before Christ. They believed strongly in keeping the Jewish laws but opposed bloodshed in attaining their freedom. While they do not appear in biblical accounts, their influence can be seen in the Pharisee and Essene postures of nonviolence. As "pious ones" the Hasidim kept their traditions regardless of the consequences. During the Maccabean period, a thousand such Jews refused to move from their city on the Sabbath. As a result the Syrians murdered them and no Hasidim resisted.   ■

MACCABEANS □ Fighting heroically, the Jews tried desperately to overthrow Greek and Syrian dominance during the Maccabean revolt, which began under the leadership of an elderly priest named

Mattathias. At his death in 166 B.C., his sons continued the revolt. Of the five, Judas proved the best leader and soon was called Judas Maccabeus, Maccabeus meaning "to hammer."

The Maccabean rebels organized full-fledged armies and battled the Syrians successfully. Forced to negotiate, the Syrians allowed the Jews to control Jerusalem and restore worship services. Peace was short-lived, however. Judas was killed in 160 B.C. and the revolt was soon crushed.

The Maccabean rebellion remains as one of the great patriotic memories in Jewish history. The word *Maccabean* became a symbol of self-assertion, bravery, and hope. During the time of Christ, many longed to initiate a similar military revolution.   ■

SADDUCEES □ Out of the Maccabean experience arose the Sadducees, a party which confronted Jesus Christ. They emerged from the turmoil of war with a firm grip on some important parts of Jewish life. First, they controlled the temple, the heart of the Jewish faith on earth. As its guardians they exercised tremendous power over its religious practices. By the time of Christ, however, the synagogue had gained centrality. Second, after a series of corrupt transactions, they were able to purchase the office of high priest. For years they were able to hold the position by the sheer power of money. Third, they managed to secure the leadership of the ruling Sanhedrin through their monopoly on the office of high priest. This gave them control far exceeding the number of people who supported their position.

Their beliefs. The people of this group held to rigid biblical interpretations, which included the denial of parts of the Old Testament because they were non-Mosaic. Therefore, there were certain widely held doctrines they could not accept. Generally, they denied the likelihood that God was concerned with their daily lives. The will of God was something broad, having little specific personal application.

They refused any doctrine of a physical resurrection (Matt. 22:23; Mark 12:18; Luke 20:27). They felt because the doctrine was not declared in the books of Moses, it was unacceptable. This also applied to the possibility of an eternal soul. Josephus says they believed the soul perished with the body. Therefore, any concept of spiritual beings, other than God himself, was totally rejected (Acts 23:8). Under this system angels were merely poetic expressions or figments of the imagination. The Hebrew word translated "angel" has, as its primary meaning, "messenger."

Their theology led them to a deistic position which saw God as a great Creator and Lawgiver who virtually divested himself of interest in this world. Therefore the Sadducees were predisposed to reject any claims to deity by Jesus Christ. Since God seldom thought about the earth, it was doubtful that He would bother sending His Son to live here.

Their influence. Most of the Sadducees came from the monied, influential class, so even if their numbers were not great their power was considerable. Headed by an aristocratic, priestly element they appear to have balanced a formidable mixture of power, corruption and Jewish tradition that allowed them to remain in office.

When Jerusalem fell in A.D. 70, the Sadducee party collapsed, but the Pharisees still wielded influence among the Jews.

Their corruption. The Sadducees would not have appreciated the label, "corrupt." They believed themselves to be facing the political realities and employing the most logical response—cash. It was difficult to hold on to the office of high priest. From the beginning of Herod's reign to the fall of Jerusalem (108 years), there were 28 high priests, their average term being less than four years. During the Greek period, money often changed hands to secure the office of high priest. We are not certain of the exact prerequisites under Herod, but we do know that one acquired the office only if he were useful to the king.

Their confrontation with Jesus. The conflict between Jesus and the Sadducees' high priest was inevitable, for almost no common ground existed between the two; Caiaphas could accept almost none of Jesus' theology. However, this was not the heart of the problem, for normally, Caiaphas was impervious to the claims of prophets and messiahs. Nor were the miracles of particular concern. He had doubtless seen similar displays of the supposed supernatural.

The crux of the clash rested in the threat of the crowds that followed the Galilean. If those crowds became a menace, the Romans might act with force to suppress them. The situation could quickly get out of hand and result in widespread destruction of Jews. Caiaphas' fears were not totally groundless. Shortly afterwards, in A.D. 70, the Roman government did crush Israel and disperse its remaining population. The uneasy issue came to a head when Jesus brought Lazarus back from the dead (John 11:48).

Caiaphas therefore formulated the axiom that demanded the death of Jesus: It was better for one man to die than for the entire nation to perish (John 11:49, 50).

Caiaphas' plan, however, did not work. After the crucifixion and resurrection of Christ, the following only grew, much to the high priest's frustration (Acts 5:4–17). It is ironic that resurrection, the very idea which the Sadducees rejected, was the factor which caused their consternation.   ∎

PHARISEES □ The Sadducees locked horns with Jesus over the question of pragmatism; the Pharisees opposed Jesus because of His interpretation of the law and claim to deity. The Pharisees could not tolerate His adherence to the spirit, rather than the letter, of the law. He in turn refused to go along with their strict, nit-picking concept of the law.

At the core of their conflict was a drastically different concept of God. The Pharisees saw Him as easily angered and unforgiving. Jesus saw His Father as loving and compassionate. The two ideas could not coexist.

Their popularity. The Pharisees were a party or society which probably never numbered more than 6,000. However, their real strength came from their support from the common man. While most people did not belong to the group, many were very sympathetic to their ideals.

Their strengths. Throughout hundreds of years of defeat and deportation, the Pharisaic position had served Israel well. Even before they were an official group, their exacting views of the law held the nation together. The Pharisees were more nationalistic than the Sadducees and quicker to defy foreign elements. They accepted the entire Old Testament as the Word of God, not just the Books of Moses. When Israel had trouble maintaining its identity, men of Pharisaic persuasion began schools to educate their young and prevent a falling away into pagan faiths. The Pharisees carried the banner of evangelism and converted Gentiles to Judaism. Jesus, however, was not impressed with those missionary ventures (Matt. 23:15).

Tithing was such an important rule that they meticulously offered ten percent of every small object in their lives (Matt. 23:23). However, in doing so they failed to practice the things that were really important to God: justice, mercy and faith.

They joined in the enthusiasm for the coming Messiah. Unfortunately, they were so confident in their own preconceptions that they could not recognize the Messiah when He came.

Despite their admirable efforts to maintain exactitude in Jewish practice, they did not fare well in the New Testament writings, especially in the gospel record.

Paul the Pharisee. The famous apostle is good evidence of both the strength and the weakness of Pharisaism. The Pharisees helped Paul gain a zealous love for God. However, his resultant fanaticism led him to destroy God's people.

After Paul had become a Christian, he looked back at the balance of his experience as a Pharisee as good. Before the Sanhedrin he proclaimed loudly and proudly that he was a member of the esteemed Pharisees (Acts 23:6).

Fence builders. As protectors they felt responsible to define the boundaries which would allow Jews to live safely before God. Thus their teachers built fences which would corral believers snugly within the borders of biblically acceptable behavior. For instance, the Bible told them to fast once a year (Lev. 23:27–29), but by the time of Christ the Pharisees were ceremoniously fasting twice a week (Matt. 6:16–18). In their attempting to outdo the Old Testament, the Pharisees perverted the ceremony of the washing of hands. Instead of a simple ceremony believers were expected to perform the ritual before each meal. They specified an exact amount of water; it was to run down to the wrists or be nullified. They were aghast that Jesus would not comply to this rule (Mark 7:5).

Repeatedly they insisted on improving on God's laws. They

thought obedience to God consisted mostly in details and not in love.

Conflict with Jesus. Not every Pharisee fit into this distorted mold. Some vigorously complained about these petty practices and refused to keep the multiplicity of laws. It seems most of the ones who encountered Jesus were not of this variety.   ■

SANHEDRIN □ Under certain periods of the Roman occupation, the Jews were allowed much latitude in governing themselves. It worked to the empire's advantage to have local people direct their own affairs. As long as their actions did not conflict with Roman laws and goals, there remained an uneasy truce.

The supreme council which governed Jewish religious matters was the Sanhedrin. The extent of its power depended greatly on the personality and courage of the council in session and the current attitude of Rome. At times its decisions influenced Judaism all over the world. On other occasions its pronouncements were taken seriously only by the people living in Judea. When Jesus entered the province of Judea, the council exercised its authority over Him. When He was in Galilee, its opinions were of little import.

The council tried to pattern itself after the group of elders formed by Moses when he was governing Israel—as a practical consideration he appointed elders to share the burden of ruling the people (Ex. 18:25). Although its origin probably goes back farther in history, it probably met for the first time during the Greek rule before Christ. When the Romans conquered they allowed the council to continue. Herod the Great, appointed by Augustus, decided to reorganize the Sanhedrin when he came to power, so he had all of its members executed. The king felt more secure appointing a council that was amenable to his administration.

Both Sadducees and Pharisees were represented in the council, its membership comprised of high priests, former high priests, members of the high priests' families, and heads of families or tribes called elders and scribes (legal authorities).

A total of 70 or 71 made up the body, depending on how they were counted. The reigning high priest served as its chairman. It is believed that once a member of the council, the individual could serve for life.

Council meetings. The council sat in a semicircle in order to see each other and converse. Two clerks stood in the room to record votes.

Only 23 of the 70 had to be present to hold court. Of those, 12 votes could acquit a prisoner. If he was convicted, more council members could be summoned to hear the case further.

An accused man was expected to appear before the court wearing mourning clothes. His behavior was to be contrite out of respect for the authority of the court.

Conflict with Christ. There can be no doubt that the Sanhedrin exercised rightful jurisdiction over Jesus when He was tried. Because Jesus' "crimes" were of a religious nature, the council had the authority to call Him into account and to render a verdict.

Whatever technical rules may have been violated during the trial of Jesus, one breach is inescapable: there was no fair attempt to ascertain His guilt or innocence. The leaders initiated the trial for the purpose of finding a way to convict the Galilean (John 11:53).

The guilty verdict against Jesus was rendered without a single dissenting voice (Mark 14:64; Luke 23:1). This means that Nicodemus, a member of the Sanhedrin, either was absent when the vote was taken or voted for the execution of Jesus. In light of his defense (John 7:50–52), it is likely that Nicodemus was absent. Joseph of Arimathea, also a member of the Sanhedrin, must not have voted either (Luke 23:50, 51). It may be that not every council member had been invited to the trial. ■

CHAPTER 19

THE IMPORTANCE OF THE SYNAGOGUE

The synagogue was extremely important in the time of Christ, serving as the center of religious education and the spiritual lighthouse of Jewish community life.

We do not know when the first synagogue began, but we are fairly certain as to why the concept was initiated. The Jews faced many serious threats to their existence. Over the centuries they had been murdered, deported and infiltrated by people who held only contempt for Jews. If they were to survive and maintain their spiritual identity, some form of educational and religious center had to develop.

Most likely the synagogue began when some of the Jews in exile decided to organize and teach their children about God, lest

Capernaum, a busy fishing port on the Sea of Galilee in the time of Christ, is where Jesus spent much of His time in ministry. This handsome synagogue at Capernaum, dating from the third century A.D., is typical of the many synagogues where Jesus read the Scriptures and taught. TW

they forget and be swallowed up by the pagan religions around them. Over a long period of time these educational facilities became more effective, more sophisticated and eventually matured into the synagogue. To the credit of the Pharisees, they led in the development of Jewish education and became strong forces behind the synagogue movement.

A few notable historians disagree with this premise. They argue that the synagogue was born in the bosom of Moses. However, it is far more likely that it evolved as an answer to specific needs and then became part of the fabric of Judaism.

When Jesus began His ministry, the synagogue could not be ignored as a force in Israel. Other than the temple in Jerusalem, no religious institution in Israel held such importance. The advantage of a synagogue was that it was in close proximity to the common person. Consequently much of the early church's initial impact was felt in synagogue services.

DIVERSITY □ Synagogues might be compared with the present diversity among Christian churches. While there were similarities between most synagogues, there were also notable differences between congregations and between regions. Ten Jewish males were necessary to form a synagogue, but beyond this standard they were free to establish their own structure and format.

The Synagogue of the Libertines or Freedmen (Acts 6:9) may have been comprised of former Roman slaves. Consequently they had their own background and perspective. Some synagogues allowed meetings concerning political intrigue and insurrection against Rome. Others were very traditional, staid and noncontroversial.

A synagogue, especially outside of Israel, might have people from diverse backgrounds. Often, converted Gentiles made up part of the congregation.

Architecture of the buildings could differ drastically. Large buildings as well as small were popular. Square buildings, rectangular ones, huge columns, or simple decor were all common. Attempts by Jewish leaders to standardize the sizes, shapes of (even doors), and behavior in synagogues were unsuccessful. The decorations, designs and layout of many synagogues suggest a blending with foreign artistic ideas.

Although there was no guarantee that any two synagogues would look exactly alike, there were a few basic features that could be found in most. Four items of furniture, in particular, were usually standard in a synagogue:

Chest. Called the Torah shrine, its purpose was to hold the scrolls of Scripture. If portable, the chest could be brought into the room when meetings were scheduled. In this case a special place was marked and reserved for the chest. There is debate over whether or not the chest ever stayed permanently in the synagogue. The New Testament makes no mention of the chest.

The bema. Scriptures were read from this elevated platform, often equipped with a reading stand, and even elaborately detailed with a wooden canopy and rails. Ezra apparently stood on one of these when he read the scrolls (Neh. 8:4, 5).

A *bema* may not have been found in every synagogue; indeed it is seldom mentioned and then not treated with particular sacredness. The only New Testament reference which might be construed to refer to this is found in Matt. 23:2: "Moses' seat" could have been part of a local *bema*.

This word is used elsewhere to indicate an elevated platform or judgment seat (John 19:13; Acts 12:21). The apostle Paul tells us that we must all appear before the judgment seat, the *bema*, of Jesus Christ (2 Cor. 5:10), but it probably has no direct reference to the synagogue item. The word was commonly used to suggest an elevated position or a place to put a throne.

Benches. Seating arrangements in synagogues varied, but most had benches lining two or three of the walls. In the center there may have been mats for sitting and at times possibly chairs.

Ancient writers, as did Jesus, mention chairs, which may have resembled benches. Jesus spoke of the Pharisees who loved the most important seats in the synagogues (Matt. 23:6). Participants were separated according to sex.

Lamps of menorah. Lights were prominent in the synagogue, both for practical use and as a symbol of the presence of God. There was no one specified place where they had to be located, so they were doubtless arranged differently in each place.   ■

Israeli Purim service in the synagogue of Yavneh, a religious kibbutz between Gedera and Ashdod. The *bema* is in the center of the photo.   WZPS

LEADERSHIP □ Most of a synagogue's affairs were managed by a committee of ten elders. It was their job to oversee synagogue life and select those who would be in charge of the activities. Two officials were expected to provide the main leadership, though this number often varied.

Ruler of the synagogue. This general overseer is found in the New Testament. He was expected to maintain smooth order in the services or other meetings. He needed to assign people to read the Scriptures and lead in prayer. When a visitor came to the synagogue, the ruler invited him to address the congregation, as was done at Pisidian Antioch (Acts 13:15). Jesus was invited to speak in synagogues as He traveled about (Luke 4:14, 15). Such a ruler objected to Christ's audacity to heal on the Sabbath (Luke 13:14).

Attendant of the synagogue. Called a *hazzan*, this was the person who worked in the synagogue and received a salary. When the Scriptures were to be read, he removed the appropriate scrolls from the chest and afterward returned them. Jesus handed the Isaiah scroll to the attendant after reading to the congregation (Luke 4:20).

The attendant's job included teaching the children, especially if the congregation was small. He also blew the trumpet three times at the beginning and ending of the Sabbath. His duties extended to funerals and mourning feasts as well. When the synagogue levied a punishment, it was his job to carry it out. In some cases he actually administered the beating, but at other times he may only have read the Scriptures during the scourging (Mark 13:9).

It was not uncommon for the attendant to live in part of the synagogue.

Not every attendant was a godly person. Some were known to save the prestigious seats for those who offered a small gift. Such men may be the objects of James' scorn when He condemned the practice of selective seating. In some congregations the wealthy were given the best benches, and the poor had to stand at the back or sit on the floor at someone's feet (James 2:1–4).   ■

SERVICES □ Considering the pluralism that existed among Jews, it is impossible to define a standard order of service. Nevertheless, there were certain ingredients that would have been found in most.

Shema. As an affirmation of their faith in one God, the congregation recited a passage from the writings of Moses (Deut. 6:4, 5). The *shema* is the central credal statement of the faith. Monotheism was the cornerstone of Judaism and conflicted with the polytheistic religions that surrounded Israel.

Several prayers of thanksgiving also were used, interspersed with hearty "Amens."

Reading the scrolls. The Scriptures were at the heart of the synagogue services. Jews believed God had revealed His will in written form; consequently literacy and the scrolls were paramount. Those who recorded their experiences in the synagogue, especially around the New Testament era, noted the centrality of the Scriptures.

Often someone would then explain the Scriptures. Occasionally young people were invited to render their interpretations. If an honored or respected visitor was in their midst, he was invited to speak.

Paul, with his gifts and training, was able to use the visitor policy to great advantage. In his travels Paul was often invited to speak in a synagogue (Acts 13:14–41). The apostle accepted these opportunities readily, for to the new believers Christianity was a natural growth out of Judaism; Jesus was the fulfillment of the promises given to Moses, David and the prophets. Therefore, the first people to hear about this good news should be the Jews, and the best place to tell them would be in the synagogues.

The Jews were quite liberal in allowing people to interpret the Scriptures. They did not look to a select few gifted, trained or anointed leaders. Most any Jewish man was eligible to present his insights concerning the Word of God.   ■

CELEBRATIONS □ Feasts and festivals were celebrated with great enthusiasm in the same buildings where sermons and prayers resounded. Some of these observances corresponded to celebrations in the temple. However, others were instituted in local synagogues in accordance with the local culture and interests. Since many of the synagogues were located in agricultural areas, their festival themes centered on thanksgiving and harvests.   ■

OTHER USES □ Synagogues were often used for meetings which had little to do with Scripture and celebration. Jesus told His disciples that they would be taken before men to judge their actions; those judges would frequently hold court in the synagogues (Luke 12:11), and the guilty could be beaten by the rulers of those synagogues (Matt. 10:17).

Josephus tells us that political rallies were held in the synagogue of Tiberias. In some ways they resembled the black churches of America which became strong political bases as well as spiritual centers.   ■

CHRISTIAN USE OF SYNAGOGUES □ At first the Christians had difficulty finding their niche in the contemporary religious structure. They met extensively at the temple but were repeatedly harassed for their teachings and practices (Acts 4:1), even though they considered themselves the logical conclusion of dedicated Judaism. That logic escaped most Jews, however.

Much of the teaching of Jesus was done inside synagogues. He not only explained the Scriptures there but also healed the sick (Matt. 4:23; 9:35). The healing of the shriveled hand on the Sabbath and its resulting debate occurred inside the synagogue (Matt. 12:9–14). In Jesus' hometown synagogue, they questioned His identity and ability (Matt. 13:53–58); consequently He chose not to perform many miracles there.

As the church formed, the strength of the synagogue worked both in its favor and against it. Before his conversion, Paul used the synagogues as a vehicle to persecute Christians (Acts 9:2). After his encounter with Christ, Paul stood in the same institutions to announce the gospel (Acts 9:20). Paul preached in a synagogue in Thessalonica for three Sabbaths and gained converts. Unbelieving Jews responded by inciting a riot (Acts 17:1-5).

Two rulers of synagogues played prominent roles in the ministry of Paul. The two possibly succeeded each other at Corinth. One was Crispus, who with his entire family came to believe in Jesus Christ (Acts 18:8). Sosthenes, the other ruler, attempted to have Paul's case heard by Gallio, proconsul of Achaia. When he failed, the Greeks turned on him and beat him (Acts 18:17).   ■

Community dances and festivals (here during Feast of the Tabernacles) provided one of the socially-acceptable ways for young Jewish men and women to mix and to get to know each other.
CD

CHAPTER 20

FEASTS AND FESTIVALS

The long, rich history of Israel gave rise to many occasions for celebration. Often these took a week to vent deep and sincere feelings.

Festivals in Israel had several good purposes. Some were moving worship experiences. Here penitent sinners reached out for forgiveness and the blessing of God. Here was opportunity to cleanse the soul and start again. Other festivals were just as worshipful but geared toward robust thanksgiving. When crops were good and flocks had multiplied, the people had extremely grateful hearts. They expressed this to God by dancing in the streets. Their singing and playing of musical instruments were offerings to a God who had blessed in abundance. Some of their festivals had times to fold hands or meditate. But more often their style was to rejoice with music, food and laughing hearts.

Always the festivals were educational. Each of their seven or more annual feasts taught something about their history, their victories, hopes, despair. The festivals gave a glimpse of a God who performed miracles, who produced lush fields, who loved and forgave. Often celebrating left a greater impression on one's mind than many books and classes.

Festivals have become teaching tools in the Christian experience as well. The communion service is a lesson based on the Passover ceremony. Christmas and Easter have become festivals with the potential to remind, humble and express gratitude. ∎

PASSOVER □ This extremely important feast has its origins deeply rooted in Jewish history. It spanned Old Testament history and spread into Christianity as part of the foundation of worship among believers in the early church.

When? This was an annual feast celebrated on the 14th of Nisan. On our calendar this is March–April.

Why? Its great historical significance is found in the Exodus, the great redemptive act by which Israel became God's people. That they might escape the plague of the death of the firstborn, God had instructed the Jews to put blood on the sides and tops of their doorframes (Ex. 12:7). Very careful instructions were given concerning how the sheep or goats were to be eaten. That night God

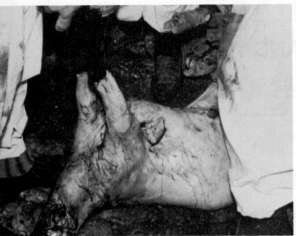

The Passover lamb, according to instructions in Exodus 12, is to be a male yearling, to be slaughtered between evenings, and roasted over a fire without having a bone broken. The Samaritans, who annually offer sacrifices on Mt. Gerizim, pour hot water over the carcass, strip off the fleece, extract the fat, and clean and salt the sacrificial lamb before spitting it on a rod and roasting. RI

passed over Egypt and killed every firstborn male, man or animal. If blood was sprinkled on the doorframes, God would pass over and not bring death to that house. As a highlight of their deliverance and protection by God, the Israelites observed this feast.

How? The means of commemorating this outstanding event changed markedly over the centuries. The instructions for the first Passover in Exodus 12 depict God's original plan for the feast.

1. *A lamb.* The animal was to be a male yearling, and it was to be slaughtered between the evenings. Its blood was to be smeared on the doorframes and the lintel of the house (a lintel is the board over the top of the door). Without breaking any of its bones, the lamb was to be roasted over a fire with its head, legs and entrails intact. The meal was to be eaten that night with unleavened bread and bitter herbs, and any meat not eaten that night was to be destroyed in the morning by burning.

The meal was to be eaten quickly, and the participant was to be dressed in sandals, with walking stick in hand and loins girded. This was a reminder of God's swift deliverance.

2. *Festival of Unleavened Bread.* Part of the Passover celebration was the Feast of Unleavened Bread. This was an agricultural celebration which may have existed long before the first Passover. It was scheduled to last for one week, beginning on the fourteenth of Nisan. The Passover feast took place on the first day of the Feast of Unleavened Bread.

The Passover feast was a mixture of joy and solemnity, celebrated in the home. The Feast of Unleavened Bread was a community festival.

The New Testament Passover. Time and social change had their effect on all of Israel, and the Passover was no exception. By the time of Christ, certain revisions in the feast had become firmly established.

Now huge crowds were expected to journey to Jerusalem to celebrate at the temple. This caused considerable strain on the city as well as on the pilgrims. Jerusalem responded by becoming an even larger commercial center. Great supplies of vegetables and spices were gathered into the marketplaces, including dandelions, snakeroot, lettuce and pepperroot. Likewise, large stocks of fruit and wine were necessary. Wine was expected to be drunk in large amounts, each adult consuming four cups with the Passover. The festivities consumed much from the olive, grape and grainfields in the surrounding areas.

The city also needed to furnish enormous numbers of animals to be used for feeding the throngs and as sacrifices. Josephus claims that as many as a quarter of a million animals were needed for sacrifice. Although his numbers were probably exaggerated, we are certainly justified in assuming that the actual number was immense.

These men are making *matza shmura* (watched matza), an unleavened bread. The process must be completed in under 18 minutes so that no leavening may occur. The Book of Exodus mentions *"uggot" matzot*.   WB

This represented one of the important changes in the Passover. For 600 years before Christ, the Passover lamb was expected to be slain in Jerusalem. Consequently, this turned the event into a public pilgrimage rather than a family celebration. Such a sudden influx of people put a heavy strain on the housing facilities in Jerusalem. Inns were scarce so homes were opened to relatives, friends and even strangers. Campsites were crowded with tents.

All who could travel were expected to be in Jerusalem for the Passover. This explains why Jesus' family made the trip every year to celebrate the Passover (Luke 2:41). It is worth noting that Jesus attended, though it was not required by the original Mosaic law to celebrate at Jerusalem. The rabbis said a Jew had to start attending at the age of 13, but Jesus was there at least by the age of 12 (Luke 2:42). Laws exempted many of the handicapped, aged and children.

1. *Celebration.* Some of the proceedings at Jerusalem were solemn and worshipful, such as the first part of Passover, but the rest of the week was dedicated to joyful celebration. The best in foods and drinks were bought and consumed with great pleasure. Like modern conventioners, the travelers spent money freely, spurred on by the fact that the law encouraged them to buy freely on such an occasion (Deut. 14:26).

A robust business was conducted in perfumes, and ladies were treated lavishly to beautiful cloth and white linen. Some of this party spirit may have come from the Greek and Roman influence. The Talmud calls the Passover "as savory as an olive."

2. *Jesus as the Lamb.* From the beginning of His ministry, Jesus was described as the Lamb of God who would take away the sin of the world (John 1:36). He fulfilled that role when He was led to the cross and offered as a sacrifice.

There are some difficulties in harmonizing the crucifixion and possibly the Last Supper with the Passover feast. Whatever the struggles in paralleling the dates, it is obvious that as Paul taught, Jesus died as our Passover lamb (1 Cor. 5:7). Jesus did meet some of the qualifications for the Passover lamb such as not having a bone broken (Ex. 12:46; Num. 9:12; Ps. 34:20; John 19:36). However, it is possible to accept that Jesus died for the sins of the world without the details dovetailing all the criteria of the Passover.　■

PENTECOST □ Fifty days after the barley harvest celebration of Passover came the wheat harvest, which was celebrated at Pentecost, also called the Feast of Weeks.

When? The 50 days from Passover have been calculated several ways, the method being a source of disagreement between Pharisees and Sadducees. Many counted from the last day of the Passover feast.

Why? Because of their dependence on agriculture, the Jews were thankful for the grain of the fields. The practice carried over from the time of Moses (Ex. 34:22).

How? The Old Testament specified several components of the offering made at this time (Lev. 23:15–22). They were (1) a morning and evening sacrifice of grain; (2) an animal offering of seven lambs, one bullock, and two rams; (3) loaves of bread baked *with* yeast; (4) a goat for a sin offering; and (5) two lambs for a peace offering.

After the Exile, Jews were expected to observe this festival in Jerusalem at the temple. It became the second of three great annual pilgrimages to that city. Besides its religious ceremonies, this was another festive occasion with much eating, drinking and music.

Christian significance. This day has special meaning in Christian history because it marked the launching of a new phase in the history of the gospel. After the ascension of Jesus Christ, the believers returned to Jerusalem to await further instructions. As they were meeting in one place, the Holy Spirit filled them, and the Christians began to speak in other tongues (Acts 2:1–4). Many scholars contend that this was the official birth of the Christian Church.

The ancient festival of Pentecost worked to the advantage of the Christians because Jerusalem was packed with pilgrims. Consequently Jews from throughout the world saw a manifestation of the power of God and heard the Good News (Acts 2:5ff.). Three thousand of that crowd believed in Jesus Christ and received bap-

This booth, built for the celebration of the Feast of Booths, is on a modern home in the Jewish Quarter of the Old City of Jerusalem.   JJ

tism (Acts 2:41). They then returned to their homelands with the message they had accepted.   ■

FEAST OF BOOTHS □ This was the third agricultural feast that sent hundreds of thousands of pilgrims pouring into Jerusalem. Over the centuries it carried many titles, including Feast of Tabernacles, Feast of Tents, Feast of Ingathering and the Feast of the Lord.

Why? In the early fall, the harvest of the grapes and olives was commemorated with this special feast. Of all of Israel's festivals this one most resembles the American Thanksgiving Day. During possibly the most carefree of the seasons, it was an opportunity to have the greatest fun.

The Feast of Booths most closely approximates the American Thanksgiving Day celebration. Pilgrims stream to Jerusalem for the celebration. This booth is built near the Wailing (Western) Wall in Jerusalem, which can be seen in the background.   JJ

Young Israeli women carry palm branches through the streets of Jerusalem in a modern-day observance of the ancient Feast of Booths.   CD

When? The date fluctuated depending on weather conditions and the completion of the harvest—harvest was not considered finished until the pressing was completed. A standard date was finally set on the 15th of Tishri, comparable to our September–October.

Where? When efforts were made to centralize the festivals the Feast of Booths was also moved to Jerusalem. These festivals were so well attended that many of the cities around Judea were left practically empty. Jeremiah tells of one city that had a mere 50 inhabitants during this season. Many participants brought booths, huts or tents from their fields to spend the cool nights in Jerusalem.

How? This feast had two distinct aspects. Part of it was for worship and thanksgiving. Trumpets were blown to assemble the crowds who would then watch a procession of priests travel to the Pool of Siloam and each dip from it a pitcher of water, then march back to the temple and pour the water on the altar. The purpose of this ritual may have been to thank God for water and to ask for more during the winter season, for rain was essential to bountiful spring and summer crops. Many of the celebrants carried palm trees or branches in recognition of a good harvest.

Reportedly the priests during the New Testament period took this opportunity to denounce the worship of the sun, for at one time priests had bowed with their backs to the temple and faced the sun in worship (Ezek. 8:16). In repudiation of this abomination, the priests now bowed facing the temple with their backs to the sun.

Shofarim usher in the New Year at Jerusalem's Wailing (Western) Wall, part of the celebration of Rosh ha-Shanah.   WZPS

A second highlight of the celebration was the celebrating. At night throngs joined in dancing, singing, marching with torches and eating. It was a time to show gratitude by enjoying life and togetherness (Lev. 23:33–43).

Christian significance. This was the feast which Jesus' brothers and sisters dared Him to attend (John 7:1–9). After rejecting their taunts, He later went secretly into Jerusalem for the celebration. Jesus taught during the festival and received heated opposition from the Pharisees. It was during this time that Jesus called the thirsty to come to Him and drink (John 7:37). This may have been in reference to water sacrifice made during the feast.   ∎

THE NEW YEAR □ Did the Israelites of the Old Testament celebrate the beginning of a new year? There appears to be no easy answer to that question. The major biblical historians make no mention of it as a feast or an observance, but there is some evidence that it became a celebration shortly after the New Testament period.

Originally, the year was probably begun in the month of Tishri, which is our September–October. At the time of the Exodus the new year was changed to Nisan, our March–April (Ex. 12:2).

The fall date seems to have returned to official use during the Exile, under the influence of the Babylonian calendar. It was probable that the Jews eventually adopted the Babylonian reckoning for their new year and celebrated it at the September–October date. *Rosh ha-Shanah*, the Hebrew name for this comparatively new festival, means "the head of the year." It is unlikely that it was celebrated during biblical times, but later Judaism grouped it with *Yom Kippur* which followed nine days later and called them the "Days of Awe."   ∎

YOM KIPPUR □ This observance has special significance both in Jewish and in Christian theology. The Bible describes Jesus Christ as fulfilling the function of the high priest during this religious rite. It was a spiritual event of such magnitude that all one had to say was "that day," and the average Jew knew what was meant. Also known as the "Day of Atonement" it was a time of introspection, national repentance and cleansing from sins. After deep feelings of remorse and solemnity, the celebrants soon gave themselves to the Feast of Booths.

When? It took place in October just prior to the Feast of Booths. The author of Acts uses this observance as a point of reference when he describes Paul's sailing trip as coming after the Fast (Acts 27:9). Jewish readers would have instantly placed the trip in October.

Why? The purpose was to pause and consider one's sinful condition. A person did this also in the greater context of Israel's general spiritual state, for he considered himself part of the whole, a nation as well as persons before God.

Having inventoried his soul before God, he then had his sins taken away and accepted the forgiveness of YAHWEH.

How? There were both personal and priestly responsibilities in the ceremony. The personal aspect included a day of fasting. No one was allowed to work. A serious countenance was expected and anyone who refused to comply faced possible execution.

On this occasion the high priest made his appearance in the Holy of Holies, the only time during the year he entered that part of the temple. Once there he made a sacrifice of the mixed blood of a bull and a goat.

The priest then administered the amazing rite of the scapegoat, which had been selected by lot. According to the Old Testament, the goat was called Azazel, which means scapegoat (Lev. 16:8–10). Placing both hands on the goat's head, the priest then confessed the sins of Israel. Symbolically, the priest transferred Israel's transgressions onto the goat, then prayed for forgiveness. When the ceremony was complete the goat was led, by another man, into a part of the desert where no one lived. As a symbol, the scapegoat carried away the sins of Israel and its people, to be remembered no more (Lev. 16:21, 22). No one was allowed to care for the goat in any way. It was gone and to be forgotten. The priest then washed his hands and cleansed himself. The act was complete and Israel's sins were forgiven.

Christian significance. The outward exercise of sacrificing animals could not in itself bring the forgiveness of sins. Forgiveness was a spiritual act and could be initiated only by God. The unrepentant could not be cleansed by fasting or sacrifices.

At best the sacrifices were only shadows or symbols of what was to come (Heb. 10:1ff.). We become holy, forgiven, only through the sacrificial body of Jesus Christ himself (Heb. 10:10), and are therefore free to approach God because of the blood which Christ has offered (Heb. 10:19).

Christ not only eternally fulfilled the role of the sacrifice, but He also served as the high priest, for He made the offering which has paid for our sins. Since He was a priest as no other could have been, and a sacrifice as none other could have been, there is no need to repeat the sacrifice. It has been accomplished once and for all (Heb. 7:27). Jesus was the only priest who did not need to sacrifice for His own sins. He was the perfect priest (Heb. 7:28). When His work was finished as high priest, He then sat at the right hand of the Majesty in heaven (Heb. 8:1). Christ became a high priest because God named Him high priest after the order of Melchizedek (Heb. 5:5, 6). Consequently, the symbol is no longer necessary. The perfect has come and the act of atonement has been fulfilled completely in Jesus Christ.   ■

HANUKKAH □ This happy celebration appears under names such as Feast of Dedication, Feast of Lights, Feast of Maccabeus, Feast of Illumination, and Festival of Rededication.

Why? The festival dates back to 164 B.C. when Judas Maccabeus cleansed and rebuilt the temple. Antiochus Epiphanes, a Syrian ruler, had desecrated the temple by attacking it and setting up his own form of worship. He had outlawed the Jewish religious laws and insisted that the Jews abandon their religion or die. He had called the temple "Jupiter Olympus," used the altar for a pagan sacrifice, then demanded that such a sacrifice be offered every month on the 25th to correspond with the date of his birth.

While Antiochus was away fighting other battles, the Jews revolted under Judas Maccabeus. The war ended in a stalemate so the two sides negotiated for peace and the Jews regained the temple. Soon it was cleansed and worship was restored.

When? Normally it was observed on the 25th of Chisley, which is comparable to our November–December.

How? It was not necessary to travel to Jerusalem for this feast, so most people observed it in the local towns. The emphasis was on joy, happiness and a good time with one's family. Actual formulas for celebrating differed widely. Many of the families displayed extra lights in their windows. They sang, danced in the streets, and played musical instruments long into the evening. It was a victory party and well worth celebrating with great energy.

Tradition says Judas Maccabeus found a cruse of oil with one day's supply and the oil miraculously lasted for eight days. This explains the extensive use of light in their homes and synagogues. Consequently, the lights were kept burning for eight days during the celebration. Later, a custom of lighting one new candle a day was established.

Mourning during this time was strictly forbidden. It was a happy season to remember a joyful occasion.

Christian significance. This celebration has not been carried over into the Christian faith, and except for one instance (Jesus in Solomon's Colonnade during the time of the Feast of Dedication—John 10:22) is not mentioned in the New Testament. ■

PURIM □ During the post-exilic period, the Jews added this joyous celebration to their list of festive occasions. Another history lesson, it reminded the Jews of their miraculous deliverance from a planned genocide.

Why? During the time of Esther, Haman the Agagite, prime minister of Persia, developed a vicious hatred toward the Jews residing in that nation. Haman had taken himself a bit too seriously and had demanded that everyone bow down to him (Esther 3:2). Mordecai, a Jew, refused to bow and thus infuriated Haman against the Jews. He thus conspired to have Mordecai executed by hanging him and having a general slaughter of the Jews authorized. To his surprise Queen Esther turned the tables and Haman was hanged on his own gallows (Esther 7:9, 10).

Mordecai, who was named prime minister, sent out letters encouraging the Jews to celebrate this deliverance regularly (Esther 9:20ff.).

When? Mordecai instructed the people to celebrate on the 14th and 15th days of Adar (Esther 9:20–22). This corresponds to February–March.

Where? This feast could be celebrated anywhere and did not

call for a journey to Jerusalem.

How? As with all Jewish holidays, this is a religious festival, but it is primarily a time of mirth and solemness. It focuses on liberty and freedom and often is celebrated with singing, plays, food and music.

Even the formal services are joyful and animated. The book of Esther is read in the synagogue

Cases for Esther scrolls used in the festival of Purim (from left): Yemen, eighteenth century; Turkey, nineteenth century; Iraq, nineteenth century; Morocco, nineteenth century; Persia, nineteenth century; Turkey, eighteenth century. JLAT

with a generous supply of hisses and derogatory remarks whenever Haman's name is read. Some will groan, "Let his name be blotted out." Even the children join in by blowing noisemakers and shaking rattles.

Christian significance. This celebration has not carried over into the Christian experience. Some scholars have speculated that the "feast of the Jews" mentioned in John 5:1 refers to Purim, but this is very improbable. ∎

CHAPTER 21

MUSIC

To understand the Jews of Bible times, we must see them as a people who loved music. It was not, however, the spectator music to which we are accustomed. Not content to just listen, many Jews played instruments, sang and danced. Practically any occasion or gathering was reason enough to make music together.

The music varied from well-rehearsed choral and instrumental music to that of spontaneous street dancing. The people took life seriously but they also knew how to have fun. The laws of God frequently gave instruction which encouraged the Jews to enjoy themselves.

In the earliest chapters of the Bible, we find music taking a prominent role. Lamech's three children became the fathers of three segments of society: herdsmen, craftsmen and *musicians* (Gen. 4:20–22).

Music became an effective means of communicating to both God and fellowmen. The Jews expressed their deepest emotions in poetry intended to be sung. Hebrew poetic structure was not dependent on rhyme but on thought patterns, statements of harmony or antithesis. It would be accurate to picture the early psalms as being sung, usually with musical accompaniment.

Special occasions were not necessary to get a group singing. Even work parties might burst into song as they labored. When God promised Moses water, he gathered the people together and they sang about the well that God gave and the princes dug (Num. 21:16, 17).

Later when the temple was being rebuilt, the priests were eager to have music. They played trumpets and cymbals and chorused praises to God. The music centered on thanksgiving, and when the foundation was completed all the people shouted (Ezra 3:10, 11).

Many musicians were skilled and highly trained. Harpists and cymbal players were specifically named and appointed as musicians (1 Chron. 25:1, 5). Others were well-trained singers such as the 288 singers for the tabernacle (1 Chron. 25:7).

Israel's musicians were so skilled that when Sennacherib, king of Assyria, attacked Israel, he demanded male and female musicians as a token of peace.

GOD'S USE OF MUSIC □ It would be hard to identify all the times God used music for His own purposes. He definitely used the soothing power of music (David's harp) to chase an evil spirit from Saul (1 Sam. 16:23).

God also used Moses' song to warn the people of Israel to avoid those who were trying to corrupt them (Deut. 31:30ff.).   ■

SPECIAL CELEBRATIONS □ Important occasions gave the Jews added reasons to sing. Jehoshaphat assembled the people to sing praises to God and extol His holiness as God miraculously thwarted the Moabites and the Ammonites (2 Chron. 20:20ff.).

After the famous crossing of the Red Sea, Moses and the children of Israel gleefully sang praises to God because He had thrown both horse and his rider into the sea (Ex. 15).

When the captured Ark was finally returned, the Jews sang and played to express their great joy (1 Chron. 16). They brought out the lyres and harps; cymbals resounded and trumpets blared. David celebrated the occasion by writing a psalm of thanksgiving. At the end of the hymn the people shouted "Amen" and praised the Lord.

Some of the songs became part of their tradition and folklore. The exploits of David as he defeated the Philistines were sung by the women, much to the dismay of Saul (1 Sam. 18:6, 7). This song was probably sung in an antiphonal style. A main singer or small group would sing, "Saul has slain his thousands"; in response a choir would sing, "And David his tens of thousands."   ■

SONGWRITERS □ Writing music was not originally a commercial venture as it is today. Soloists usually sang their own compositions. Choirs probably did not use harmony but sang in unison. This is not to suggest that they did not practice. Both soloists and groups spent many hours rehearsing the music.

One of the Bible's most famous songwriters was the multitalented King Solomon who wrote 1,005 songs (1 Kings 4:32).   ■

THE INSTRUMENTS USED □ *Pipe.* This was a wind instrument, an ancient ancestor of the clarinet. It was made of wood and had a hole for pitch control. The high tone made it ideal for funerals and weddings (Matt. 9:23; Isa. 30:29).

Lyre. David played this wood-based, stringed instrument. Almug was one of the woods used to construct the lyre (1 Kings 10:12) which had from 3 to 12 strings. In Josephus' time it had 10 strings. The Hebrew word for lyre is *kinnor*.

Flute. Similar to the pipe, it was made from wood or bone and was a favorite of shepherds. It was not normally used in the temple.

Trumpet. A straight tube with a bell-shaped end, it was often made of silver or copper. At least two silver trumpets were required for a temple service. Sometimes there were 120 trumpets playing in the temple (2 Chron. 5:12).

This man is blowing the shofar, or ram's horn, one of the oldest musical instruments known to man. The shofar is mentioned 63 times in the Bible and was used by the Jews to call to battle or assembly, or to sound an alarm.   AJW

Shofar. Blown in the synagogues, it was a curved instrument made of ram's horn. This was the instrument—the Hebrew in this instance is *yobel*—used when the walls of Jericho fell (Josh. 6:20). Gideon had the *shofar* played to put fright into the Midianites (Judg. 7:16–22). A cow's horn could not be used for a *shofar.*

Harp. Strings were stretched across a jar or skin bottle to make this instrument; however, some were made of wood or metal. Men usually played the 10-20 stringed instrument.

Timbrel. Also known as a tamborine, it was a handheld drum made of skins stretched over a wooden hoop. Not allowed in the temple, it was nevertheless a favorite for dances and feasts. David had it played at the return of the Ark to Jerusalem (2 Sam. 6:5).

Cymbals. An essential part of the percussion section, cymbals were much like the ones we use today. Like other rhythm instruments, they were usually played at celebrations rather than at worship services.   ■

BANDS AND ORCHESTRAS □ Groups of organized musicians were plentiful in Israel and in other nations. Nebuchadnezzar loved to employ musical groups, as did David (2 Sam. 6:5) and other Jewish leaders.   ■

DANCING □ With so much rhythmic music being played in Israel, the average Jew had trouble standing still. Not a particularly staid or reserved people, they believed in freely expressing both sadness and joy. Their wails of anguish were often loud as were their cries of thanksgiving and joy.

As David danced before the Lord (2 Sam. 6:14) so did Miriam and all the women (Ex. 15:20). The Jews danced at harvest festivals (Judg. 21:19ff.).

During New Testament times children danced in the streets (Luke 7:32); the guests at the party for the returned Prodigal Son also danced (Luke 15:25). The exact form of the dances is not known but, as with most folk dances, men and women probably did not dance together as partners.   ■

The shofar, or "ram's horn," was primarily an instrument to give signals and to announce special occasions rather than to supply music. It was made from the curved horn of a ram. The finished shophar is at the top; the raw ram's horn at the bottom.   EHLE

THE CHRISTIAN ERA □ Singing remained an integral part of the worship and inspirational experience for Christians. Jesus himself sang during the normal worship services. At the Last Supper, before going to the Mount of Olives, Jesus and His disciples sang (Matt. 26:30). They probably sang Psalms 115–118 or Psalms 113–114, as was the custom during the Passover.

During times of distress, it would appear that Christians found strength by singing. In the Philippian jail, while other prisoners groaned and cursed, Paul and Silas sought comfort in prayer, praise and singing (Acts 16:25).   ■

ENCOURAGEMENT TO SING □ The value of singing was strongly endorsed by the early believers. They saw it useful as an expression toward God and others, and for their personal benefit.

Paul addressed the subject of music in at least three separate passages: Eph. 5:18, 19; 1 Cor. 14:15; Col. 3:16. He encouraged Christians to sing psalms, hymns and other spiritual songs. Paul wanted believers to both sing and make music.

During the days of the tribulation of Revelation, several significant musical experiences are noted. The 24 elders sing "You are worthy to take the scroll. . ." (Rev. 5:9). At the end of tribulation the 144,000 sing "a new song" (Rev. 14:3), and the overcomers sing the Song of Moses at the end of tribulation (Rev. 15:3).

The Jews had a divine concept of music, that something so lovely must have come from heaven. It was thus incorporated into festivals, the temple, synagogues and then moved naturally into the church.   ■

CHAPTER 22

SUPERSTITIONS AND MAGIC

When one reads about the daily life of the Jews and early Christians, he is impressed with the great amount of dabbling into the supernatural. They knew there were many unexplainable wonders in the world, and they also recognized that forces were at work which could not be seen or touched. When these attitudes were combined with ignorance, the result was a readiness to use magic. An uninformed acknowledgment of forces beyond their control logically led them into superstition.

In their defense we must not forget that the practice of magic was widespread around them. The Egyptians not only believed in magic but practiced it commonly. It was the ability of the Egyptian magicians to duplicate miracles which allowed Pharaoh to harden his heart and resist Moses' demands. Consequently, the Jews had little trouble believing in supernatural forces.

The ancient Jews and early Christians were much like people in our culture. They believed in God but also found a need to appease other forces. Many early Christians would have understood walking around a ladder, avoiding black cats or throwing salt over one's shoulder. Early Christians frequently practiced similar rituals. Their attitudes are difficult to decipher, but we can wonder, did they go to worship because they wanted to meet with God or because they were afraid evil would visit them if they did not? Did they wear the sign of the fish as a testimony or because it obligated God to protect them? Certainly both were true. Some comprehended the freedom in Christ and others kept seeking lucky charms. ■

The Egyptian god Bes.   EHLE

AMULETS □ Since ancient times people have believed that someone can wear or possess an object that will ward off evil and bring good fortune. The use of charms was popular not only among pagan religions but was quite well received among many Jews. The use of amulets was not restricted to the early years of ignorance, however; in a number of circles their use is still accepted.

Some Jewish leaders and followers carried amulets. These people held monotheistic faith but frequently felt that other spirits and forces had to be appeased, consoled or invoked. Consequently, much Jewish thinking and theology is a complicated mixture. It seems as if they were fighting to trust solely in God and yet felt that these other spirits could not be ignored.

Often an amulet might carry an inscription of the key phrase necessary to dispel evil. Other objects were in the shape of sacred figures such as fertility gods. Such are found in great abundance by archaeologists, testifying to their wide use. They could be in the form of earrings, shells, stones, rings, necklaces, gems or statues.

Even later Jewish traditions recommended protective amulets. The tractate Sabbath speaks of carrying a fox tooth or a locust egg when traveling on the Sabbath. The Maccabeans, a militant group of Jews during the Intertestamental Period, carried amulets for good luck.

It was easy to cross over the fine line between an object that reminded one of his faith and an object which brought good luck. The Jews repeatedly had this problem. They put the *mezuzah* on their doorpost to remind them of the Passover sacrifice, but some treated it as a help for their faith, while others began to see it as a charm.

The same confusion is evident in the matter of phylacteries.

Beginning in about the second century B.C., Hebrew men wore phylacteries on their heads and forearms. The small leather boxes, bound by thongs, contained passages of scripture from Exodus and Deuteronomy.   EHLE

Pharisees tied these small boxes of scripture verses to their wrists or foreheads, supposedly as a symbol of keeping God's Word near their heart and mind. In reality many felt God would give them good luck for wearing them.

Rabbinical writings are filled with superstitious advice. It was believed that people could cast spells strong enough to end a person's life, so therefore it behooved a person to wear ribbons, jewelry, or phylacteries.

Because of the wide acceptance of amulets, these objects continued to haunt post-apostolic Christianity for centuries, even to this present day. Some wore the symbol of the fish as a charm. Others wore ribbons of scripture verses around their necks. Later they amassed huge collections of wood, reportedly part of the original cross. Nails were claimed to have come from the same place. The assembling of these relics, and the importance and power assigned to them, is very similar to the use of charms.

Jesus Christ accepted the fact that ungodly powers did exist and those who employed them would claim many followers (Matt. 24:24).

From its beginning Israel fought a losing battle against amulets. Only sporadically did godly leaders win and totally remove them. Even Jacob collected the family idols and earrings at Shechem and buried them (Gen. 35:4).   ∎

TERAPHIM □ Pagan influences caused the Jews to use household gods called teraphim, which were either small or large statues, or representations of the power that the gods possessed. These statues were plentiful among the Jews and were not necessarily considered contradictory to Judaism. This was true despite the fact that the Bible clearly condemns images of God (Ex. 20:4).

When Rachel left her father's house to join Jacob, her new husband, she stole the family teraphim (Gen. 31:19) from Laban. Laban furiously pursued Jacob and Rachel in hope

This clay bird, from around 500 B.C., is another example of a common household idol. Many were made to look like birds or animals.   EHLE

of recovering his teraphim.

Saul's daughter Michal made use of an idol so large it could be placed in a bed and covered over to resemble a person. She did this to help David escape the wrath of Saul (1 Sam. 19:13).

As with other pagan practices that were popular in Israel, teraphim posed great difficulty for kings who attempted to extract them from the nation. Only after the Exile was their use abandoned.   ■

MAGIC BOWLS □ Many of the ancients believed that good luck came from inscribing sayings inside their clay bowls. Archaeological evidence indicates that people of Jewish and Christian backgrounds practiced this form of magic. This was "white" magic because the owner's request was aimed at bringing good fortune rather than bad. The incantations were written inside a bowl, beginning on the outer rim and progressing toward the center. Often the bowl was used for eating. Some were crudely fashioned and possibly never used except for magic.

There are some strong reasons to believe they were kept by Jews, and even Christians. First is the frequent appearance of the name of God, YHWH. A second evidence is complete scripture passages written in the bowls. The most frequently quoted passage is Zech. 3:2 in which the Lord is called to rebuke Satan.

The evidence for Christians using the bowls is less clear, but

A number of "cultic" or otherwise unique vessels appeared in the fully-developed Iron Age (ca. 900–600 B.C.) such as the Kernos at the bottom right. As part of the libation ceremony, liquid could be introduced through the mouth of the upright head, circulated through the hollow ring, then emptied into the bowl from the mouth of the horizontal head. It is not clear whether the rattle (top, right) and animal figurines (bottom) were toys or for cultic use. The two censers at the top (left and center) were for burning incense, perhaps in cultic ceremonies.   DM

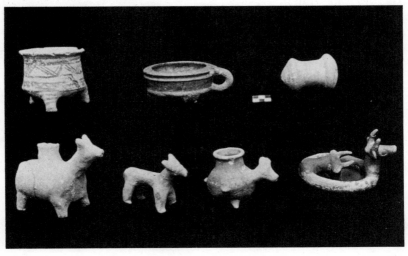

there is some basis for the theory. Apparent excerpts from several New Testament passages appear. However, these are not as obvious as the Old Testament quotations. There are also several possibly Christian names present, including Peter and Jesus. The question of Christian use is not fully resolved, but the fact that the inscriptions are in Aramaic and that some call on the names of Gabriel and Michael certainly leave open that possibility. ■

SPELLS □ Spells were attempts to affect life, for better or worse, by sayings or incantations. Sometimes they were vocal, other times they were written. They were used prolifically throughout biblical history. Josephus tells us that even great men such as Solomon made use of the practice (Ant. 8.2.5).

Much faith was placed in curses and blessings of this nature, and there are many evidences that they had power. It is believed that the witch at Endor used this means to beckon Samuel from the dead (1 Sam. 28:7ff.).

The early Christians found the widespread use of spells difficult to combat. They were written on jewelry, and even household items. The elimination of the use of spells and their accompanying charms opened the way for God's blessing (Acts 19:19, 20). ■

LIVER READING □ For centuries many people have considered the reading of an animal's liver as a highly dependable form of occult guidance. Called hepatoscopy, this method of reading the future was viewed as a science which required extensive training. Many clay models of livers have been discovered with complete

This clay replica of a sheep's liver, inscribed with magical incantations, was frequently used in quasi-medical rituals. For centuries people received guidance through the science of hepatoscopy, or the reading of an animal's liver.   REI

instructions written on them, describing the type of event a specific color or shape would predict.

We cannot be certain that the Jews used this form of divination but many nations around them did. A biblical example of this is the allusion to the king of Babylon having a liver read (Ezek. 21:21). However, the Hittites, Greeks and Romans also considered this as a reliable practice.   ■

WATER READING □ It was believed that after mixing more than one liquid, a person could understand the future by the shapes that were created. Too much darkness or a failure to mix might be a good omen.

While the technique was not generally accepted in Israel, some infer that Joseph may have acquired this art in Egypt (Gen. 44:5, 15). The Babylonians also practiced it.   ■

ARROW READING □ Another Babylonian favorite (Ezek. 21:21) was to shake arrows and throw them on the ground. Their formation would indicate which action to take.

We do find an unusual use of arrows by the prophet Elisha in 2 Kings 13:18, 19, but this was probably a prophetic, symbolic act, rather than divination.   ■

CASTING LOTS □ Several objects could qualify as lots, including sticks, dice (usually knucklebones) or even pebbles. These were in use throughout biblical history and probably changed according to time and place.

Lots were used by both believers and pagans, both looking for supernatural guidance as a result. No form of divining more clearly demonstrates the difficulties in drawing the fine line between magic and godly intervention. The Urim and Thummim, for instance, which were used to discern God's will, may have been a form of casting lots. We know that Judas Iscariot's replacement was selected by lot and everyone accepted it as the will of God (Acts 1:26). The nation of Israel used lots to identify a guilty man (Josh. 7:14ff.). The Jews and early Christians did not doubt God's ability to express His will through the common casting of lots (Prov. 16:33).   ■

ASTROLOGY □ The strong condemnation of astrology by Old Testament writers did not fully deter Israel from practicing it. Babylonians and other peoples surrounding Israel held tremendous stock in consulting the stars. The prophets attempted to expose the hypocrisy and futility of this occult matter (Isa. 47:13; Jer. 10:2). Some writings among the Qumran Scrolls suggest the use of astrology in the post-exilic period.

God used a group of apparent astrologers (the magi) who followed the star of Bethlehem (Matt. 2:1–12). The best historical data suggests they probably traveled from as far away as Babylon or Persia.

Although the prophets condemned the practice, they did not say there was no basis for belief in astrology. And the Scriptures say God clearly used the stars as signs to convey messages (Gen. 1:14; Matt. 2:9). This may have contributed to the Jews' susceptibility to accept the practice. ∎

NECROMANCY—TALKING WITH THE DEAD □ For many centuries this has been a popular means of discovering the future and appears to enjoy considerable interest in our time also. Numerous and elaborate schemes have been devised to communicate with persons beyond the grave. However, the Bible consistently condemns the practice.

Saul, during his reign, vacillated by first banishing every medium (one who claims to consult the dead), but later tried to contact the deceased Samuel (1 Sam. 28:7ff.). This was clear evidence of his spiritual decline.

The prophets viewed some of the attempts to contact the dead as just muttering, and possibly a bit of ventriloquism (Isa. 8:19). ∎

DREAMS □ A great deal of significance was placed on divine guidance through dreams, and some interpretations were legitimate. Joseph and Daniel, for example, were used by God to interpret dreams. However, elaborate systems were devised to help the dreamer understand his dream's implications. Consequently many people went to extremes hoping even to cause a dream that might help them cope with their situation. ∎

JACOB'S STRIPED SHEEP □ An amazing feat was accomplished in breeding sheep according to Gen. 30:37–43. Jacob peeled the bark off some rods and placed them in the watering troughs. The sheep who mated in front of the peeled rods later gave birth to spotted sheep. This is called sympathetic magic. The explanation probably lies in a combination of folk magic and animal husbandry. The ancients frequently used magic to guarantee results. ∎

NEW TESTAMENT MAGIC □ The Bible contains many accounts of the supernatural, the bizarre and the unexplainable. It would be convenient if we could dismiss all the acts of magic as fraud, based on ignorance. However, that would be too simplistic. Without pretending to understand them fully, let us consider some of the instances of magic which confronted the early church.

Simon Magus (Acts 8:9–24). He was a working magician who lived in Samaria. The population was amazed at his astonishing ability, though the Scripture does not say exactly what that included. When Simon saw the miracles performed by the apostles, he offered to purchase the power of the Holy Spirit. Peter condemned the man for treating God's gift as a power to be bought and sold. This was the origin of the term Simony.

Elymas Bar-Jesus (Acts 13:6ff.). On the island of Paphos, Elymas the sorcerer tried to turn the proconsul away from believing in Christ. Paul denounced the man as a dispenser of deceit and trickery.

The Girl at Philippi (Acts 16:16ff.). This slave girl made money for her owners by telling fortunes. When she saw Paul and his companions, she began to follow them, shouting that they were servants of God. The girl was "possessed" by a spirit of divination. When Paul finally tired of the poor advertising, he pivoted and commanded the spirit to leave her. It immediately vacated her body, but this caused an outcry from those who made money from her magical talents.

Sons of Sceva (Acts 19:14–16). On occasion some bystanders tried to imitate the power which the followers of Christ displayed. Such were the seven sons of Sceva who tried to use the name of Jesus to cast demons out of others. The almost comical result was that the spirit attacked them, beat them and sent the men running away naked and bloody. ∎

CHAPTER 23

FUNERALS

Respect for the dead was of great importance to Jewish families. They were determined to avoid the extremes of other groups; the Jews could not accept contempt for the body common among the Greeks, nor could they embrace the near worship that prevailed in Egypt.

Although a spiritually minded people, the Jews did not divorce themseves from honor for the temporal. The cleansing and preparation of a body for burial was significant and considered a demonstration of love.

Over the centuries of Israel's history, funeral practices changed markedly. There was no set of laws concerning the burial of the dead, though some basic guidelines existed. People were controlled more by customs, which changed gradually through the years.

BURIAL DURING THE TIME OF THE PATRIARCHS □
The most notable grave in ancient Israel was the cave of Machpelah which Abraham bought from Ephron. It was probably a large cave and tradition places it beneath the *Haram el-Khalil* mosque at Hebron. Several major Bible characters were laid to rest there, including Sarah, Abraham, Isaac, Rebekah, Leah, Jacob and probably others. As late as A.D. 1119, the bones of the patriarchs were claimed to have been seen on this site. For a while a church stood on the location, but today it is covered by the mosque, Haram el-Khalil.

The Bible describes Machpelah as resting among fields dotted liberally with trees (Gen. 23:17). Ephron, the owner, offered the free use of the cave to Abraham, but the patriarch insisted on paying 400 shekels for its purchase. This may be similar to bargaining rhetoric in the present Middle East, where such a free offer is a courteous response which indicates a willingness to haggle over price.

Jacob and Joseph give us a glimpse of how important burial was to the early Jews. The elderly Jacob, who was in Egypt when he died, requested burial in Canaan in a crypt he had dug at Machpelah (Gen. 49:30; 50:5). Joseph had Jacob's body embalmed in the Egyptian fashion and carried it back to the promised land for burial. Joseph prophesied on his deathbed that his own bones were to be buried in Israel (Gen. 50:25; Josh. 24:32). ∎

EMBALMING □ The general rule was to bury a person as soon as possible after death (Deut. 21:22, 23). Yet exceptions were made with Jacob and Joseph (Gen. 50:2, 26).

Since the Jews expected the body to go its natural way and be reclaimed by the earth, they saw no need to embalm. They did not practice it extensively; almost none of the Jewish bodies which have been exhumed were embalmed. Their laws prohibiting the touching of a corpse (Num. 5:1–4) may have discouraged the practice, but of itself may not have prevented it.

The period of mourning for Egyptian royalty was 70 days, the first 40 devoted to embalming. Jacob, as the prime minister's father, was accorded this honor (Gen. 50:3). The body was opened and many organs were placed in jars, except for the heart which was left undisturbed. Chemicals, salts and spices were packed in the cavity and the cadaver was wrapped tightly in linen.   ■

SPICES AND LINENS □ The Jews prepared a body for burial, not with preservation in mind, but to allow it to decompose as easily as possible. To control the odors while the body decayed, generous amounts of perfumes and spices were placed inside the wrappings. Spices might also be laid next to the body. Funeral customs in early Israel involved periodic visits to the tomb during the first year. This may explain the perfume.

The quality of perfumes depended greatly on the income of the family. The condition of the bier, the design of the ossuary box, the type of tomb, the linens, the number of mourners and musicians, were all dependent on the amount of money available. Funeral expenses may be a problem which has never escaped man.

The men who buried Jesus, Joseph of Arimathea and Nicodemus, were people of means who provided an expensive burial for the Messiah. They packed the body with 75 pounds of myrrh and aloes. This practice had a long history. King Asa was laid on his funeral bed, saturated with lavish perfumes (2 Chron. 16:14). ■

COFFINS □ Containers that we think of as coffins were not common in ancient times. Instead, the people used ossuary boxes, designed to hold the bones after a body had decomposed. First the body was laid on a slab and packed with spices to fight the odor. After completing its decaying process, the bones were collected and placed in the ossuary box which was then stored in the cave or tomb. Many of these tombs held several ossuary boxes.

Ossuary boxes were made of clay and ranged from 20 to 30 inches in length. They were one to one and one-half feet wide and a little over a foot deep. Hundreds of such boxes containing either Jewish or Christian remains, have been unearthed. The bones of famous Christians may be among those retrieved, for several familiar names have been found on the boxes. The ossuaries used were not plain boxes. Artistic designs frequently were carved into the clay sides, depicting flowers or the deceased's name. They were not uniform in shape, often fashioned in the form of small houses or other objects. The description of Christ's body in the tomb indicates the usual customs were followed. The spices were wrapped with the body, and it was placed on a slab until the women could return after the Sabbath to complete preparations.

Lazarus' body was expected to be in an advanced form of decomposition after four days, and a strong odor would have been normal (John 11:39). ■

FUNERAL BIERS □ Funeral processions were common among the Jews. The body was carried on a wooden bier often consisting of little more than flat boards. The use of biers certainly goes back as far as King David (2 Sam. 3:31), and they were still being used during the time of Jesus Christ. It was one of these biers that Jesus touched, restoring a dead boy to life. Miraculously the lad sat up immediately and began to talk (Luke 7:11–15).

A bier carried a symbol to indicate the deceased's occupation or social status. If a young lady had been engaged, a canopy might cover her bier. Wealthy families supposedly used more elaborate biers than those with less money. ■

PROCESSIONS □ A funeral march was hardly quiet, for the typical Jew believed in venting his emotions by loud wailing, beating on his chest and even tearing his clothes.

In the crowded procession one would expect to find three main features.

Mourners. Without shame the Jewish community gave themselves to unbridled grief. Friends, relatives and even professional

These Roman Age ossuaries from Jerusalem are typical of the clay boxes, often carved with ornate artistic designs, which were used to house the remains of those who died. BAS

mourners joined in expressing a bitter farewell. The mourners at Jairus' house did not appreciate Jesus' efforts to run them off, probably because they did not want to lose their wages (Matt. 9:24). These professionals might call out the names of the deceased's family members to add a personal touch and enhance the sadness. Even the poorest family was expected to hire at least one mourner.

Singers. Many of the psalms and other traditional songs lent themselves readily to funeral processions. Especially when important people such as King Josiah died, sad songs were written to soothe broken hearts. Such songs were sung later as memories persisted (2 Chron. 35:25).

King David wrote and compiled funeral songs to commemorate the passing of people he loved. He made no attempt to hide deep remorse. These songs were collected and were probably added to the Book of Jashar (2 Sam. 1:18).

Musical instruments. The most common ancient funeral instrument among many nations was the flute. This was also true of the Jews. Often the players of instruments walked at the rear of the procession.

Since the Bible does not dictate funeral procedures, a number of rabbis accepted that responsibility. They laid down rules as to how flutes were to be used as well as the correct amount of mourners. Biblical laws restricted themselves to practices that were contributed by paganism. Consequently, the Bible forbade mourners from cutting themselves (Lev. 19:28) or shaving their eyelashes or eyebrows (Deut. 14:1).

Other acts associated with funerals and mourning included the custom of mourners tearing their clothes to show exasperation. The tear, a symbol of despair, was not usually large. Barclay tells us that 39 laws had been compiled to govern proper tearing of clothing by mourners.

Another act of mourning was that of putting ashes on one's head, face or clothing. Ashes, especially when mixed with dust, were demonstrations of deep humiliation before God and man.

Shaving one's head, fasting and meditating in total silence were also acceptable displays of grief.　　　　　　　　　　　　　■

CREMATION □ The Bible does not appear to concern itself with the question of cremation. Examples of the disposing of bodies with fire usually have to do with judgment (Josh. 7:25).

Two facts are obvious about the subject. First, Jews and early Christians did not normally practice cremation. Second, later Jewish teachers condemned cremation. However, since they condemned so many things, their statements add little to our understanding of the subject.　　　　　　　　　　　　　■

TOMBS □ Caves were the first tombs. In time the caves were refined into crypts. Shelves were chiseled into the walls to receive the filled ossuary boxes. Frequently there would be room for a dozen or more relatives. A stone slab might occupy the center of the floor to hold the body until it decomposed. This was the place where Jesus was laid inside the tomb (Luke 23:55).

The tomb which Jesus occupied had been hewn out of the rock (Matt. 27:60); this was often done, especially in limestone. Whether the entire tomb was dug out or merely improvements made on the interior is not certain. Some of the tombs were carved below ground level and thus required steps.

A large stone had to be rolled across the entrance of the tomb to protect the corpse from scavenging animals (e.g. dogs) or thieves. Such stones were round enough to roll and were set in grooves to hold them.

An entrance stone might be carved elaborately, if the family were wealthy. Carvings included pictures, names and possibly words of comfort. Greeks and Romans sometimes chose to carve pillars around the entrance. Some Jewish families, such as the one which King Josiah saw, also put carvings on tombs (2 Kings 23:17). Josiah wanted to know what the peculiar appearance of the tomb-stone meant.

At times it was ceremonially unclean for a Jew to touch a tomb. This may have been why they were whitewashed with lime (Matt. 23:27)—so they could be identified easily and not accidentally touched.

The narrative of the death of Lazarus in John 11 provides an excellent description of first-century funeral practices. ∎

Tombs in New Testament times were often cut from rock, with a round stone set in a groove which could roll in front of the opening.
RI

CHAPTER 24

SOCIAL CONFLICTS AND PREJUDICES

When Jesus lived in Israel, He was surrounded by bigotry and was himself slandered by others. Often when a Jew in Bible times heard the word Gentile, an ugly feeling stirred inside him. The word Samaritan also could make a Judean's blood boil. Similarly, when Caiaphas heard the name Jesus, his heart probably raced from the adrenaline of hate.

It is important to try and comprehend the prejudices that controlled people's emotions. A person's prejudices indicate how he feels, what are his impulses, what he might do if free to do it. It is impossible to know fully the feelings of someone in Bible times, but we can attempt to understand what thoughts went through his mind.

The prophet Jonah is a prime example of a man operating on the basis of his bigotry. Called by God to preach repentance to Nineveh, the prophet refused because he hated to see God's grace extended to his bitter enemies (Jon. 4:1–3).

EXCLUSIVISM □ Many Jews felt they were not only God's chosen people but also His only people. Naturally this led to feelings of undue pride and superiority, rather than humility and gratitude. Some Jews became insufferable because of this. Not all Jews developed such attitudes. Some realized that God was also working among others and that often His blessing spilled over into other nations. They remembered that God had promised to bless all nations through Abraham (Gen. 12:2, 3). The ageless problem has been that a concern for godliness too frequently results in spiritual pride rather than humility. ∎

RACISM □ There is amazingly little said in the Bible about color or racial distinctions. Even less mention is given to questions of prejudice based on skin color. There is hardly any reference to the subject. We therefore cannot be certain how light or dark an Israelite's complexion might have been. It is generally assumed to be a medium color.

A few people in the Bible seem to have had a dark complexion but most cases would be difficult to prove (e.g., Song of Sol. 1:5, 6). One of the clearest references to black skin is found in the description of a Christian at Antioch (Acts 13:1). Simeon is called Niger, which is Latin for black. It may be that he was from Africa.

The Ethiopian eunuch was probably from Cush in northern Africa and was not necessarily very dark skinned (Acts 8:26ff.).

While there may have been cases of bigotry on the basis of race, there is no clear case of it in the Bible. There also is no definite example of segregation on the grounds of color. ■

RELIGIOUS PREJUDICES □
When Israel invaded Canaan, they had specific instructions to kill everyone because of the terrible practices of the pagan religions there (Josh. 8:24–27; 10:28; 23:6–13). During this time, war and religion were tightly intertwined. If the Israelites were to survive as a nation, they had to eliminate the pagan nations that would destroy them.

This worked for the Jews as long as they could keep themselves fairly isolated. However, the continued contact with other

The Ethiopian eunuch (Acts 8:26) was probably from Cush in northern Africa and may, or may not, have had dark skin. This monk is part of an Ethiopian monastery which still functions within the Old City of Jerusalem. TW

countries and invasion by conquering empires made attempts at purity nearly impossible. During the major captivities, Israel suffered a great amount of religious mixture. Many who were carried away to Assyria and Babylon intermarried and did not return, adopting the religions of their new lands. Likewise, many who were not carried off intermarried with those who came to Israel and inhabited it (their offspring are known as the Samaritans). Consequently, by the time of Ezra and Nehemiah and the return to the land (459 B.C.), religious and physical purity were hot issues. Ezra tore his tunic in despair over the large number of intermarriages (Ezra 9:1–3). These strong feelings against interreligious marriage were to create hardship and even bloodshed for many centuries. Even today it is an uncomfortable subject for many.

It is important to appreciate these deep-rooted feelings in order to understand the resentments that came later. Some groups, such as Samaritans, and Gentiles in general, were never completely acceptable to Jews because of this. Jesus and the apostles fought these feelings. However, many Jews and early Christians were operating with these historic emotions and found prejudice difficult to eliminate. ∎

TERRITORIES □ *Samaritans.* The Jews had maintained a high degree of purity, but were surrounded by a cosmopolitan mix. Jesus was born into this world where Jews were often intolerant of that mixture. Consequently, He began to minister in the midst of icy cold prejudices, constantly addressing those prejudices in word and action.

One of the most serious tensions existed inside Israel's borders. Directly to the north of Judea were the much hated people of Samaria. Samaritans were the objects of prejudices held by Jews from centuries past. It was generally believed that Samaritans were descended from the people brought into Israel by the king of Assyria. They intermarried with Israelites and set up idols in the Jewish places of worship (2 Kings 17:24–29). Years later the Samaritans opposed Ezra when he tried to reestablish and rebuild the nation (Ezra 4).

When Jesus began His ministry, the relationship between the Jews and the Samaritans had continued in open hostility. Jews traveling through Samaria were frequently attacked. A hundred years before Christ, the Jews destroyed the Samaritan temple on Mount Gerizim. During the night a group of Samaritans strewed human bones over the porch of the Jerusalem temple. Soon after Christ's ascension, raids were conducted on Samaritan villages in retaliation for the murder of a Jewish traveler.

We need to appreciate the heated emotions involved when the Jews called Jesus Christ a Samaritan and demon-possessed (John 8:48). They were insulting Him as severely as they knew how.

Christ's disciples were willing to perpetuate the old prejudices. Their solution to Samaritan hostility was for God to pour fire on their enemies (Luke 9:52–54). Jesus, on the other hand, risked His reputation by associating with Samaritans (John 4:7) and telling a story in which a Samaritan was the hero and the Jews the villains (Luke 10:30–37).

Christ directly addressed the question of prejudice during His lifetime. By association, by word and by action Jesus placed a hated people in a good light, even though His contemporaries were bound to be angered.

Greeks and Romans. Of even greater magnitude was the Jews' resentment toward Gentiles in general. There was usually a mutual feeling of distrust. Many Greeks and Romans cared little for this small nation of people with an eccentric, monotheistic religion, whose value system was at considerable odds with most pagan practices. However, Judaism's morality attracted many sensitive, upright Gentiles, and especially Romans who longed for a return to the virtues upon which Rome was founded.

Jewish feelings had been intensified by the centuries of Greek and Roman military occupation. Not only had the Jews been denied their freedom as a nation, but their religious practices had often been denounced and insulted. Men such as Antiochus IV (Epiphanes) slaughtered Jews, sold others into slavery, stole from the temple, and sacrificed pigs on the altar. Pontius Pilate serves as another example of a leader who offended the Jews; as Roman procurator of Judea, Pilate angered the Jews by using standards with images, an affront to most Jews, and reportedly used temple money to build an aqueduct. The result was an uprising of tens of thousands of Jews. Pilate retaliated and killed many demonstrators. "Greek" and "Roman" were unpleasant sounds in the ears of most Jews.

This Roman statue stands near a road unearthed in Caesarea in 1954. The statue dates from the second and third century and is of white marble and reddish porphyry. TW

Strangely enough, this animosity did not prevent the Pharisees from attempting to convert the Gentiles (Matt. 23:15). However, this very act of evangelism caused strain. Some Jews were reluctant to accept these new believers as full Jews, or to accept Gentiles who had married Jews (and the resulting offspring).

The latent and often visible Jewish disdain for Gentiles surfaced in the early days of the church; a large number of Christians had carried ugly emotional baggage into their new faith. One of the first serious divisions in the church was over the question of nationality and prejudice. The Greek Jews complained that their widows were not receiving their fair share of the distributions (Acts 6:1). Their accusation was against the "full" Jews.

The problem never completely disappeared during the time of the New Testament. There was frequent debate over whether a Gentile had to become a Jew in order to become a Christian (Acts

15; Gal. 6:12–16). Jews found it hard to accept Gentiles as equals. Frequently, it was just as difficult for Gentiles to believe that Jews were their equals. Some modern commentators argue that the book of Romans was written to correct Gentiles who felt that Jews, because of their rejection of Christ, had no place in the kingdom of God.

Galileans. Jesus grew up in Galilee, an area known for its feisty independence. The people there were different than their traditional cousins south in Judea. Their interpretations of Jewish law and practice marked them as only slightly better than apostates.

Out of Galilee came some of the most tenacious resistance to Roman occupation, and Pilate even killed some as they worshiped (Luke 13:1). The Zealots were founded by a Galilean, Judas, who repeatedly revolted against foreign presence (Acts 5:37). He eventually was killed and his followers dispersed. Pilate had frequent clashes with this underground movement.

Jesus selected at least one Zealot (Simon) as one of His disciples, and he remained faithful to Christ even after the resurrection (Luke 6:15; Acts 1:13).

Not only were Galileans distasteful to the Romans, but the Jerusalem Jews found them extremely repugnant. Galileans were strong willed and determined to worship God as they understood the Scriptures. This may help explain Christ's immediate dislike for the Pharisees. The Galileans battled these moral policemen on practically every detail. They fought over the use of olive oil, dietary habits and over the celebration of festivals. Some Galileans considered their hate for the Pharisees practically a birthright.

Not only were the Galileans' activities considered repugnant but also their personal habits. They were popularly viewed as ignorant, uncultured, earthy and crude. Once prejudice reigns, it seems that its victims can do little that is commendable. These feelings were only intensified by the difference in accent (Mark 14:70). Jesus most likely spoke not only Aramaic but the distinctive brogue of Galilean Aramaic.

These differences are important when we consider Christ and His disciples. Some of the hate they received was based, not on religious or practical considerations, but on the basis of their regional origin. Jesus, Peter, James and others were the victims of whatever prejudices were directed toward Galileans during this time.

Early Christianity was so closely tied to Galilee that it was sometimes called a Galilean religion. Julian demanded that Christ be called the "Galilean God." Indeed, the angel which addressed the disciples at Christ's ascension called them "men of Galilee" (Acts 1:11). ■

NAZARETH □ When Philip told Nathanael that Jesus was from Nazareth, Nathanael scoffed, doubting that anything good could come from there (John 1:46). In all likelihood Nathanael was not voicing a widely held prejudice against people from that town, but reflecting a prejudice against small towns. He did not expect a person of the Messiah's magnitude to come from a remote village which was not a theological or philosophical center. ∎

RICH AND POOR □ As in other societies, there was a strong feeling of division between the wealthy and the poor. The poor often spoke harshly of those who had money, and at the same time treated the prosperous with special care. Both attitudes speak to a sense of inequality. Wealth was a status symbol and often people held respectable positions in the community solely on that basis. Christianity addressed these feelings and tried to correct them.

Jesus spoke often against showing deference to the wealthy. He said their money was not an advantage and could even prove to be a curse. Therefore we need not envy or hate the rich, for few of the wealthy would be willing to make the sacrifices necessary to enter the kingdom of God (Matt. 19:23). Indeed, those who followed Christ had to be willing to sell everything (Matt. 19:21).

Jesus did not see wealth as a sign of God's blessing. Quite the contrary, He seems to have at least a skeptical attitude toward riches. Primarily He discusses the subject in terms of warnings and suspicions rather than praise.

Despite Jesus' refusal to be impressed with wealth, several people of means became His followers. It appears that Joseph of Arimathea and probably Nicodemus were men of means, and the women who contributed to Jesus' ministry possibly had greater finances than the average. Zacchaeus appears to have accumulated a substantial fortune. It may be that some of the wealthy were attracted to Jesus because he relieved them of the burden of possessing money. He was willing to deal with them outside the realm of prejudice for or against their wealth.

The apostle James gave clear warning against showing prejudice for the wealthy (James 2:1–7). His attitude toward the rich was based on his assertion that the wealthy exploited the poor and worsened their condition. ∎

ILLEGITIMATE CHILDREN □ Throughout Israel's history, a child born out of wedlock received cold, even hostile treatment. The term "bastard," which is used in the KJV and other versions, could refer to one whose parents were not married to each other or to the offspring of a union with a foreigner. A child of a foreign marriage or illegitimate union was forbidden entrance into the assembly (Deut. 23:2). However, some feel the original intent of the passage may have been to exclude the children born of encounters with Philistine prostitutes. Whatever the purpose, extreme bigotry was shown against many hapless children.

Later rabbis created rules to govern such children's lives. Some forbade them from marrying except to proselytes, freed slaves or Jews with severe deformities. Bastards could not hold offices except under limited conditions. Some people felt that bastards had no part in redemption.

It is out of this context that the term bastard received such an ugly connotation and left lifelong scars on a child. The word carried such coarseness that anyone inaccurately calling someone a bastard could be beaten with 39 stripes.   ■

WOMEN □ In a patriarchal society, it was easy to discriminate against women. Women could therefore fall into a position of inferiority and some men were eager to put them there.

We have discussed this problem in chapter seven. These attitudes prevailed over the centuries of Jewish history. Generally women were discouraged from seeking much education, attempting a career or venturing into business. However, some made successful ventures into the world of men.   ■

OCCUPATIONS □ Frequently a person was considered inferior purely on the basis of his job. The types of such jobs and the degree with which they were disliked changed with the times.

Some of the hated professions may not surprise us. Dung-collectors, tanners, animal drivers and usurers were social outcasts. Tax collectors were despised and butchers were sometimes considered on the fringe of proper society. Pigeon trainers, herdsmen, weavers, and goldsmiths appear on lists compiled by Jeremias. One such list includes doctors as a despised vocation.   ■

JEWISH PROSELYTES □ When a Gentile converted to Judaism, the results were not always ideal. Many Jews, highly suspicious of proselytes, added burdensome religious luggage on the unsuspecting newcomers. Christ's accusation that Pharisees made life difficult for converts is far from hyperbole (Matt. 23:4, 15).

Some converts were rejected by Jewish leaders as unacceptable because of their background or the means of their conversion. They were considered genetically blemished (Deut. 23:2, 3) and hence unqualified for religious leadership. Proselytes were counted by some Jews as bastards. It was falsely assumed that all heathen women engaged as prostitutes; therefore no Gentile child could be sure who his father was. Consequently he was to be treated as fatherless.

In theory the convert was to be welcomed into the faith as if he were being born for the first time. In actuality his past was frequently held against him. This is not to say that all converts were made to feel uncomfortable. However, it is to suggest that many proselytes did not understand the full implications of becoming a Jew, including having to face the anti-Gentile attitude that existed.   ■

JEWS □ The Israelites were not strangers to prejudice. They had broad experience both as victims and perpetrators of bigotry. There is no single reason why so many nations and individuals have hated the Jews. Some have despised them even though they have never met a Jew. Such is the nature of prejudice. Others used the Jews as scapegoats for their ills much as the Nazis did in our century.

Two Jewish characteristics have often brought them trouble, as they did in the time of Jesus. First was their blunt rejection of paganism and the culture that accompanied it. Daniel was a prime example of a Jew persecuted for refusal to compromise. Second, they were despised because they were not understood. It is the problem of being different. Since people did not know what they were like, they hated them.

Haman typified the insane rage that has been poured out against Israel (Esther 3–5). He wanted to execute all Jews because one of them refused to bow to him.   ■

CHRISTIANS □ Christianity was born out of prejudice and hate. Jesus was persecuted and "legally" murdered as was John the Baptist before Him. They were despised because what they did and taught antagonized the Jewish establishment.

The apostle Paul experienced wearing both suits of prejudice. He first hounded Christians because of their faith (Acts 8:1–3) and later became the prime target of many Jewish leaders because of his new faith.

Tradition indicates many of the early church leaders were martyred. Stephen, James, Peter and Paul were each believed to have been killed for their faith and John was exiled to Patmos. He may have been the only one of the original twelve to die a natural death.

At first Christianity was considered a sect of Judaism, and because of the size of the movement and its peculiarities, it was open game to hatemongers. Christians were vulnerable because of the same general difficulties the Jews faced: their refutation of paganism and distorted knowledge about their beliefs. One early rumor charged that Christians ate flesh and drank blood during communion.

The Romans soon set out to destroy the Christian Church in several famous persecutions. Under Nero, the Flavian rulers, Trajan and Diocletian, the church was attacked for over 50 years, costing many lives.   ■

CHAPTER 25

CRIME AND PUNISHMENT

L aw and order in the best sense of the words were high priorities in Israel. In order for the majority of the population to live in peace, the lawless minority had to be kept in check. If fair laws were not enforced, chaos and violence soon resulted.

Not all laws were carefully preserved. Some have no examples in history of ever having been enforced. Nevertheless, many were effective and generally Israel functioned well under its legal system.

The civil law of Israel was considered a commandment from God, for it was given as part of the covenant. If a law was violated, that crime constituted a sin against both God and the community. Violation threatened the national existence of Israel, so there was great pressure to correct the situation and punish the offender.

The punishments prescribed may seem unnecessarily harsh in our time, but where no physical harm had been inflicted in the crime, there was no physical punishment. The death penalty was invoked against crimes considered treasonous against God, the King. If possible, the criminal was to be kept in the community where he could support his own family, and then work to reimburse the victim for losses plus punitive damages.

Over the centuries the laws that governed Israel changed as new laws were added and old laws gained fresh interpretations. Some laws arose from passages that had never before been considered as laws. Rabbis, attempting to keep the law relevant, added large bodies of laws to explain and expand the existing laws as Israel moved from rural to urban life. Jesus Christ chose to ignore many of these latter statutes.

CITIES OF REFUGE □ In early Israel when someone accidentally killed a person, his own life was in danger. If a relative of the dead person found the one who had caused the accident, the relative was bound by custom to kill him. The "eye for an eye" of justice was the responsibility of the tribe or family, and thus could lead to long, bloody feuds.

Consequently, six cities were established as cities of refuge. If the person who caused the accident entered one of these cities, he could not be harmed by the relative. A relative was still free to kill the man if he caught him outside the city. Therefore good roads were built to give speedy access to these places and the cities that were chosen were evenly spaced throughout the country. Before the person could flee to one of these cities, he had to face a trial by the local elders, who would rule if the death was accidental. If they decided the death was murder, there was no protection for the person (Num. 35:24). Once the congregation ruled that the death was accidental, the person must try to get safely to a city of refuge. Once inside the city, he had to remain there. If he was caught outside the walls, the relative was free to kill him with impunity. However, this danger lasted only until the high priest died. At that time the ac-

This is the marketplace of the modern city of Hebron, in the hills of Judah about 20 miles south of Jerusalem, which has a population of about 40,000 people. Ancient Hebron was one of six "cities of refuge" given in Numbers 35, to which a person who unintentionally killed another could flee and gain protection until he stood trial.   TW

cused person was able to leave the city without fear of harm. Should the relative then kill him, the relative would be guilty of murder. The text is unclear as to exactly which high priest was intended (Num. 35:28; Josh. 20:6), although it probably refers to whichever man was high priest at the time of the murder.

The six cities of refuge named in Deut. 4:41–43 were Kedesh, Shechem, Hebron, Golan, Ramoth and Bezer (three on each side of the Jordan). We have no stories of the cities actually being used for refuge.

Israel was not the only nation to have such a program to provide safety for fugitives. However, the Jews limited their protection to accidental deaths.   ∎

JUDGES AND COURTS □ During ancient Israel's long history, its judicial system underwent a series of drastic changes. Its earliest forms were little more than revenge taken by individuals. This practice eventually gave way to leaders and elders serving as judges over the people.

Moses had difficulty finding a correct balance. At one time he attempted to make all the judgments for the entire nation, which kept him busy from morning until night. Jethro, his father-in-law, persuaded Moses to divide the people into groups and appoint judges over them. After this only the most difficult cases were brought to the leaders (Ex. 18:13–26). This system worked well, eventually leading to elders judging in open-air courts at public places such as the city gates (Deut. 25:7). Deborah, one of Israel's great judges, held court in an area that became known as the Palm of Deborah (Judg. 4:5).

When Kings David and Solomon reigned, they retained final judicial authority but appointed 6,000 judges to handle most cases (1 Chron. 23:4). Jehoshaphat enlarged that system with Levites, priests and clan leaders (2 Chron. 19:8). After the collapse of the monarchy, a wide gap existed in the justice system, so after the Exile King Artaxerxes instructed Ezra to establish judges to administer the law (Ezra 7:25).

The Sanhedrin of the New Testament most likely grew out of Moses' judicial system of 70 elders. The Sanhedrin were 70 men who met within the temple in the hall of polished stones. They met regularly on Mondays and Thursdays and needed 23 members to deliberate. The Sanhedrin reigned in the religious courts at Jerusalem and Judea, but they also imagined their powers to extend to Jews all over the world. They sent Paul outside the borders of Judea to arrest Christian Jews wherever he could find them (Acts 9:1, 2). Jews in Rome later looked to Judea for a confirmation of Paul's innocence (Acts 28:21).

Other courts existed to make decisions at lower levels. Towns had small Sanhedrins consisting of 23 judges, as well as local courts with limited powers. The most severe punishment they could administer was 39 stripes.

There were two types of judges. Practically any Jew could sit in judgment over civil matters, but in criminal cases only priests, Levites and members of levitical families could judge. A number of assistants crowded around a judge and helped carry out his orders. Jesus advised us to settle our problems quickly and stay out of courts, lest we find ourselves turned over to a judge's assistant and thrown into prison (Matt. 5:25).

People were not easily taken to court because of built-in hazards. For instance, if the accused was found to be innocent or the accuser a false witness, the latter could receive the penalty intended for the accused (Deut. 19:16–21). This law alone probably reduced litigation drastically.

Because all law was considered religious law, a Jewish court was dependent on Scripture and its traditional interpretations. The average court also had a huge amount of oath-taking, witnesses swearing by God, by heaven, by Jerusalem, by the temple, etc. Oaths were spoken so loosely and without meaning that Jesus denounced the practice (Matt. 5:33–37). He told people to say yes or no and skip all useless claims. He was also referring to the Pharisees' habit of playing games with oaths and using them as excuses to lie (Matt. 23:16–22).

Court lawyers, as we know them, did not exist. Witnesses were the nearest thing to lawyers their system had.

The court systems were not tightly controlled, and justice was not always fairly dispersed. Despite the ability or honesty of the judge, however, Paul instructed believers to respect them as God's appointed officers (Rom. 13:1–7). ∎

TYPES OF CRIMES □ *Religious crimes.* Few practices held as much potential for national destruction as that of following false gods and idols. Israel's history is riddled with the horrendous results of spiritual defilement. Idolatry was strongly condemned from the early days of the nation's existence (Ex. 20:3–5). However, because they were surrounded by idol worshipers and because of their human weaknesses, the Jews frequently incorporated their practices into their worship.

Some idol worship consisted of devotion to carved images and little more. Objects from simple sticks to golden mice were used in religious practices (1 Sam. 6:4). It is possible that some actually worshiped Baal-Zebub, the god of flies, and may have had a statue of a huge fly (2 Kings 1:2). Some scholars feel Baal-Zebub was a pun intended to make fun of Baal-Zebul. Not only were man-made images worshiped but also a large array of natural objects, including the sun, moon, lightning and animals.

Idolatry was not only immoral because it denied the nature of God, but also because it often was physically immoral. Some of the pagan practices in Canaan included sexual performances (see chapter nine), and others called for the sacrifice of human infants (2 Kings 21:6).

In New Testament times some Christian converts came from an idolatrous background (Acts 15:29; 17:23).

The penalties for idol building and worship were severe in Old Testament times. The person was to be put to death, and often by his own relatives (Deut. 13:6–9).

Violent crimes. Certain laws were given to protect the physical well-being of each human being. Jewish law offered broader sanctions than the laws of many other societies.

A person could not be physically hurt without punishment to the perpetrator. If an individual assaulted and injured someone during an argument, he had to pay for any loss of income or medical fees resulting from the injury (Ex. 21:18, 19).

Accidental injuries were also covered. If someone dug a ditch and through neglect another person fell into it, the owner was held liable. A homeowner had to build a protective rail around his roof (Deut. 22:8). If two men fought and inadvertently caused a pregnant woman to miscarry, they were to make restitution (Ex. 21:22–23).

These laws also gave protection to slaves. If an owner caused physical harm, he was held accountable (Ex. 21:26, 27).

Assault against one's parent was punishable by death (Ex. 21:15). Kidnapping, which was sometimes done for the purpose of selling a person into slavery, was likewise condemned. When the offender was caught, punishment was death (Ex. 21:16).

Laws concerning rape and prosecution of the attacker are quite detailed (Deut. 22:23–30). If the rape took place in the city and the girl did not scream when attacked, both she and the man were to be stoned. If found guilty, the man might have to pay 50 shekels or marry the girl. If he had to marry her, he could never divorce her.

Material crimes. While the Jews placed a high value on property, they tried to keep it in perspective. They could not execute a person for stealing an ox or killing a sheep as some societies allowed. Their system of repayment also made jails and prisons less necessary. The penalty for stealing a sheep was repayment of four sheep. If an ox was taken, five oxen were demanded in return (Ex. 22:1). Should he be incapable of paying his penalty, the thief could be sold into slavery until the debt was paid (Ex. 22:2, 3).

A thief's life was protected. If he was caught robbing a home in the daylight, he could not be killed by the property owner. However, if he was breaking in during the night, the property owner could kill him without penalty (Ex. 22:2, 3). A thief could be freed by repaying the value of the item stolen plus a 20% penalty (Num. 5:7). If a man burned the crops of a neighbor, he had to replace them (Ex. 22:6). Because God had directed the apportionment of land, landmark boundaries were sacred. Anyone who deceitfully removed one was cursed by the people (Deut. 27:17). A long life was promised to those who had a fair set of weights (Deut. 25:15), and we might assume a shortened life for those with dishonest weights.

Ethical-moral crimes. Any attempt at lying, cheating, greed, sexual unfaithfulness or sexual perversion was considered a basic dishonesty to oneself, to others and to God.

Leviticus gives a considerable list of sexual relations which are strictly forbidden (18:1–29). Non- and extra-marital sexual unions as well as relations with animals are spelled out and condemned. If a person violated these rules, he was to be cut off from the population.

Lying is condemned in all its forms, not only verbal lying, but also deceit and fraud.   ■

PUNISHMENT □ Several methods of punishment were used under Jewish laws. The frequency of their use differed according to the times and situations. The following are the most prominent ones.

Eye for an eye. Called the *lex talionis,* it was also applied under other ancient laws such as the Babylonian and Assyrian. It prevented a person from taking a life in reaction to losing a hand, etc. (Lev. 24:19, 20; Deut. 19:21). The biblical law defines the limits of retaliation—eye for an eye or a tooth for a tooth, hand for a hand, etc. (Ex. 21:23–25), but never more than the original injury. Some believe this was later restricted to court verdicts, but initially it applied to personal vengeance.

Christ's interpretation of this law prohibits personal retaliation (Matt. 5:38, 39). It can be argued that Moses, in regard to fellow

Israelites (Lev. 19:18), and Solomon (Prov. 24:29) also condemned individual revenge. Jesus told us we do not have the right to go through life returning tit for tat; penalties must be reserved for courts and judges. The New Testament does not defend vigilante justice.

Corporal punishment. A criminal could be beaten with a maximum of 40 stripes (Deut. 25:1–3). For fear that one might offend God the number was later restricted to 39, in case someone miscounted. When the crime was less severe, a smaller number of lashes could be inflicted. Both the Sanhedrin and local congregations practiced this type of punishment during the time of Christ (Matt. 10:17). On five separate occasions the apostle Paul was beaten with 39 stripes (2 Cor. 11:24) and each time may have almost died. Normally the victim was placed face down on the ground and beaten with rods while his hands and feet were held. Members of the court usually observed to insure it was done properly. Later in history leather straps made of calf's hide were used instead of rods.

Financial punishment. Monetary penalties were paid to the person who had been hurt or defrauded, instead of paying the court. Theft (Ex. 22:1–4), death caused by an animal (Ex. 21:29, 30), and causing a miscarriage (Ex. 21:22) were some of the crimes which carried a financial punishment.

Capital punishment. Several forms of capital punishment were sanctioned by Jewish law. We have instruction to execute by stoning, by sword, and by burning.

Stoning. This method was the most widely prescribed in ancient Israel. A long list of crimes could be punished with this type of execution, including adultery, infant sacrifice, blasphemy, witchcraft, violation of the Sabbath, rejection of parents and treason. The group of executioners often included several members of the community, with the witnesses throwing the first

The Church of St. Stephen, belonging to the Greek Orthodox Sect, is built over the spot at the foot of the Mount of Olives where the first-century martyr, Stephen, was stoned to death (Acts 7:54–60). TW

stones (Deut. 17:7). The stoning of Stephen was probably a mob murder rather than an official execution (Acts 7:57, 58). However, it is possible that this execution did follow legal guidelines (i.e., F. F. Bruce, Acts, *The International Commentary of the New Testament*, p. 169). By any standard, stoning appears a gruesome way to die. The Sanhedrin had a method that apparently was supposed to ease the pain; they insisted the victim first be pushed down a cliff to stun him.

When some priests and teachers tried to trick Jesus, He turned the tables on them by asking them a question, which if they did not answer carefully might have caused them to be stoned by an angry mob. They decided to avoid answering (Luke 20:1–8). Jesus saved a woman caught in adultery from being stoned by another mob (John 7:53—8:11); the validity of this text is questioned by some experts, however.

Sword. An entire community of idol worshipers was to be executed by the sword (Deut. 13:15), as were those who worshiped the golden calf (Ex. 32:27).

It is also likely that the family that avenged the blood of a murdered relative used a sword to dispatch the victim when they found him on the road (Num. 35:19–21). Many people were killed with swords, and while we might question how formal the executions were, they definitely were carried out.

In the New Testament two men were formally executed with swords: John the Baptist (Mark 6:27) and James the brother of John (Acts 12:2).

Burning. At least two situations in Scripture called for execution by burning. If a man married a woman and her mother at the same time, he was to be executed in this manner (Lev. 20:14). Likewise, if a priest's daughter became a prostitute possibly in connection with Canaanite fertility rites, she was to be burned to death (Lev. 21:9).

In the execution of Achan and his family, the guilty were first stoned, then burned (Josh. 7:25).   ∎

PRISONS □ Most of Israel's punishments for crime were designed without prisons in mind. The Israelites would have seen our present penal system of incarceration as counterproductive. Their major concerns were to repay the victim and place the punished person back into society. During much of Israel's history, their mobile lifestyle made the general use of prisons impractical. If they considered a person unsafe for society, he was likely to be executed. When the Israelites found a man who had broken the law, they incarcerated him only until they had decided what to do (Num. 15:34). After the nation settled in the land and had selected a king, prisons became more numerous. Some of these were houses or merely crude holes in the ground. In these cases the care of the prisoner was minimal.

Surrounding nations may have made extensive use of prisons

earlier than Israel. There are biblical accounts of Jews being confined in prisons of foreign powers: Samson by the Philistines (Judg. 16:21), Jehoiachin by the Babylonians (2 Kings 25:27), etc.

Solomon did not feel the need for a prison when he dealt with Shimei ben Gera (1 Kings 2:36, 37). The king simply told the man to stay in the city of Jerusalem or be executed. It appears Solomon was looking for an opportunity to avenge his father's humiliation (2 Sam. 16:5ff.).

Historians tell us the attitude toward imprisonment changed under Ezra and Nehemiah when authorities began imprisoning people for their debts. Prisons were miserable experiences. Prisoners might be placed in stocks, forced to perform hard labor, chained, beaten, underfed and kept in dark, damp cells. These deprivations are what concerned Jesus when He told His followers to visit those who were in prison (Matt. 25:34–36).

Jesus advised His disciples to keep short accounts with creditors to avoid falling into the hands of the judicial system (Matt. 5:25, 26). A stay in a debtors' prison was a miserable affair.

The disciples were virtually promised imprisonment (Luke 21:12), and many saw it come true. John the Baptist, Peter, James, John, Paul, Silas and many unnamed disciples experienced the fulfillment of this prophecy, and some a number of times. Usually the apostles were imprisoned in Jewish facilities. John the Baptist reportedly was imprisoned at Herod's fortress near the Dead Sea. Herod locked up Peter at Antonia and Paul was later detained there.

This dungeon is on the lower floor of the Church of St. Peter in Gallicantu on the eastern slope of Mount Zion, which is built over the traditional site of the domestic quarters of Caiaphas, the High Priest, where Peter is said to have denied his Master. Remains in this prison include a flagellation post, with rings for binding the hands, hewn stone basins for vinegar and salt water, and footrests. It is possible that a pit in the corner may have been for the confinement of condemned prisoners.   TW

Paul was also a prisoner in Herod's castle at Caesarea. In Philippi, Paul and Silas were held in a Roman jail. Later Paul suffered house arrest in Rome.   ∎

CIVIL DISOBEDIENCE □ Throughout biblical history, individuals and groups found it necessary to rise up and disobey the ruling authority. Some of those involved were selfish in their motives. Others exercised defiance in the name of God. Many of both types persevered and succeeded. Others died for their convictions. Moses was a champion of civil disobedience in the name of God (Ex. 3:10). Jeremiah was beaten and jailed for the message he preached (Jer. 20:1, 2). Daniel defied an executive order and continued his prayer habits (Dan. 6:6ff.).

When Israel was occupied by the Greeks and Romans, there were many Jewish uprisings which led to considerable bloodshed and caused much controversy among the people. Because of deep conflicts over religious practices, the Maccabees led a successful revolt of 3,000 Jews against the Syrian Army and established an independent Jewish dynasty 160 years before Christ. Later the Galileans were still very rebellious and Pilate ruthlessly attacked some of them as they worshiped (Luke 13:1).

There were, of course, many acts of civil disobedience during Israel's history. As a frequently oppressed people with a "peculiar" religion, pockets of believers sometimes found it necessary to disobey the government. It was regarding this matter that the Pharisees tried to ensnare Jesus by sending Herodians—supporters of Herod—to quiz Him (Matt. 22:15–22). Christ refused to be trapped and told them to give to Caesar whatever he rightfully deserved. Paul agreed with Jesus that the general rule was to obey the government (Rom. 13:1–7). However, Peter's declaration to the Jewish council demonstrated that when faith and the law are in opposition, God must be obeyed (Acts 5:29).

Very little of the Jews' history was spent in total tranquillity. Invasion, exile, occupation, resistance, uprising and oppression were often part of their life. During Christ's time, an underground movement existed in Galilee as well as open rebellion in Judea. Some of the disciples probably had been involved with resistance organizations.   ∎

POLICE □ By the first century, several police organizations were in place and functioning. King Herod had developed his own secret police because he distrusted practically everyone. Much like the Nazi Gestapo, they infiltrated the population and listened for derogatory remarks about Herod.

The Levites formed a police unit to guard the temple area. They patrolled the grounds to make sure no one entered the forbidden places. Outside doors and the Courts of the Gentiles and of the Women were carefully guarded. The Sanhedrin controlled the police; they could order arrests and administer punishment. Apparently the temple police were the people sent to arrest Jesus (Matt. 26:47; Luke 22:47). They were accompanied by servants of the high priest and Roman soldiers (Matt. 26:51; John 18:3, 12). The temple police were probably the same ones who tried to arrest Jesus earlier in His ministry (John 7:32).

This police force arrested the apostles at the temple (Acts 4:1–4).

Roman police were sent by the magistrates to release Paul and Silas from prison at Philippi (Acts 16:35, 38). They were called lictors, and carried bundles of birch rods, known as *fasces* which symbolized their authority. The rods were used to beat prisoners. Most major Roman cities had an assembly of these police. Their general function was to carry out punishments ordered by a magistrate. As servants of the magistrate, they traveled with him and heralded his arrival. They were distinguished by their togas while inside the city limits and their red coats while traveling. They were not actually city or regional police but served at the pleasure of the magistrate. Apparently Paul was beaten by lictors on at least three occasions (2 Cor. 11:25).

During most ancient times, the majority of arrests and punishments were carried out by city elders or soldiers. Prior to that justice rested in the hands of avenging families and clans.   ∎

DESPOTIC RULERS □ The laws laid down by rulers varied greatly and were generally characterized by the ruler's disposition, his ability to enforce the laws and in some cases the tolerance level of the population. Some rulers were firm but fair. Others, such as Herod, could be cruel and preposterous.

Herod's concepts of crime and just punishment were often extreme, and he enforced his idiosyncrasies by a rule of fear, by compromise with self-seeking groups and by placating the Roman emperors. He faced stiff opposition from most of the Jewish population but managed to persevere for nearly 35 years. Among his atrocities were some forms of law enforcement the people appreciated: Herod had robbers executed. His subjects applauded such measures. While his powers were not absolute, they bordered on it. His ruthless authority allowed him to execute the infant boys of Bethlehem by decree (Matt. 2:16).

The Bible contains many accounts of such despots who could end life or liberty by simple pronouncement.   ∎

COEXISTENCE WITH THE ROMANS □ Generally the Romans allowed the Jews to govern themselves while the empire concerned itself only with stopping insurrection. When problems occurred, the Roman soldiers could move quickly and violently. However, they tried to avoid involvement with daily problems and matters within religious jurisdictions. The Jews could arrest a criminal and hand him over to the Romans for punishment, which is what they did in the case of Jesus Christ. The enemies of Christ knew that the charge of insurrection would spur the Romans to swift action. Consequently, they repeated the accusation often. Paul (Acts 21:38) and the apostles (Acts 5:35–39) were suspected of treason against Rome. Augustus had ruled that a Roman citizen could not be beaten or thrown into prison. This law sometimes worked for Paul (Acts 22:25–29; 2 Cor. 11:25).   ■

CRUCIFIXION □ Crucifixion as a form of execution was not unique to the Romans; the Phoenicians, Persians and Greeks had used it previously. Originally reserved for slaves, the method was eventually used as the authorities determined necessary. Roman

"Gordon's Calvary," located near the Garden Tomb, is named after General Charles Gordon who spent a year in Jerusalem studying the Bible, and, thinking he detected the outline of a skull in the hill, related it to Golgotha—the Place of the Skull—where Jesus was crucified. Whether or not it was the actual site of the crucifixion, it is in a conspicuous, public location, and those crucified on its summit would be seen by many spectators and passers-by.   TW

law stated that Roman citizens could not be crucified; however, on occasions exceptions were made, such as for deserters in the Second Punic War. In Israel the Romans applied this punishment to crimes other than sedition and disorder. Some people were crucified even for robbery (Luke 23:32).

The Via Dolorosa—the Street of Sorrow—is the route Jesus is believed to have traveled from the Judgment Hall of Pilate to Mount Calvary.   TW

The basic purpose of crucifixion was not merely execution but humiliation. Death was certainly the objective, but that could have been accomplished with far less trouble. The victim's suffering and shame was to serve as an example and deterrent.

Men were crucified with their backs to the cross and women with their faces toward it. A block of wood beneath the feet held the weight of the victim, whose hands were tied or nailed to the crossbeam.

Death came very slowly in most cases. Starvation, thirst, asphyxia and vultures each contributed to the torment and eventual demise. If death did not occur by an appropriate time, the victim might have his legs broken, eliminating the support for his body, thus speeding up asphyxiation (John 19:31–33).   ∎

ATHLETICS

Throughout their history, the Israelites were surrounded and infiltrated by other nationalities who enjoyed sports and contests. Because some sports had a pagan emphasis, many Jews resisted them. However, their attempts at separation were not entirely successful. In many cases Jews succumbed to the splendor and challenge of the athletic contests around them for the several centuries leading up to the time of Christ.

The ancient Jew was an outdoorsman who enjoyed physical challenges but probably did not participate in sports to the degree that the Greeks, Romans and even Egyptians did, but neither was he above a good contest. Old Testament authors made little mention of athletic events, but a few statements using athletics imagery suggest that these did exist (we know little about athletics in general before 100 B.C.). A prime example is an illustration used by Isaiah (22:18). The prophet suggests that God might want to roll them up as a ball and toss them into another country. This could refer to a popular sport of the time.

In Gen. 32:24 Jacob wrestles with the angel of the Lord. Some scholars think this could have been a sport of that time period.

Some Jews were excellent marksmen with the stone and sling. At one time the army had 700 left-handed sling throwers who could hit a hair (Judg. 20:16). Shepherd boys such as David became expert at this skill (1 Sam. 17:49). It is possible that slingers occasionally met to test each other's ability. Men were noted for their speed (2 Sam. 2:18), and Jeremiah

This Roman theater at Sebaste was typical of the sporting arenas Herod had built to display sporting events.   BAS suggests they pitted themselves against each other (12:5). Although devout Jews looked with some suspicion at sports and many forms of amusements, over thousands of years of history it is very likely that they at least informally competed.

By the first century A.D., the Jews had been exposed to a great amount of athletic events. The Greeks who conquered Israel around 300 B.C. were committed to sports. Their fanaticism in athletics was fueled by their quest for the ideal in all of life. Sports functioned to develop the ideal body. The Greek games, dedicated to the gods of Olympus, had been held since at least 780

This Roman amphitheater is built right on the Mediterranean seashore at Caesarea, just south of a Crusader wall. The theater was built in the second century and was unearthed in 1961. Many New Testament events took place at Caesarea, including the coming of the Holy Spirit at the "Gentile Pentecost" (Acts 10:44–48). TW

B.C. Despite resistance to and even repulsion by the games, Israel did feel their influence. In 63 B.C. the Romans occupied Israel and brought their games with them. Their interest in sports was acquired from the Greeks but took a distasteful turn as they developed their own sadistic variations.

When Herod the Great became king of Israel (37 B.C.), he strove to emulate the Graeco-Roman lifestyle, part of which was an interest in spectacles and athletics. A large part of his massive building scheme was dedicated to stadiums which would display great sporting events. Herod had witnessed the magnificent Olympic games and desired to see such sports in his own country. He had a particular fondness for wrestling and chariot racing. The king built amphitheaters and arenas across Palestine. Locations included Caesarea, Tarichaea, Samaria-Sebaste and possibly Jericho.

Generally the Jews were offended by these forms of amusement on several grounds. First, many of the games were a form of worship to pagan gods. Second, some of the prizes had images on them, which angered the Jews. Third, the Greek games were played in the nude (the Romans had less appreciation for nude sports). The more religious Jews avoided these blasphemous events. However, at the time of Christ and Paul, such strong feelings were not very common. Joshua, the high priest (also known as Jason the Vile), encouraged athletic games in Israel. For this he was accused of "perverting" the Jews with Gentile paganism.

Sports were extremely popular in ancient times, as they are today. Thinkers wrote articles to protest so much attention, time and energy being wasted on athletics. But the populace did not seem to listen. Some of the huge arenas held over 40,000 people in a day when Jerusalem's population may not have been that large. One mammoth structure, Circus Maximus, was enlarged by Nero to hold 350,000 spectators. Toward the end of the Greek empire the games began to lose their popularity. However, the Romans injected a new surge of interest and the emphasis on sports continued.

PAUL'S INTEREST IN SPORTS □ We cannot be certain where Paul witnessed athletic events, but his many references to sports show him to have been an observer. At first glance it would appear that the great apostle made a few passing remarks about sports; his terminology shows knowledge of the current practices and serves to make interesting analogies and metaphors. However, further study of his writing shows Paul may have been a sports enthusiast, for he frequently resorts to athletics for illustrations. If not, he was a well-informed individual who exploited popular imagery to make his points clear. If a writer is an accountant, one might expect to find some accounting terms sprinkled among his works. If he is a fisherman, that often surfaces. In Paul's case not only does he display a knowledge of sporting events, he also resorts often to strong expressions used in athletics. To Timothy Paul wrote that believers need to obey the rules as an athlete who competes fairly (2 Tim. 2:5). He told the Christians at Philippi to "strive together" for the faith (Phil. 1:27); borrowed directly from the arena, the term is a combination of two words, literally meaning to "athlete together" (*sun-athleo*).

As Paul says he strains toward the goal, the reader can almost see veins stretched on the runner's neck (Phil. 3:13, 14). The word for prize actually refers to the umpire who awards the prize at the end of the contest.

When he tells Christians that Epaphras is praying for them, Paul informs them that their friend is contending as one would wrestle in the arena (Col. 4:12).

While it is impossible to know the mind of Paul, these references, and others in his epistles, suggest that Paul had a keen interest in sports. If he is the author of Hebrews, the evidence is even more weighty. Christians are commended for standing their ground in a great contest or struggle (Heb. 10:32); the word meaning "athletic" is used in 2 Tim. 2:5. And in Heb. 12:1 believers are told to "run with patience the race. . . ."   ■

FIGHTING ANIMALS □ Herod the Great was fond of contests that pitted men against animals. In 10 B.C. he opened the public festivities at Caesarea with such terrifying events. They were not for his twisted taste alone; thousands of spectators jammed the arena to see them. The animals used in such "sport" included lions, bears, leopards, rhinoceros, crocodiles, tigers and elephants. In the mornings men could fight with armor. However, to enhance the excitement, unarmed men (sometimes naked) were forced into the arena. Often the crowds would throw objects at the animals to further aggravate them. Normally the victims were prisoners. Later Jewish prisoners were killed by this method when Titus assumed rule in A.D. 70.

The Romans at that time had a tremendous hunger for sadistic sport. When men were not fighting animals, they merely turned the animals on each other. Such cruelty definitely influenced men such as Herod. In some instances seals would be turned loose and a polar bear released to chase them. The crowd delighted to see the large animal eat its prey. These cruel events were witnessed by men and women, as well as boys who had been brought by an adult.

When Nero began his ruthless persecution of Christianity (A.D. 64–65), he employed similar horrors. The Roman emperor had Christians dressed in animal skins and attacked by wild dogs. He is also reported to have attached Christians to poles and used them as torches to illuminate some of his garden parties. ■

GLADIATORS □ The

Bible makes no direct reference to gladiators or their fights, but such contests were popular for at least 1,000 years. Generally, gladiators were unfortunate men pressed into fighting because they were slaves, prisoners or heavily in debt. Often they were owned by a sponsor and possibly a trainer.

This type of contest could assume many forms. Two men could fight each other or teams could square off. The weapons could include nets, swords, shields

The Colosseum is a Roman arena begun by Emperor Vespasian and finished by his son, Titus. It's marble seats held 45,000 spectators for the gladiator fights. ICI

or a trident (a three-pronged spear). They did not always fight until death, though many did. At the end of a large battle many bodies might be strewn across the ground, and the two or three remaining could be rewarded a crown of minimal value.

The most famous gladiator was Theogenes who lived around the time of Solomon. Historians say he and his opponents wore on their fists leather thongs studded with sharp, metal spikes. The two contestants would sit face to face on two stone slabs. On the signal to begin they would beat each other until one bloodied gladiator was dead. It is claimed that Theogenes faced 1,425 men and killed them all. This sport was commonly performed in Israel during the time of Christ and the apostles.   ∎

WRESTLING □ This appears to be one of the earliest, most primitive sports. With little training any two participants might square off and test their ability. As it became more sophisticated, they wore special belts and loincloths. From as early as 3000 B.C., we find pictures of wrestlers with hands on each other's belts.

Wrestling is stated or implied in various portions of the Scriptures. Among his many physical talents, Samson may have been an outstanding wrestler (Judg. 15:8). He smote the Philistines "hip and thigh." It is possible that this is an ancient wrestling term as half-nelson and flying scissors are modern terms. There are other places where wrestling may be the author's implication. The fight at Gibeon between Ishbosheth's and David's men was probably a wrestling match which ended in a bloodbath (2 Sam. 2:14). On one occasion Paul clearly used the Greek word for wrestling when he told believers they were not wrestling against flesh and blood but rather against the forces of evil (Eph. 6:12). His contemporaries could probably picture themselves face to face with evil, in a ferocious contest of strength and quickness.   ∎

BOXING □ The Greeks were fond of fistfighting similar to our present boxing. The participants wore no gloves, however, though their hands and arms were wrapped with leather strips.

Their contests had few of our present regulations. Fighters were not matched according to weight. They had no timed rounds and fighters were not confined to a ring. The object was to hit each other until one participant could no longer stand. If the match was prolonged, the judges could call a halt. In this case rigid ox leather, sometimes studded with metal, might then be put on the contestants. Often these matches ended in death or permanent injury.

We do not know what Paul thought of this sport, but we do know that he understood the terminology very well, for he speaks of himself as a boxer who doesn't just beat the air (1 Cor. 9:26). His word for box comes from the word fist, from which we derive the word pugilist. He portrayed shadow boxing as someone "skimming" or flaying the air. The apostle explains that his spiritual discipline is rigorous, not merely as someone boxing imaginary opponents. ■

THE GYMNASIUM □ The Greeks emphasized the theater, the arts and the intellect, but they also considered physical development an essential ingredient of personal wholeness. Four hundred years before Christ the Greeks developed an integrated program which stressed the mind and the body. Large learning centers, gymnasia, soon arose. A gymnasium compound consisted of a building for boxing, wrestling and other sports. Another building provided baths. Still other indoor and open-air structures were used for lectures and discussions. Some of the great thinkers of history taught at these gymnasia. At Athens, Plato taught at one, Aristotle at another and Cynosarges at the third.

The word gymnasium comes from the Greek word for naked, for young men exercised in the nude. This particularly offended the Jews and also embarrassed the circumcised Jewish young men. Consequently, some were ashamed of their Jewish heritage. Despite such antagonism, a Greek gymnasium was contructed in Jerusalem in 170 B.C. Its presence was one factor which led to the revolt by the Jewish Maccabeans. Some Jews welcomed and even asked for the structure, but others were horrified. Not only was the nudity offensive to some, but so was the wearing of broad-brimmed felt hats by the athletes. The hats were associated with the Greek god Hermes.

It is possible that Paul held no such hostility as had the Jews 200 years before. His terminology suggests familiarity with the gymnasium but without condemnation. The apostle employs the term when he encourages believers to train themselves in godliness (1 Tim. 4:7, 8). His word for train is the same as gymnastics. He concedes that some gymnastics is good for the body but that godliness is of supreme value. Paul does not shun the term or denounce the practice. While this does not prove his acceptance, it does imply that it was not an issue with him. It also implies that his readers would not be insulted by the analogy.

The writer of Hebrews uses this same word (Heb. 5:14; 12:11). Believers are to "gymnastic" themselves in order to discern good from evil. Peter reminds Christians it is possible to train oneself (gymnastically) in the ways of evil (2 Pet. 2:14). ■

RACING □ *Chariot races.* The first wheeled vehicles were heavy, slow carts, often drawn by donkeys. However, around 2,000 years before Christ a lightweight chariot that could be drawn swiftly by horses was developed in Mesopotamia. This was an effective war machine that dominated military encounters for over a thousand years and eventually became a popular racing vehicle.

Some men, such as Jehu, gained reputations for driving a chariot at breakneck speed (2 Kings 9:20).

By the first century chariot races were a regular part of the Graeco-Roman entertainment scene. Driving in these dangerous contests required considerable skill to perform the many maneuvers, and to control the powerful, spirited animals that pulled the chariot. Regular racing consisted of driving seven times around the hippodrome a two-wheeled chariot drawn by four horses. (Some chariots used two horses.) Normally the distance amounted to six miles. Few rules regulated the races. This, coupled with the speed, resulted in the death of many drivers.

If a driver was particularly skillful, he would develop crowd-pleasing stunts, much as modern rodeo riders do. Some riders would leap onto their galloping horses and then jump from horse to horse. Some could snatch a white cloth from the ground while maintaining full speed.

Riders tied the reins around their waists so they would not lose them. However, if a rider was thrown from the chariot, he could be dragged to his death or be run over by other chariots. Consequently, he carried a knife in hopes of being able to quickly cut himself loose.

Much like modern horse racing, spectators could place bets on their favorite entry and riders often became celebrities. Their pictures were publicly displayed, and some retired with considerable financial benefits.

Generally, women were not allowed to participate in these and other athletic contests, but not always. Belisiche, a woman from Macedonia, reportedly won a chariot race in the 128th Olympic Games.

Foot races. Track and field contests were popular during the era of Christ and Paul. The famous five-event pentathlon consisted of the long jump, javelin and discus throws, wrestling and the foot race. While the Romans may have altered some events, many of them remained the same.

The ancient *dromos* was a race of one lap around a track approximately 600 yards in circumference, a third longer than our present 440-yard tracks. Later, longer races were added. Paul used *dromos* to describe the spiritual race he had finished (2 Tim. 4:7). We cannot be certain with which races Paul was familiar, but we do know the Isthmian Games were held in Corinth. These were a major event, held every two years. Many cities held similar games. There were at least 150 celebrated major contests.

Paul was aware that track competition demanded intense practice. Olympic athletes had to swear they had undergone ten months of rigorous training before competing. The last month had to be under the stern eye of an Olympic instructor. Paul noted that service in the gospel demands no less discipline than the sacrificial training needed for races (1 Cor. 9:22–27).

On other occasions the apostle drew on the same analogy. If the Judaizers were correct, Paul would feel he had run the race in vain (Gal. 2:2). He had a great desire to complete the race Christ had laid before him (Acts 20:24). He insisted that God's mercy does not depend on how hard we run the race (Rom. 9:16). When Paul expressed his disappointment over those who became Judaizers, he again used the racing analogy: "You were running a good race. Who cut in on you and kept you from obeying the truth?" (Gal. 5:7).

The author of Hebrews displays a rich imagination by picturing life as a great racing track. God has marked out the race, a life of holiness. In the stands sit hordes of departed saints, cheering us on to run the race to the best of our ability (Heb. 12:1). The writer and his readers could easily picture the tens of thousands of spectators, former racers, shouting encouragement. ■

The ruins of this shopping area are from ancient Corinth of Paul's day, a bustling city of 500,000 residents. It was the site of cultural and athletic events, including the Isthmian Games. In the background is the Acro-Corinthus, a rock rising 1500 feet above the city, where the decadent and immoral worship of Aphrodite, the goddess of love, occurred.   TW

CROWNS □ There were often valuable prizes for those who triumphed in the athletic games, although the most cherished reward, the satisfaction of winning, was intangible. When the victorious athlete returned home, his community lauded him with great honor. Statues were sculpted to honor some of them.

In earlier periods, the sports programs were wholesome and the rewards simple. Often the victors were acknowledged with a fragile, leafy crown. Depending on the event and the location, the winner's crown might be made of a collection of pine leaves, wild olive leaves, parsley, celery leaves or ivy. These garlands or wreaths were taken home with tremendous pride to soon wither and discolor.

Paul made a vivid comparison by contrasting these leafy temporal crowns with the eternal rewards of God (1 Cor. 9:25). He used the same word to describe the crown of righteousness which God had in store for him (2 Tim. 4:8). His familiarity with this award is shown by his use of the term on several other occasions (Phil. 4:1; 1 Thess. 2:19). Peter (1 Pet. 5:4), James (1:12) and John (Rev. 2:10, etc.) also used the term.

In time the games degenerated and the participants were no longer content with recognition and crowns of leaves. Some of the games offered lavish gifts and prizes to the winners. Many of the contests became expensive to enter and prepare for, especially if chariots or horses were necessary. While this may have been a golden age for amateur athletics, it was not as ideal and untainted as we might imagine.

These athletic contests evolved over a period of a thousand-year history, and little is recorded of many events that were included. We do know dancing, tumbling, rope climbing, leaping and balancing were part of the games. Other unnamed sports may have been lost in history.

The Roman games came to a close under emperor Theodosius in A.D. 392.

■

SUBJECT INDEX

SUBJECT INDEX

SCRIPTURE INDEX

Scripture Index